An Atlas of Rural Protest in Britain 1548-1900

Edited by Andrew Charlesworth

University of Pennsylvania Press
Philadelphia
1983

First published 1983 in the United States by the
University of Pennsylvania Press, Philadelphia

First published 1983 in the United Kingdom by
Croom Helm, London and Canberra

Library of Congress Cataloging in Publication Data

Main entry under title:

An Atlas of rural protest in Britain 1548–1900.

  Includes index.
  1. Peasant uprisings – Great Britain – History – Maps.
I. Charlesworth, Andrew.
HD1536.G65A87   1983   912′.132242′0942   82-8362
ISBN 0-8122-7853-4   AACR2

Printed and bound in Great Britain

CONTENTS

Contents

MAPS

ACKNOWLEDGEMENTS

I was educated in a school and in a university department where my teachers were always regarded as personalities, fellow human beings, even if somewhat larger than life. That fascination for people, particularly fellow members of the academic community, has luckily never left me. I never tire of reading acknowledgements that show how a particular author is located at the centre of a particular network of friendships and acquaintances within the academic community. It is one of my greatest regrets today that university students now tend to regard their teachers as 'grey men' nine-to-five office workers. Moreover, in a work of this kind where I have persuaded so many to contribute to the atlas and where I have borrowed so freely from their and other researchers' work, I feel doubly justified in writing the type of preface I like to read and leave the methodological introduction quite properly to the first essay in the atlas. The 'grey men' who would find what follows tiresome, will at this point pass on — and safely pass on for they will not find any acknowledgement here. Such men and women have the ability to labour away on their own and so have no debts to pay. I am not of their number and could not have laboured away without the help, encouragement and in many cases friendship of the following.

First, Professor George Rudé whose book *The Crowd in History* has been an inspiration throughout all my research on rural protest and whose encouragement at various times in my researches has been most welcome. Secondly, there are the scholars whom I have corresponded with and talked with and who have freely let me use their ideas. Amongst this group are the contributors to the atlas who allowed themselves to be persuaded by a geographer to take part in the project and to allow their data to be mapped. Of these I would like to single out in particular John Martin, Eric Richards and John Walter. Equally my thanks must go to Roger Wells, Clifford Davies, John Morrill, Ian Blanchard, John Styles, Julian Cornwall, Mike Beames, Edward Thompson and the late Andrew Appleby. For a geographer venturing into this historical territory many of them will not have realised how grateful I have been for their words of encouragement, persuading me that the work was valuable to them, when I had grave doubts that I was indulging in cheap and easy map correlations and comparisons.

At the University of Liverpool I must thank my two heads of department, Dick Lawton and Mansell Prothero, for their continued encouragement of my work in this somewhat esoteric geographical study. From the high standard of the maps it is clear the debt I owe to the staff of the Drawing Office, Alan Hodgkiss, master cartographer and his right-hand women, Julie Isaac and Sandra

Mather. The clarity of the reproduction of the maps is due to the skill of the Faculty Photographic Unit, Douglas Birch and his right-hand men Chris Roberts and Ian Qualtrough. Betti Thomson deciphered my handwriting with an ease that makes me envious every time I have to do the same with a nineteenth-century letter. I would also like to thank the University of Liverpool for allowing me a term's study leave to complete the atlas.

The Nuffield Foundation provided funds to employ a part-time research assistant and travelling expenses without which the atlas could not have been expanded from its original exhibition format. Liz Steel bravely took on the job of research assistant and managed to keep me organised and on schedule whilst in that post. Five others have helped in research tasks in various ways: Vince Budd, Jenny Donovan, Mark Edwards, Rosalind Jordan and Chris Roche.

I would also like to thank the staffs of the British Library, the Newspaper Library at Colindale, the National Library of Wales, Gloucester City Library, the Public Record Office and Norfolk County Record Office for the assistance they have given me and my research assistants. A particular debt of gratitude goes to Ann Rowlands and Christine Jones in the Inter-Library Loan Office in the Sydney Jones Library at the University of Liverpool.

Peter Sowden at Croom Helm has given good advice in shaping the whole atlas, has encouraged me throughout the project and was sympathetic when unforeseen difficulties arose. Frances Kelly has steered me through the multiform problems of editing a piece of work with so many contributors.

Lastly, my wife Jean, without whom the labouring away day after day in isolation would have been to no avail.

In the course of preparing this atlas, I have consulted numerous theses and books with great profit. To all these scholars I acknowledge the enormous debt of gratitude I owe them. The following, however, must be singled out for particular mention.

D.G.C. Allan, 'Agrarian Discontent Under the Early Stuarts and During the Last Decade of Elizabeth', unpublished MSc (Econ) thesis, University of London, 1950.

D.J.V. Jones, 'Popular Disturbances in Wales 1790-1832', unpublished PhD thesis, University of Wales, 1965; *Before Rebecca* (London, 1973).

K.J. Logue, *Popular Disturbances in Scotland 1780-1815* (Edinburgh, 1979).

T.L. Richardson, 'The Standard of Living Controversy 1790-1840 with Specific Reference to Agricultural Labourers in Seven English Counties', unpublished PhD thesis, University of Hull, 1977.

J.G. Rule, 'The Labouring Miner in Cornwall c1740-1870', unpublished PhD thesis, University of Warwick, 1971.

R.A.E. Wells, 'The Grain Crises in England 1794-96, 1799-1801', unpublished D.Phil thesis, University of York, 1978.

I must also thank the following for permission to use material that has appeared elsewhere: the editors of the Historical Geography Research Paper series for Map 44 from my *Social Protest in a Rural Society*, HGR series 1 (Norwich, 1979), Frank Cass & Co Ltd for permission to reproduce parts of my article 'The Development of the English Rural Proletariat and Social Protest 1700-1850: A Comment', *Journal of Peasant Studies, 8* (1980) pp. 101-11; and Dr Joan Thirsk and Cambridge University Press for material derived from Figure 1 in J. Thirsk (ed.), *Agrarian History of England and Wales vol. IV: 1500-1640* (Cambridge, 1967).

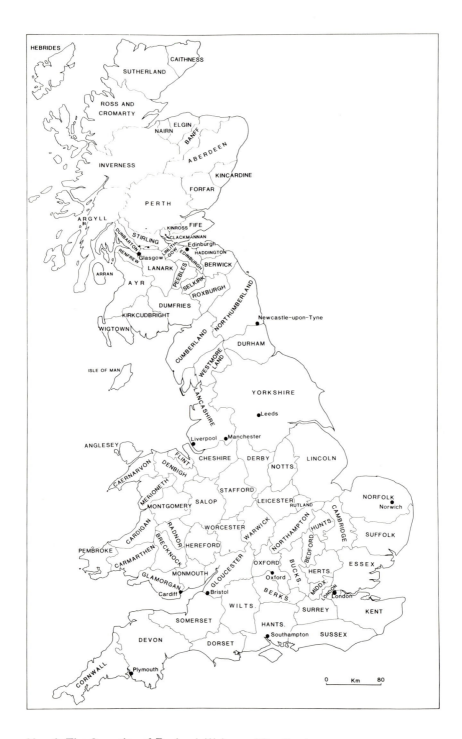

Map 1. The Counties of England, Wales and Scotland

1 INTRODUCTION

Two of the aims of Rudé's pioneering work of 1964, *The Crowd in History: A Study of Popular Disturbances in France and England 1730-1848*, were, one, to place the crowd in its geographical setting and, two, to encourage others to undertake studies of popular disturbances in other places and in other periods.[1] The latter aim has been amply fulfilled by the subsequent volume of papers, books and theses on social protest in the past. Out of that growing body of studies of social protest this work focuses on direct collective actions that occurred in or were of the countryside but were not directly related to industrial, religious or political issues. The crowds that interest us are those, as defined by Rule, that 'have a common purpose in achieving a certain end' (be it removal of enclosure hedges, the prevention of drainage of their land or fixing a fair price for food in the market place) and 'seeking to achieve it by acting in a collective manner'.[2] Thus all protests that could have been done by individuals, arson, threatening letter, malicious damage to hedges and fences, all such covert and anonymous acts will not be considered except where it aids our understanding of direct collective actions. In the text 'direct collective action' will not, however, be widely used. The phrase is somewhat cumbersome. Moreover, the contemporary usage of the term 'riot' and the need for some variation of terminology mean that 'riot', 'disturbance' and 'collective protest' will be used, although restricting the former two terms for occasions where collective violence took place. Moreover, I have chosen to focus on the major episodes of direct collective action so as to avoid maps on which there is little information.

The particular direct collective actions that interest us are those over the issues of land, food, labour, poor law, tithes, turnpikes and militia recruitment. There is also a section on the Clubmen disturbances of the Civil War, which were the reaction of rural communities to the presence of military troops demanding quarter or provisions in their regions. Thus their resistance, like so many other of the collective protests considered in the atlas, was couched in terms of a defence of local institutions and local rights.

One of the major series of collective protests examined in the atlas are food riots. Given that one of our contentions is that in the main food riots were not staged by agricultural workers, it may seem confusing to wish to include it in an atlas of rural protest. Why then do so? First, food riots often did occur in rural areas, even if they were the direct collective actions of proto-industrial and industrial workers and artisans. Secondly, this was a major form of protest *of* the countryside, in that the direct collective actions involved the agricultural produce of the countryside. Thirdly, it was felt that the evidence of the geography of food riots aids a critique of a chronological sequence of collective protest, such as that developed by the Hammonds, with agricultural labourers first involved in enclosure riots, then at the centre of food riots and finally in protests over wages and attacks on agricultural machinery.[3] Fourthly, the sequential chronology of land, food and labour protests, that is seen clearest for England, is partly related to the rise, expansion and transformation of agrarian capitalism.

Once having selected this set of protests I decided that for most types of direct collective action it was more meaningful to examine the full range of locations in which they occurred rather than differentiate, often somewhat arbitrarily, between the rural and urban variants of the protest. The collective protests this particularly concerned were food riots, turnpike disturbances and protests over the enclosure of town common fields. This inclusiveness is valuable not only in avoiding the arbitrariness of selection but also it allows comparisons to be made when there are regional variations in the types of communities involved in the protests. For example, turnpike riots were the work of small farmers in Scotland and Wales, whereas in Yorkshire they were undertaken by industrial workers; during the series of Bristol turnpike disturbances at one time farmers and colliers came together. In the case of food and land protests in England in the eighteenth century it emphasises that both types of riot in town and country were mainly staged by industrial workers, thus highlighting the lack of directive collective actions by agricultural labourers for most of that century.

The three countries that make up the mainland of Britain — England, Wales and Scotland — form the geographical frame of reference of the atlas. Given the propensity of historians to study only one nation at a time, it was felt this combination of three countries was sufficiently adventurous. To have attempted to encompass the Irish experience as well would have stretched my resources too far.

The time period covered by the atlas is somewhat arbitrary. The end point is taken as 1900, although not in any way to suggest that direct collective actions died out after that date in the countryside: the Highland Land War was to be carried on into the twentieth century with campaigns of land seizures and in terms of the government's response to the crofters' demands was to be a fairly successful tactic. Food riots occurred in West Cumberland in 1917 during a time when there was a return in some aspects to the food scarcities of the last years of the eighteenth and first years of the nineteenth centuries. Yet by 1900 there is a sense in England and Wales that of the three major protests that had dominated the countryside over the last three and a half centuries, food and land disturbances had run their course, whilst labour issues were by then pursued by trade unions. Indeed, one of the reasons for taking the time span as far as 1900 was to chart such changes. The starting point of the atlas is more logical. It is taken as the crisis years of 1548-52, which are regarded by many as a turning point in the history of class relations in lowland English rural society.

Few social historians have, however, emulated Rudé's pioneering example of complementing their studies with relatively detailed maps of the social protest movement being investigated. Even Rudé himself, when collaborating with Hobsbawm in their 1969 study of the Captain Swing riots of 1830-1, found the cost too high to provide their research with 'the cartography without which it must remain incomplete'.[4] As Hobsbawm and Rudé noted, historians find it difficult to write in a manner different from that which their historical training has afforded them. This is particularly evident when they come to undertake research on social protest in rural society. Narrative skills that can describe the storming of the Bastille can only be effective for events on a much larger scale if the narrator has mapped the temporal sequence of events in the greatest detail possible. Thus, despite the increasing bulk of studies on rural protest, the geography of such disturbances is still largely unknown. The primary purpose of the atlas is then to act as a much needed complement to the research already undertaken by historians.

In the atlas there are three types of map: those that show the geography of rural protest from a national or regional viewpoint, those that focus on the locality of a particular series of protest in detail and those that attempt to plot the spread of certain series of rural protests. The latter are important because as Bohstedt has noted charting the spatial diffusion of a set of riots is often the only information we have from which to infer the mode of communication of rioting from one area to another.[5] Bohstedt's comment indicates that the mapping of social protest can be more than just a supplement to research undertaken. The very act of mapping can yield new insights and stimulate the formation of new hypotheses. To aid this process there are in the atlas three interpretative essays on the geography of the three major protests of the countryside: land, food and labour collective protests. In particular the shifting patterns of the geography of land and food riots and the emergence of labour disturbances predominantly in southern and eastern England have been considered. In these essays a comparative approach has been adopted because the geography of collective protests 'does not contain within itself an explanation of its own causation'.[6] One needs to be able to offer some explanation or hypotheses why some areas did not have direct collective actions over particular issues.

At this point, however, one should be made fully aware of the dangers of placing too great a reliance on the precision of the maps presented here. This is what Gould means when he says that the map imposes a stricter discipline upon us than we care to admit.[7] Once symbols are placed in one area and another is left blank, then an inference is drawn that the former region was riotous, the latter tranquil. This lends to the maps an air of stark precision in terms of areal dichotomies: black/white, presence/absence. The discipline of the act of mapping requires that we spell out how reliable and precise are the spatial patterns that the map highlights and at what scale can inferences about the map patterns be drawn with confidence.

First, it is unlikely that the maps are either comprehensive or fully accurate. They attempt to summarise the presently available findings of research on rural protest. It has not been possible, except in one or two instances, to do any more than draw together in a summary form this material. New research and new source material coming to light will undoubtedly alter the picture. There are acknowledged gaps in the evidence on rural protest where no research has so far been undertaken by scholars. The most glaring of these are the lack of research on rural protest in Wales between 1640 and 1780, in Scotland before 1680 and in England between 1552 and 1596. Such lacunae have obviously shaped the nature of the atlas with its early focus on England. It is unlikely, however, that any major series of rural protest, comparable to, say, the Midland Revolt of 1607, has not been uncovered to date and, so, many of the inferences drawn relate to the shift in the spatial distribution of such major revolts.

Secondly, as a number of historians have indicated in their work, the available sources of evidence — official and private papers, newspapers and legal records — are not without their pitfalls for reconstructing the geography of rural protest.[8] Walter notes that the sixteenth- and seventeenth-century reports of food riots by the authorities can be misleading because 'the authorities too readily translated the threat of disorder into evidence of riot and reports, when not vague and generalised, employed the stereotyped shorthand of "food riot" which might obscure a more complex reality'. For the eighteenth century, on the other hand, Wells points out that many JPs refrained from reporting local disturbances to central government, not wishing to admit any problems in their ability to keep order. In extreme crises such as 1795 or in towns where disorder was endemic, demonstrations and minor riots were similarly not reported to higher authorities. Again, as Wells notes, some of the press might maintain a conspiracy of silence during such crises and as newspapers often depended on each other's local news, examining other newspapers cannot always get round that problem. There are, moreover, pitfalls with legal records. As Wells, Walter and Neeson note, charges of theft and assault, often brought against a few people, can hide a riot by a whole crowd. Furthermore, as Walter and Beloff indicate, the curtness of an indictment for riotous assembly may conceal to the researcher the particular type of riot that had taken place. Conversely, because the contemporary legal definition of a riot only required three people to be present, as Hay stresses, such an indictment could also be simply a personal assault or a relatively limited trespass. Legal cases may not have been instituted, as Wells and Neeson point out, because witnesses and informers were not willing to come forward in communities which supported the protestors' actions. With regard to private papers, on the one hand, as Hay notes, we are now at the mercy of their coming to light. On the other hand, as Beloff's comments reveal, it is completely random whether riots were recorded in private papers. It depended whether the person wished to act as a chronicler for the locality. If there had been more people like Anthony Wood of Oxford, who recorded in such detail events there in the seventeenth century, our knowledge of collective protests would be much enhanced.

The problems of this material are greatest when the sources are not used in combination and reliance is placed on a few national sources. This leads to a further limitation on the accuracy of the maps. In preparing the atlas I have had to rely at times on surveys of a more general nature where only a few national sources, a selection of newspapers, the *Gentleman's Magazine* and the *Annual Register* have been used. This creates problems of variability in the accuracy of the levels of social protest between maps and at times within the same map. A good example would be the land protest map of 1740-79 which draws both on Neeson's detailed study of enclosure collective protests in Northamptonshire and Wearmouth's general survey of riots for the whole of England. It is difficult to give anything other than an impressionistic measure of the variability this introduces to a particular map. The reader should consult the list of references accompanying the map to see what combination of these types of study has been used. Thus the maps must be treated as a summary of work on an active research frontier rather than a definitive account of the geography of rural protest. It is one of my hopes that the maps will stimulate others to do more detailed research in the blank areas to establish an even more accurate record of social protest.

The quiescence of particular communities is not, however, just a matter of their not yet finding a researcher. It also has to be seen in the context of the complex reality out of which direct collective action came which, as Walter noted, the authorities' reports often obscured. There are two aspects that need to be considered: first, what Brewer and Styles call a 'negotiative process' between the crowd and the authorities and, secondly, the use of repressive measures against direct collective action when the negotiative process broke down.[9]

In the negotiative process, in which the crowd sought redress for some grievance, be it the taking away of either common rights or customary winter employment or the setting of unfair prices in the market place, collective negotiating or bargaining by riot or demonstration was but one form; petitioning, litigation, threatening letter and arson were others. The escalation to direct collective action was most often the result of the lack of responsiveness by those in authority. Thus in certain settlements an early positive response on the part of the authorities to the aggrieved party's demands, such as the putting aside of threshing machines or instructing tenants to sell wheat at the customary price, could mean that in terms of direct collective action nothing happened there and the map would be blank. One of the clearest examples of this variation in response over a short distance is the contrast between King's Sedgemoor and Alder Moor on the Somerset Levels in the 1630s and 1640s. These two moors, less than four miles apart, were both to be drained in the 1630s. In the former case the political pressure of the commoners on the commissioners successfully delayed the drainage scheme, whilst in the latter moor opposition was swept aside, the drainage was completed, only to be destroyed by the commoners in the troubled times of the 1640s.

Such variations in response would cause problems if they were not taken into account in an explanation of local variations in direct collective action: why certain villages or towns remained quiet during a major period of social tension whilst their neighbours saw demonstrations and riots. Rarely, in the atlas, however, does the scale of analysis focus down to such a detailed level. Neeson's study is an exception but she attempts to record these variations in the occurrence of certain of the legal and extra-legal forms of the negotiating process in enclosed parishes in Northamptonshire between 1760 and 1800. For these variations of responsiveness to be a major difficulty one would have to contend that they occurred at the regional scale. The only clear examples of this was abandonment of the use of threshing machines by many farmers as a precaution against disorder in the Swing protests of 1830-1.

Similarly one needs to remember that the presence of the military or the implementation of other repressive measures by the authorities could prevent the crowd from taking direct collective action. Yet the implications of this for the spatial patterning of collective protests varied over time and with the areas within which disturbances took place. Before the nineteenth century, with limited military resources, the authorities tended to operate a 'horse and stable door' policy.[10] Troops were only summoned if there was a breakdown of the negotiative process, that is, rioting would have to occur before troops were called into an area. This meant that although the reoccurrence of disturbances in an area was most likely prevented, the spread of the protests to new areas and settlements was often not halted. In the early-nineteenth century there seems to have been a relative shift in emphasis from repression to preventing such spatial diffusion of collective protests. Regional strategies began to be devised accordingly. One might have expected that as the nineteenth century progressed the use of military force would have more effectively contained the spread of rioting. This was somewhat nullified by the fact that protests after 1830 occurred for the most part on the remote periphery of Britain and by the terrain and settlement patterns of the regions where disturbances occurred: the hilly terrain of south-west Wales where the Rebecca riots took place, the dispersed fishing communities of the far north of Scotland through which the food riots of 1847 spread, the scattered islands of the Inner and Outer Isles of Scotland where the Highland Land War was fought out.

From this it should be clear that most of the maps in the atlas should not be used as the basis for a local or county study of variations in the level of rural protest. In the three main interpretative essays that accompany the protests over land, food and labour, I have directed my attention to the major regional variations. I and my fellow contributors have tried to incorporate into the individual commentaries at appropriate points some of the points noted above on the concessionary and repressive measures taken by the authorities. Indeed, the essay on food rioting sets out explicitly to underline the complex reality within which food disturbances must be viewed if they are to be properly understood. The atlas is thus but the first step towards an understanding of the historical geography of class conflict in the countryside.

Notes

1. Rudé (1964), p. 15.
2. Rule (1971), p. 118.
3. Hammond and Hammond (1911).
4. Hobsbawm and Rudé (1973), p. xvi.
5. Bohstedt (1972), p. 175.
6. This point is made by Richards, with regard to the problems of explanation of any riot episode, in Richards (1981).
7. Gould (1964), p. 123.
8. This paragraph is mainly based on three surveys of the sources for evidence of social protest: Wells (1978a), pp. 68-72; Hay (1975a), pp. 262-5; Neeson (1977), pp. 363-71; a personal communication from John Walter; and the brief note in Beloff (1938), p. 70.
9. Brewer and Styles (1980), p. 17.
10. See, for example, Hayter (1978). This excellent account should be followed by similar accounts for other periods.

2 THE GEOGRAPHY OF LAND PROTESTS 1548-1860

2.1 LOWLAND ENGLAND 1520-95

Most participants in the debate on the rise of agrarian capitalism are in agreement that agrarian capitalism made significant advances in lowland England in the sixteenth century. By this they mean that this region saw the appearance of the classic tripartite social structure; landlord — tenant farmer — landless wage labourer, and the concomitant development of a co-operative relationship between landlord and tenant farmer. What is in dispute is how such a social structure and the ending of the feudal antagonism between lord and peasant came about and what social repercussions ensued during the transformation. The two main contributors to the debate are Tawney and Kerridge; the former seeing the transformation being accompanied by clamour and peasant revolts, the latter seeing agrarian capitalism arising silently as the old feudal tenures gave way to the new capitalist doctrine of estates.

Tawney saw the sixteenth century as an increasingly commercial age.[1] In such an age landlords sought to maximise their rent roll by creating large leasehold farms. These large farms were leased to capitalist tenant farmers, men as commercially minded as their landlords. Theirs was a co-operative partnership, for capitalist tenants were guaranteed a reasonable share of the increased revenue from their capital investments and landlords were guaranteed a much higher rent than they could have obtained from their customary tenancies. This all, however, depended on the amalgamation of the latter holdings.

> To carry out this new policy they [the landlords] had to get rid of small tenants. When the tenants held at will, or were lessees for a short term of years, lords could do this without difficulty. When they were copyholders for one life or more, they could do it more slowly; but still they could do it in time. When they were copyholders with an estate of inheritance, lords had only two alternatives — to induce them to accept leases, or to raise the fines for admission.[2]

Thus Tawney gives us a probable sequence of which tenancies would be the first to be engrossed, consolidated and enclosed and which the last. The end product of this process, it should be emphasised, was the large leasehold farm granted on fair terms to a capitalist tenant not liable to be dismissed at a moment's notice. Tawney's capitalist tenant had as his first and most heartfelt need security of property and tenure. Without it he would not have invested in new innovations and improvements.

Kerridge has offered one of the most sustained rebuttals of Tawney's interpretation.[3] It suffers, however, from both personal attacks on Tawney and tendentious misrepresentation of Tawney on certain points. These have tended to blunt the force of Kerridge's arguments. He sees the rise of agrarian capitalism also as a partnership but this time long-term co-operation between the landlord and his tenants is extended to all the tenantry who had security of tenure in law. In this he agrees with Tawney's assessment of the varying degrees of security of tenure except over the question of copyhold of inheritance. Kerridge holds that landlords could not raise the entry fines arbitrarily in order to displace such tenants from their land. The fines had to be 'reasonable'.

With such security of tenure most of the tenantry were able to improve their land and to innovate without fear of imminent eviction or of fines that could be so levied as to cream away all their profits from such improvements and innovations. Given such a secure environment and given that certain farming regions favoured large enterprises, the family farm of the middling peasantry would decline and the capital farm of the enterprising peasant advance simply because of the advantages of the lower working costs of the latter type of farm.[4] The landlord might here and there help the process along particularly with regard to demesne land, land that would usually be in the hands of tenants at will or let on short leases, but that was all.[5] Kerridge thus denies the landlord the key role that Tawney and subsequent historians have accorded him in sixteenth-century agrarian change.

To be fair, Tawney also noted such a process of the small capitalist preparing the way for the great but argued that it was too slow a process of attrition for the degree of alarm, protest and legislation that he saw aroused and produced in the sixteenth century.[6] Kerridge's counter argument is that there were not the numerous cases of customary copyholders being ousted and left without remedy that Tawney would lead us to expect. He sees the alarm of the pamphleteers as exaggerated.[7] Also, he almost completely ignores protests and riots.

The two interpretations would seem irreconcilable. Given Tawney's conditional hypothesis relating the advent of large-scale capitalist agriculture to outbreaks of social protest, it would seem that the geography of land protests could help to resolve the debate. It is, however, paradoxical that the century, for which the debate has raged most fiercely and for which there is considerable knowledge of its agricultural geography, is also one in which our knowledge of land protests is relatively limited. There is a historiographical nescience between the peasant revolts of the late-fourteenth and early-fifteenth century and the Midland Revolt of 1607, only broken by the research of Manning and our knowledge of the crisis years of 1548-52.[8] Even in the case of the latter revolts too much attention has been focused on Kett's rebellion in Norfolk.

The evidence on social protest that can, however, be discerned for the period 1520-1607 is not wholly consistent with either interpretation. First, there appears to be a varying level of social tension in southern, eastern and east

Midland England between 1520 and 1600. Between 1520 and 1554 there was a considerable amount of social discontent; complaints of high entry fines and of the rackrenting of 'covetous' landlords abound; enclosure rioting increased. The culmination of these tensions in rural society was the disturbances of 1548-52. After that crisis what is noteworthy is the lack of tension until the mid-1590s. Secondly, when social discontent again broke to the surface, a new geography of land protests was revealed. The revolts of 1548-52 had been centred in southern and eastern England, the disturbances in the east and west Midlands had been peripheral and muted. The attempted rising of 1596 and the Midland Revolt of 1607 were focused on the clay valelands of the east Midlands. There was no spread of the rioting into southern and eastern England. Indeed from the 1550s onwards, certain farming regions of southern and eastern England were never to see major protests over the issue of land again, not even in the turbulent days of the Civil War. Thirdly, because so much attention is usually accorded to southern, eastern and east Midland England, it needs to be emphasised that throughout the whole period 1520-1607 certain regions in lowland England were relatively quiescent. This suggests that the two theses may be compatible in that they could be two models that fit the evidence best for different time periods and different regional experiences.

Such a synthesis is possible if the revolts of 1548-52 are viewed from a new perspective, that is, they were part of the long struggle of the peasantry against seigneurial power rather than, as Tawney described them, a reaction against agrarian capitalism. What evidence is there for such an interpretation?

It can be argued that between 1520 and 1550 the strategies the lords and the gentry adopted were not in order to clear their properties to make way for the large leashold farmer.[9] Rather they were staging a seigneurial reaction just as the reviving land market put power back into their hands. The tactics employed were adapted to the particular circumstances the lords and the gentry had to deal with in the first half of the sixteenth century: that is, they were confronted with a tenantry that had made gains both tenurially and materially during the fifteenth century. They were no longer dealing with a peasantry mainly composed of bondmen, though numbers of the latter were still far from negligible, particularly on monastic estates.[10] The lords and gentry seem to have adopted two main strategies. First, they moved back into direct farming by using demesne and particularly common pastures for sheep and probably cattle farming.[11] By this means they could both benefit from the profits from pastoral farming at the expense of their tenants and undermine the economic security of their tenants. This tactic was seen in its most extreme form in the foldcourse system of the sheep-corn regions of Norfolk and Suffolk.[12] The second strategy was to increase rents and entry fines, and press their tenurial claims to the full. At times and in certain areas, the lords may even have preferred to turn out the graziers on their favourable leases in order to let out holdings at new rents to their tenantry, now the balance of advantage had shifted back to the lord.[13] As Brenner has argued, they had taken in much of this land in the fifteenth century and leased it to graziers to prevent the tenants converting it into freehold.[14] They had not taken it as a premeditated step towards agrarian capitalism. The strategy of the lords throughout the fifteenth century had been to conserve their tenures for better days.[15] There is no reason to suppose that lords in the early-sixteenth century had changed their attitudes to tenures. They did not grant a general manumission for bondmen when a bill was presented in the House of Lords in 1537.[16] During this period the Duke of Norfolk was using 'muche more extremitie than his Auncestoures did' towards his bondmen.[17] It was not habit that made the lords cling to these most conservative tenures. Thus the lords and gentry were using every opportunity to claw back some of the gains their tenantry had made in the previous 120 years.

The hostility towards the lords and gentry underpins the whole of the 1548-52 crisis. As Manning notes, by 1549 the enclosure riot had become more specifically anti-aristocratic.[18] Deer parks throughout southern and eastern England were attacked (Maps 14 and 15 underestimate these attacks because at times it is difficult to separate out enclosure riots from deer park attacks as both involve hedge breaking). MacCulloch has gone so far as to suggest that Kett's revolt was in part a popular celebration of the fall from power in 1545 of that most conservative aristocrat, the Duke of Norfolk. The bondmen grievance in the Norfolk list of articles, which has for so long been regarded as either anachronistic or a borrowing from the German Peasants' War, was a real grievance against the Howard family's residual seigneurial power. One mark of their conservatism had been the retention of bondmen on their estates.[19] In the atmosphere of renewed and revitalised seigneurial rights in the second quarter of the sixteenth century, the very presence of bondmen amongst freer men could be seen as a warning of a possible future return to such villeinage for all men. One step on the way to this was the buying up of freehold land by the manorial lords in order to convert it into the more insecure copyhold (Norfolk article 21).[20] The peasants feared the revival of the power of the manorial lords particularly the potential for class alliance between the gentry and the lords (Norfolk article 25). In Kent the peasants may have seen the gentry's move to have their lands disgavelled in the same light. It aligned the gentry with the lords and separated them from the customs of the peasant community. Moreover, disgavelling may have been regarded as part of a general attack on peasant rights and customs.[21]

A revival of seigneurial rights and power necessarily entailed a greater inter-ference in village society and economy. Indeed the tenor of the Norfolk list of articles is for a complete withdrawal of the lords and the gentry from village and peasant life. As regards the commons, the lords of the manor were to keep their beasts off them and only freeholders and copyholders were to have the profits from them. In the wood pasture region of East Anglia, where most of the land had long been enclosed, the peasantry feared the lords and gentry enclosing the commons and hence the enclosure attacks there. In the sheep-corn area enclosure was not a threat to the tenants. They wanted a radical curb on the exploitation of the foldcourse system by 'lords knyght esquyer' and 'gentle-man'. Indeed MacCulloch suggested that the ambiguous article on enclosure can possibly be interpreted as achieving the same end, if the word 'saffron' is seen as a scribal error of 'sovereign'. Such 'sovereign', that is, freehold, land once enclosed would act as a defence against the lords' ability to exploit their foldcourse rights.[22] In the case of disgavelling by the Kentish gentry it allowed them to engross land at the expense of the peasantry. Peasants also objected to seigneurial interference in fishing rights (Norfolk article 171). In Kent a similar seigneurial perquisite, an oyster bed, was destroyed.[23] Deer parks were not only attacked as symbols of seigneurial power, since emparkments for pleasure also interfered in the economy of the neighbouring village communities. First, there were the depredations of deer on their crops; secondly, the parks themselves, as even Kerridge admits, drew hostility from country-folk because they took away good farm land from the village.[24]

This, of course, brings us to the question of 'enclosure'. The revolts of 1549 have been seen as a reaction against the early stages of rural capitalism: engrossment, consolidation and enclosure.[25] The hedge breaking incidents scattered across southern and eastern England have been used as the evidence for such a reaction. However, care needs to be taken with both the term 'enclosure' and the incidents themselves. First, there is the question of the enclosure commissions set up by Somerset and said by many to have stimulated the peasant unrest. To the government 'enclosure' was a portmanteau covering a whole range of agrarian issues that concerned them. As Hales pointed out to the Earl of Warwick, 'I mean not here hedging lands but decaying tillage and husbandry'. The commissions were to investigate the latter not the former. They were thus to investigate a wider range of agrarian grievances.[26] It was for that reason that the Kent rebels requested that a commission came to their county, as part of the concessions wrung from the government.[27] Secondly, hedge breaking incidents were not always defensive acts nor always staged to bring to light the enclosing activities of a local lord. They were part of the peasantry's armoury of assertive tactics in their struggle with manorial lords. Hedge breaking and trespass were used to bring legal suits to court.[28] In 1548-52 it is also likely that they were used to draw the government's attention to a particular area. A government that was concerned with the decay of tillage and the unrestrained extension of pastoral farming because of its effect on internal security and the military capacity of the state, could be seen as a useful ally of the peasantry against the oppression of the lords and gentry.

If enclosure *per se* has been overstressed in the troubles of 1548-52, then the repeated calls for lower rents and reasonable fines (Norfolk article 14) have, on the other hand, been ignored. Rackrenting was noted as one of the principal grievances of the Kent rebels and by the Buckinghamshire rebels in 1552. In a 1550 Act, the government had singled out meetings of those who combined to reduce rents[29] — these were the rebels' demands to halt rent exploitation by the lords and gentry. They were probably most vocally articulated by the one group in peasant society most likely to benefit from a lowering of rents and fines: the yeomanry and the enterprising middling peasantry.

Although so far the collective term 'peasantry' has been employed, by the

1540s the communities of southern and eastern England had already undergone a certain degree of internal differentiation. Yet so long as there was the threat of arbitrary action by lords or gentry, the peasantry would close ranks and mobilise for direct collective action. That is why we find the yeomanry and the enterprising middling peasant as leaders of the revolts.[30] They had most to lose from the lords and gentry renewing their active intervention in the village economy, pressing their seigneurial rights to the full, embarking on another campaign of rackrenting. They had made gains before the 1520s; they did not wish to see these taken away. If the lords and the gentry could be beaten back the yeomanry could consolidate their gains and even improve their lot. That is why they were prepared to put themselves at the head of a peasantry from whom they were beginning to grow apart.

An interpretation of the revolts of 1548-52 in southern, eastern and east Midland England as a defence against a seigneurial reaction is also supported by the geography of the protests. First, there is the regional division between the relatively quiescent west and the turbulent south and east. In many areas of the west Midlands manorial lords were weak and were faced with the corresponding strength of numerous freeholders. Moreover, there was much sparsely populated wasteland still to be cleared.[31] Thus the ability of the lords to press their demands were limited.

In other areas of the west Midlands, as Dyer has shown for the Bishop of Worcester's estates, the peasantry, partly through their continued assertiveness in the fifteenth and early-sixteenth centuries, had already successfully challenged the lords' power before the 1540s. The estate hesitated to take full advantage of the revival of the land market from the 1520s. In 1533 one such attempt at new rent exactions was promptly met by a rent strike.[32] Similarly Hatcher's account of the Duchy of Cornwall before 1500 suggests a region where seigneurial power is of less importance, given the existence of such features as a free land market and the constant mobility of tenants between farming and industry. Moreover, Coate notes a traditional assertiveness on the part of the Cornish tenantry in the seventeenth century. Thus it is perhaps clear why the men of the south-west in 1549 were preoccupied with protesting over other issues unrelated to the lords' and gentry's interference in the agrarian economy and the exploitation of seigneurial rights to the full.[33] In southern and eastern England and the east Midlands, the three most completely manorialised regions in England, and on the great estates of Kent and East Anglia, on the other hand, seigneurial power was still extant.[34] Lords there had been in the best position to conserve their seigneurial rights and tenures for the days when the balance of advantage shifted back to them.

Secondly, it seems on reflection paradoxical that the most vehement protests came from Norfolk and Suffolk and Kent, regions that also had the greatest number of freeholders in southern and eastern England, a much greater strength of freeholders than existed in the east Midlands, where the protests were muted and peripheral to the main revolt. This paradox is removed if one remembers that in 1381 and 1450 the peasant revolts were centred in the same regions.

What fuelled all these risings was the contradictory nature of rural society in southern and eastern England: the juxtaposition of powerful lay and ecclesiastical estates with a freer peasantry.[35] The presence of the conservative lords nearby was a reminder that what few seigneurial rights the free peasantry might have to respect were not just irksome, they were potentially threatening. Hence the response of the Norfolk peasantry to the house of Howard and hence the degree of protest when the lords and the gentry seemed to be moving against the free peasantry from the 1520s onwards.

In 1548-52 the peasant assemblages were either dispersed by the granting of concessions or crushed by military force. Indeed most commentators have seen the events of 1548-52 as a defeat for the peasantry. Yet, like 1381, though the battle was lost, the long struggle against the lords and the gentry was won. The continued assertiveness of the peasantry and changed economic circumstances meant that the lords and the gentry backed down from their attack on the peasant community. First, on the issue of security and tenure, as they had done before 1552, the tenantry, particularly the yeomanry, continued to take cases to court. As a result of these cases the courts developed 'principles concerning the admission of copyhold custom in common law courts' and 'what constituted an unreasonable fine'.[36] On the issue of rents the lords seemed to have held off from pressing their demands, for between the late 1550s and the 1570s rents lagged behind prices.[37] It was not in the lords' interest to press the yeomen too far because that would always leave them as the natural leaders of any future peasant revolts. Thirdly, in 1549 there began a 24-year boom in corn prices and in 1550 a contraction in cloth exports.[38] The urge towards increased wool production slackened considerably. This had two results: first, there was a retreat from large-scale sheep farming. In Norfolk, for example, Simpson notes the ending of the growth in the size of flocks. Several flockmasters subsided into rentiers; others reduced the size of flocks or moved to cattle-farming. Friction over the foldcourse subsided in the second half of the sixteenth century.[39] Secondly, lords were more likely to let out land in arable tenancies and, as we have noted, at rents suited to the yeomen.

The peasantry's resolve in the face of the seigneurial reaction between 1520 and 1550, particularly in the 1540s, thus represents a divide for many of the yeomanry and middling peasants of southern and eastern England: were they to hold on to and build on the gains they had made in the fifteenth and early-sixteenth centuries or were they to be pushed back for another century or more to a state of impoverishment such as their counterparts in many areas of continental Western Europe were experiencing? Moreover, it marks a turning point for the peasantry as a whole because once the lords and gentry had been successfully challenged and retreated from direct interference in the village economy, this allowed the yeomen and the more enterprising middling peasant room to expand their holdings and accumulate wealth. Economic circumstances would now begin to sift through the ranks of the middling peasantry. Whilst some would be lucky and prosper to become yeomen, others would be unlucky and fall back to be smallholders or even landless.

In certain regions, such as the sheep-corn areas or those clay vales with good market opportunities for corn, the lower working costs of the larger farm and the greater capital reserves of the more prosperous farmer would ensure the steady growth in the capital farm and the demise of the family farm.[40] The mechanism of accumulation of holdings would be gradual dependent on how and when land of the middling peasant came on the market. Usually the middling peasant gave up his holding or sold off part of it through either failure of heirs, economic misfortune or indebtedness. In particular the farmer on a smaller acreage was more liable to run into financial difficulties as a result of a bad harvest.[41]

As Batho remarks: 'In the early sixteenth century the yeomen were in many counties no more than an "emerging class" . . . their average wealth doubled between the time of Elizabeth and the Civil War.'[42] During the same time span the warp and weft of the old medieval peasant community would be finally unwound only to be woven into a new pattern of social order and control by the new leaders of the village, the successful and prosperous yeomen. The innovations and improvements that constitute Kerridge's sixteenth-century agricultural revolution were henceforth increasingly adopted without fear that their increased profits would be siphoned off by lords and gentry in rent exploitation.[43] Agrarian capitalism with its increasingly polarised social order was from then on brought forward silently over most of southern and eastern England.

Thus Kerridge is correct in his interpretation of a quiescent agrarian capitalistic development but only for the second half of the sixteenth century. It would seem that Tawney's original equation of the rise of the great capitalist estate and outbreaks of social protest needs modification. The protests of 1548-52 were not a reaction to the rise of agrarian capitalism, quite the reverse. As Kerridge rightly points out, Tawney's sixteenth century with its 'nagging fear of sudden confiscation' and 'unjust expropriations' was 'the face of rural society before the advent of agrarian capitalism'.[44]

Notes

1. Tawney (1912).
2. Ibid., p. 310.
3. Kerridge (1969).
4. Kerridge (1951), ch. 9.
5. Kerridge (1969), p. 90.
6. Tawney (1912), pp. 178-9.
7. Kerridge (1969), p. 92, ch. 6.
8. See Manning (1974), pp. 120-33 and (1977), pp. 18-40. (Professor Manning is now researching the period 1550-1607). Martin's study of peasant struggles does not add much to our knowledge of the incidence of sixteenth-century protest, as it is based on already published material, see Martin (1979), ch. 11.
9. Blanchard notes the lack of eviction during this period. Blanchard (1970), p. 438n1.
10. Kerridge (1969), p. 90.
11. Bush (1975), p. 59n107.
12. Allison (1957), pp. 22-3, 28-30.

13. See Blanchard's arguments on this question. Blanchard (1970), pp.436-41; cf. Bush (1975), p. 59n107.
14. Brenner (1976), pp. 61-2.
15. Searle (1974), pp. 368-75.
16. Kerridge (1969), p. 91.
17. Quoted in MacCulloch (1979), p. 56.
18. Manning (1974), p. 38.
19. MacCulloch (1979), p. 55.
20. The list of articles is printed in Russell (1859), pp. 48-56.
21. Clark (1977), p. 424n39.
22. The above is based on MacCulloch (1979), pp. 36-59.
23. Clark (1977), p. 79.
24. Kerridge (1969), p. 102.
25. Tawney (1912); Bindoff (1949).
26. Bush (1975), pp. 44-5.
27. Clark (1977), p. 79.
28. Blanchard (1970), p. 440; Kerridge (1969), p. 82.
29. Clark (1977), p. 80; Strype (1822), Anno 1552 1-2; Blanchard (1970), p. 441.
30. Davies (1969), pp. 43-4. I would like to thank Dr Davies for allowing me to see the English original transcript of this article. Tawney (1912), pp. 326, 331. For the yeoman as protagonist in Tudor rural society, see Campbell (1942), and as leader of the rest of the peasantry, ibid., pp. 141-2.
31. Thirsk (1967), p. 107; Hey (1974), pp. 8-10.
32. Dyer (1977), ch. 12. This was written before Dr Dyer's book based on his doctoral thesis was available: Dyer (1980).
33. Hatcher (1970), ch. 9; Coate (1928), pp. 150-1. Dodgshon has noted the greater degree of personal freedom and the presence of freer non-customary economic relationships in the peripheral areas of southern Britain: Dodgshon (1978).
34. For a description of the geography of feudal England, see Martin (1979), pp. 132-7.
35. See comparable arguments for the revolts of 1381 in Hilton (1973), ch. 6 and in Martin (1979), ch. 6. Unfortunately, there is no fully researched and published account of the rising of 1450.
36. Croot and Parker (1978), p. 40. This article in particular has helped to shape a number of my ideas on the importance of the yeomanry in agrarian development. Kerridge (1969), p. 39; Tawney (1912), p. 296n3; Campbell (1942), pp. 135-6, 141-2, 366-8.
37. I. Blanchard, personal communication.
38. Bowden (1967), p. 635; Beresford and Hurst (1971), p. 19.
39. Simpson (1958), p. 92.
40. Kerridge (1951), ch. 9; Bowden (1967), pp. 650-8; Spufford (1974), pp. 50-3, 165; Wrightson and Levine (1979), pp. 20-1, 24-31.
41. Spufford (1974), pp. 76-85, 90-2.
42. Batho (1967), p. 305.
43. Kerridge (1967); Blanchard (1970), p. 440n8.
44. Kerridge (1969), pp. 92, 93.

2.2 LOWLAND ENGLAND 1596-1710

In sharp contrast to the quiescence of the previous 40 years, this period was the most disturbed for protests over the issue of land for lowland England. Indeed one could argue that the seventeenth century is Tawney's real century. Here was his archetypal landlord, with his falling income, seeing his salvation in promoting capitalist agriculture, sweeping away his tenantry to make way for the large leasehold farm and in so doing meeting with fierce opposition. Even so this statement needs to be qualified. Landlords only employed this strategy in those areas where agrarian capitalism was not already developing. There agrarian capitalism continued its silent progress. Two further qualifications also need to be made. Violent opposition was not always encountered when the tenantry were evicted. Secondly, it was not always the legal tenantry who opposed tenurial and agrarian change; often it was the commoners with no legal right to pasturage and the landless who put up the sternest resistance.

The landlords, including the Crown, set about their clearances of small farmers and commoners in four major farming regions: the clay vales of the Midlands, the lowlands of north-east England, the fenland and the royal forests. This was, however, part of the landlords' overall re-evaluation of their properties, commenced in the 1580s, to safeguard themselves against inflation. This entailed a marked rise in rents and entry fines; a general reduction in the length of leases, especially in the south and east where the demand for land was greatest; and a closer scrutiny of land titles as more scientific methods of surveying of estates were adopted. Rent rolls on estate after estate doubled, trebled and quadrupled in a matter of decades.[1] The prosperous yeomanry of southern and eastern England were, thus, not exempted from such treatment. Yet this time there was no violent reaction, as there had been in 1548-52, for by the end of the six-teenth century the yeomanry could withstand such rent increases because of the productivity changes, the result of a half century of uninterrupted agricultural improvement and innovation.[2] The end product of the agrarian and social revolution that the tenantry in southern and eastern England had undergone was the ability of the yeomanry to pay commercial rents for their property. Any attempt by the landlords to take more than their fair share of these profits would now mean that the yeoman would no longer invest to gain greater pro-ductivity and hence profits would be lowered. This would then entail a decline in rent for the landlord. The interest of the landlord and tenant were now consistent: co-operation meant that both gained.[3] Thus, one longstanding antagonism had been removed from rural society by the assertiveness of the yeomanry class throughout the sixteenth century. How were new antagonisms averted in the divided village community of yeomanry and commoners and landless labourers? The quiescence of these communities was only partly a question of the gradualism of the expansion of agrarian capitalism.

This antagonism was driven underground by the nature of the new order of village society. The first process by which this was achieved related to the labour force and its organisation on the capital farm, where the labour force was reduced, particularly if up-and-down husbandry was adopted. The excess labour force migrated to other areas of the county where there was industry or labour-intensive agriculture; the labour force that remained was often housed as farm servants on the farm and under the farmer's paternalistic eye (see p. 132).[4] The second process relates to changes in the village itself. The emergence of the yeomanry as the leading members of village society, 'the better sort', has been documented by Wrightson and Levine. By the second decade of the seventeenth century, in Terling in Essex, there was a 'quite conscious attempt by the leaders of the parish to impose upon the community a social discipline that would preserve social stability, while at the same time bringing the comportment of the villagers more firmly into conformity with their own novel conceptions or order and reformation'. Through the poor law, the attack on alehouses, the quarter sessions and the church courts this was achieved — the poor were made to be deserving and orderly. The hierarchical paternalism of social control was gradually stamped upon the villages of lowland England,[5] and the remarkable success of these changes was shown by the events of the Civil War. The political turmoil and the breakdown of authority would seem the ideal time for the landless and cottagers to seize land but there were no major peasant revolts in the sheep-corn and clay vales of eastern England. Only where such an ordered society had failed to be established by 1642 could men take advantage of the times.

Why then had agrarian capitalism and its attendant hierarchical society not evolved 'naturally' in the regions where the landlords had to go over the heads of their tenants to bring about agrarian and tenurial change? In Northumberland the development of a prosperous agricultural base had been checked by border raiding and the troubles of 1536 and 1569. In the long peace after 1569 there had also been the division of tenements into uneconomic smallholdings under the pressure of population increase and with the landlord's blessing. More tenants were then thought to mean an increasing rent-roll, but such rent exploitation resulted in progressive impoverishment. Climatically Northumberland was not suited to large-scale corn production; indeed, the county was not self-supporting in corn and had to be supplied from Yorkshire and East Anglia. Thus in Northumberland before the 1590s there had been no real development of capitalist agriculture or of a differentiated tenantry.[6]

In the second region, the clay lands of the Midlands, the distance from a large city with its attendant demand for corn and the suitability of clayland for mixed rather than sheep-corn husbandry had ensured that the freehold communities in the region would preserve their equitable social structures. The open parishes on even poorer soils had extensive and fragmented freehold. Unlike the tenantry of the Northumberland lowlands, these communities had been under threat of enclosure throughout the fifteenth and sixteenth centuries. They had not been enclosed by 1607 because, in the case of the prosperous freehold communities, they had been able to resist such attempts and, in the case of the open parishes, they had proved unattractive to a potential encloser because of the dispersed nature of their holdings and the poor quality of their soils.[7] In the third and fourth regions the fen country and the forests, weak manorial control, the unstinted rights to commonland and the varied natural resources of such environments all helped to sustain the small peasant farmer, the cottager and the artisan and in increasing numbers in the sixteenth and early-seventeenth centuries. The fenland in particular saw an extreme fragmentation of the medieval tenements. In the forests the growth of population tended to be based on the use of commons often without any legal rights to such usage.[8] The populations of all four regions would seem to have had a stake in the future continuance of their communities in their present state. One therefore might have expected resistance in all these areas; yet in the north-east there was no resistance to their landlords' action. A comparison of the north-east and the Midlands may help to explain why this was so.

Perhaps the crucial difference concerns the very nature of the two rural societies: the potential mix of communities who could have protested over the enclosures. In the Midlands the protestors were drawn from an alliance of different rural communities and town artisans. The freeholders, who partici-pated in the riots, unlike the tenants-at-will of Northumberland, could not be dismissed from their land at short notice as punishment for having taken part in the disturbances. Protestors in the Midlands also came from the open parishes and the adjacent forest areas, neither of which type of community occurred in Northumberland. The different agrarian regime in Northumberland meant that the town artisans of Newcastle were less affected by the enclosures and conver-sion to pasture in terms of employment and grain supplies than their counterparts in Leicester, Coventry and Northampton. Thirdly, there was the servility of the Northumberland peasantry that had prevented the emergence of any tradition of class conflict between lords and tenants. Even when the royal policy had been to protect northern tenants from the rent exploitation of their lords, the tenantry of Northumberland had failed to call on the Crown's support.[9] The threat of border raids and warfare and the charisma of the Earl of Northumberland may have preserved the ideology of servile dependence much longer than one would expect. The peasantry of County Durham, just that further removed from the border, were much more assertive (see pp. 21-2). In the Midlands the freehold communities owed their very survival to successful conflicts first with manorial lords and later potential enclosers. The men of the open parishes and the forests and town artisans were part of the 'ungovernable multitudes' the Tudor and Stuart authorities feared as potential sources of disorder within society. Thus the nature of Northumberland rural society and the class relations within that society militated against a violent reaction to the evictions and enclosures.

Some historians have pointed to certain communal organisations as the crucial element in the mobilisation of the fen and forest men to direct collective action, for example, in the fens, the court of sewers.[10] These organisations were not as crucial, however, as the fact that the protestors were 'masterless men'.

One region that can pertinently be compared on this point with the fenland was the marshland. As Thirsk points out, the similarities between the two regions was striking. The marshlands were ill-drained lowlands with large areas of common grazing, although not as extensive as in the true fen. The cottagers grew hemp and further supplemented their income from fishing and fowling. Indeed in the sixteenth-century Lincolnshire marshlands the peasantry were the most prosperous in the whole county. There, however, the similarities cease. The class composition of the marshland villages differed markedly from the smallholder settlements of the fen. The farms of the marshland were larger and the villages had their gentry, squires and rich yeomen. The social polarisation increased in Lincolnshire in the seventeenth century as the native manorial lords and rich yeomen are thought to have increased the size of their holdings and as rich upland farmers began the process of integrating the marshland grazings into their own agrarian economy. As a consequence the prosperous peasant of the sixteenth century became the poorest in the county by the end of the seventeenth century. Capitalist farmers had found a use for the marshland without totally draining the region and converting it to arable.

The gradualism of the takeover of the commons and grazings and the polarised social structure of the marshland communities mitigated against outbreaks of overt protest. If, however, the Crown had pressed its claims to the coastal marshlands, as it had done with the salt marshes of the Wash, it may have been for a time a different story. The resistance of the marshmen to one such grant at North Somercotes, however, shows that it would not have been impossible. For unlike the fens of Lincolnshire, the owner of North Somercotes was only dis-possessed during the Civil War and soon had his land returned once the turmoils were over. The marshmen were not able to offer such a strength of resistance as the fenmen because of the more ordered nature of their society.[11]

Secondly, Sharp has shown that the forest rioters were in the main those on the very margins of society, the virtually landless artisans and cottagers, engaged almost full time in either the cloth or forest industries or trades.[12] They were not small peasant farmers engaged in industrial by-employments who were led by or allied to their social betters in the protests over disafforestation.[13] Such a Mousnier view, the disturbances involving the whole of the forest community and led by men of social standing, leads one to look for formal, respectable organisations to provide the springboard for the mobilisation of the forest people such as the manorial courts and arrangements for cattle drives. This is now unnecessary. The protests were planned by the 'common sort', those who the authorities at the time and certain historians have thought were 'too brutish to organize themselves into a coherent and well-directed movement'.[14]

Notes

1. Bowden (1967), p. 690; Batho (1967), p. 304.
2. Blanchard (1970), p. 435n7. I would like to thank Dr Blanchard for amplification of this point. Kerridge (1967), particularly for 'up-and-down husbandry', p. 194.
3. Batho (1967), pp. 304, 305.
4. Kerridge (1969), pp. 121, 124, 130-1.
5. Wrightson and Levine (1979), p. 137, ch. 7.
6. Butlin (1967), p. 149; Newton (1974), pp. 9, 23; Kerridge (1969), p. 59.
7. Martin (1979), ch. 17.
8. See relevant sections in Thirsk (1967).
9. Kerridge (1969), p. 59.
10. Thirsk (1967), pp. 39-40.
11. Ibid., pp. 35-6; Thirsk (1957), ch. 6.
12. Sharp (1980), chs. 4-8, 10.
13. Everitt (1967), pp. 396-465, especially p. 407; Allan (1952), pp. 76-85; Kerridge (1958-9), pp. 64-75.
14. Sharp (1980), p. 269.

2.3 UPLAND ENGLAND 1520-1650

The history of lord-tenant relations and of protests over land arising out of that relationship in upland England diverged from that of the lowlands during this period primarily because much of the region before 1603 was Border country, subject to Scottish raids and intermittently the scene of national conflict. Yet such is the size of the region that lands at a distance from the Border were less troubled by such insecurity and rural society there had less of a militaristic appearance. The Northumbrians had the longest common boundary with Scotland. As has been noted, the military feudalism this situation bred meant that the tenants were the most servile of the upland people. In the Lake District and County Durham, more secure from Border raids, the tenantry were, on the one hand, less reliant on the protection of their lord. On the other hand, the temptation for rent exploitation on the part of the lords was greater. Thus lord-tenant conflict would break to the surface at times, as in 1536-7 during the turmoil of the Pilgrimage of Grace. In County Durham in the 1570s and 1580s the Dean and Chapter of Durham Cathedral had tried to overturn the custom of their tenants, on the second occasion challenging the validity of tenant right in Weardale. They were met by staunch resistance from their tenants. The Council in the North were sympathetic to the tenants' case and found in their favour: ever since the Pilgrimage of Grace the Council had feared the effect of disaffection between lord and tenant on border defence. Moreover, they feared that rent exploitation would prevent peasants from equipping themselves for Border service.[1] This attitude prevailed until the Union of Crowns in 1603. Indeed Appleby notes, and all his examples come from after 1537, that in the Lake District when enclosing the waste the lords sought to co-operate with their more substantial tenants. They did this by, for example, leasing the wastes to the latter who then could sublet the enclosures to the landless. Thus the more substantial tenants shared in the benefits of enclosing the wastes and hence strengthened the loyalty and service between the lord and his followers.[2]

After 1603, however, the tendency to see men as entries on a rent roll predominated: co-operation between lord and tenant was no longer necessary. As Appleby points out, one might have expected that this would have been the moment for the lords in Cumberland and Westmorland to evict their tenants to make way for large pasture farms, as landlords had done in lowland Northumberland. They did not, however, because unlike the landowners near the Tyne valley, they had no nearby booming market for pastoral products. The whole of the Lake District, both upland and lowland, was relatively isolated from the major sheep and cattlemarkets, particularly since the decline of the woollen industry from the mid-sixteenth century. Thus the protests that were to follow the landlords' change of attitude to their tenantry were not because they attempted to bring in agrarian capitalism rather it was because they pressed their rent exploitation to the full. This was the basis for their attempt to undermine the favourable tenure of tenant right both in the Lake District and in Weardale in upland County Durham and in the manors of Wark and Harbottle in upland west Northumberland. They were part of a seigneurial reaction and led to a resistance to defend their tenures by most of the tenantry.[3]

Historians have been somewhat cavalier in their use of the term 'tenant right'. As Watts pointed out, only certain manors in the northern counties had authentic tenant right. Thus the limited number of collective protests is partly explained. Even so not all these manors saw 'tumultuous meetings' and 'combinations'. The manors of Wark and Harbottle in western Northumberland only saw passive resistance to the tenurial changes. There were probably three reasons for this surprising difference, surprising because the 'surnames' of Northumberland, like the analogous Scottish clans, seem an ideal community from which resistance should spring. First, as Watts notes, the tenants of Tynedale and Redesdale were miserably poor — a mass protest where a common purse was formed to buy the best lawyers was hardly an option open to them. It was, however, open to the wealthier tenantry of the Lake District and Weardale. Secondly, the degree of organisation in the Lake District and Weardale campaigns, the petitions, the signing of collective undertakings, the common purse, to which in Weardale £80 was subscribed all this suggests that the leaders did know upon what sure ground they stood as regards their customary tenures. Indeed, in Weardale, as just noted, they had only fought for recognition of their customary tenures some 40 years before. In west Northumberland the tenantry had no valid documentary evidence, the lack of which and the poorly kept court rolls in these manors may point to the most major difference between the two types of tenantry.[4]

The 'riding surnames' of Redesdale and Tynedale were still fighting units raiding and being raided across the Border. They had little use for such niceties of legal status because of the nature of their 'clan' society, which was still firmly based on ties of kinship and personal obligation, on true reciprocal bonds of protection and service.[5] Moreover, this clan society, like the Scottish Highland clans in the late-eighteenth and early-nineteenth centuries, had little experience of conflict with their landlords. In the Lake District and Durham the tenant right conflict was but part of a longer struggle between lord and tenant. This conclusion is important because communities of kinsmen have seemed to have an equal facility for mobilisation against a Scottish raiding party as for mobilisation against their lord's attempts to overthrow their 'custom'.[6]

Notes

1. Appleby (1975a), p. 583; James (1974), pp. 83-4.
2. Appleby (1975b), pp. 20-4.
3. Appleby (1975a), pp. 593-4; James (1974), pp. 69, 73; Appleby (1978), p. 186.
4. Watts (1971), pp. 64-87; James (1974), pp. 84-5.
5. Newton (1974), pp. 7, 9-10.
6. James (1974), p. 25.

2.4 WALES, SCOTLAND AND UPLAND ENGLAND 1650-1860

In the eighteenth century, the centre of gravity of the spatial distribution of land disturbances moved decidedly to the peripheral areas of Britain; to southern Scotland in the early part of the century and to Wales and northern Scotland in the latter part of the century. There were two reasons for this. First, the expansion of large-scale pastoral farming into the periphery required in certain regions the clearance of the tenantry. Secondly, there was a desire on the part of landowners to secure their property rights in upland wastes and commons. Yet not all pastoral capitalist agriculture required the clearance of the tenantry, nor were all upland wastes and commons the scene of disturbances. To understand more clearly the geography of land protests in the eighteenth and nineteenth centuries, therefore, it is necessary to compare those regions that did see rioting with areas that did not, but which experienced similar agrarian transformations.

In the lowlands of Galloway on the western borders of Scotland, the Levellers' Revolt of 1724 was a protest against enclosure and eviction. In the lowlands of the eastern borders there was very little overt protest against enclosure. How can these differences be explained? The key seems to lie in the nature of the contrasting developments of the dominant agrarian economies of the two regions.[1] The region of Galloway, being remote from any sizeable sources of demand for corn, had a largely undifferentiated tenantry who 'lived chiefly by tending the flocks of their more wealthy countrymen or by cultivating . . . small runrigg farms'.[2] This tenantry had not the capital to develop large-scale cattle ranching and so they had to be cleared to allow the landowners to farm directly. In the east, estate owners found it more profitable to be involved in the grain trade of the east coast rather than in pastoral farming. To do this they had three alternatives. First, they could emulate their counterparts in Eastern Europe, enserf their tenantry and practice direct grain production. The landowners, however, had long ago lost the political power to do this. Secondly, they could evict the tenantry and directly farm their estates for grain production using wage labourers and bailiffs as farm managers. Thirdly, they could co-operate with their tenantry and allow the latter to prosper for the price of increased fermes or grain rents paid to them.[3] The latter outcome is what seems to have happened which suggests that the tenantry were powerful enough to rebuff any attempts at the second alternative. This also meant that to reap the economies of scale of grain production farm sizes had to be increased. But this was done gradually and probably matched the increasing economic differentiation of the tenants.[4] The policy of co-operation between landlord and tenant, and also of gradual reduction in tenant numbers, was not only confined to the lowland Border country of the east it was also found in the upland pastoral areas. Why the policy was continued into these upland areas is not clear. It did mean, however, that when after 1750 large-scale sheep farming with its extensive sheep walks, similar to that which was to spread through the Scottish Highlands, came to the region it was accepted with hardly a murmur.[5]

In other upland regions the reasons for the reduction of tenants and the gradual engrossment of farms is clearer, as is the lessened impact on rural communities of the development of pastoral farming and the enclosure of the upland wastes. This can be most clearly illustrated if we examine the Lake District, a region whose economic development before 1650 was briefly considered in the previous section. After 1650 there were two important changes in the economy of the Lake District. First, like Galloway, the increasing demand for meat and livestock products meant that both Cumberland and Westmorland were also drawn into the national agricultural supply area. Cattle producers in the latter counties had, moreover, the comparative advantages over their counterparts in Galloway of being closer to the market and being this side of the Border thus avoiding tolls and custom dues. Yet there were no clearances in the Lake District to make way for the obvious increase in cattle production in that region. This was partly related to the securer tenure of the men of the Lake District; all Scottish tenants being tenants-at-will. More importantly, however, was the second important and contemporaneous economic change in the region: industrial and commercial development. As Appleby notes,

> by 1650 mining had expanded to the point where it provided by-employment for many smallholders. At about the same time trade with Ireland began to flourish and prompted a rapid growth in shipping along the west coast of Cumberland.

Appleby then links these changes to the reduction in the number of customary tenants that then began.

> A tenant could, if the lord demanded an excessive fine, now walk away from his customary holding and still find a living within the region.

Such an opportunity was not open to the tenantry of Galloway but was perhaps more open to the tenantry of eastern Borders with the developing east coastal trade. Moreover, as tenants left, the landlords had an easier task to engross their holdings. Thus industrial and commercial development in a region aided the gradual transformation of its agrarian structure and hence ensured that even pastoral agriculture could be introduced silently and without much overt clamour.[6]

This factor may also account partially for the quiescence of the southern Scottish Highlands and the eastern parts of south Wales in the eighteenth and early-nineteenth centuries. The expansion of nearby industrial areas required a steady stream of labour; tenants 'voting with their feet' provided such a supply. In the Lake District the link between industrial and agrarian change was even more intimate in that a number of the industrial capitalists, men like Sir John Lowther, were also 'improving' landlords. They were probably quite prepared to let agrarian change take its natural course for this very reason. In the southern Scottish Highlands the gradual nature of changes in tenurial arrangements was also related to the equally gradual transformation of the clan chiefs of that region into private property-owning landlords, as irrevocably such chiefs as

Campbell (Argyll) and Gordon (Huntley) became economically and socially linked to the increasingly-capitalist lowlands.[7] Such changes not only blunted their impact by their gradualism they also served to undermine the solidarity of communities themselves. Even when large-scale enclosures and clearances took place in these regions, as they did, the communities affected were weakened already by the loss of families through permanent migration both in terms of numbers who were left to resist and the fact that permanent migration was an accepted part of the community's life. Complaints of the hardships to commoners were made but no overt collective resistance occurred.[8]

In contrast, in the northern Scottish Highlands and in the western parts of Wales, the livelihood and whole way of life of communities was taken away and changed abruptly by clearance or enclosure for sheep farming or for capitalist slate quarrying. The profound transformation of the clan chiefs of the northern Scottish Highlands to private landlords only came in the post-1745 period so helping to pre-empt any slow agrarian change from communal agriculture to capitalist sheep farming. Thus the tenants or commoners had to migrate permanently, either to newly constructed settlements nearby or out of the area or emigrate. Or they had to become a virtually landless wage proletariat almost within the span of the passing of the enclosure act. Which of these stark and new alternatives they 'chose' was most often determined for them by the plans of their landlords. To such plans the tenantry offered collective resistance: this was the real basis of their direct collective actions.

This was even true in the northern Scottish Highlands. The traditional view of the clearances had been that they were passively accepted because of the tribal nature of clan society. There was no tradition of antagonism or conflict between clansmen and chief. This indeed did reduce the level of protests over clearance but the passivity can be exaggerated, as Richards has argued and as the comparative evidence reveals. There was more *concerted* resistance in the northern Highlands than in England during the period 1780-1831. Indeed it is the scattered protests on the west coast and the islands in the period 1835-54 that has tended to exaggerate the initial inability of the clansmen to oppose their chief-turned-landlord, because in that same region in the 1880s a most determined and aggressive opposition by the crofters was launched. It would seem that equally important in reducing the level of overt conflict in the period 1830-60 were the problems of isolation and inaccessibility of communities in the west. In the earlier period one should not underestimate the ability of the clansmen to take direct collective action when there were contacts between different areas and with the regions not dominated by clan society such as the lowlands of Easter Ross. Moreover, in terms of the ability of the authorities to contain such protests by police or troops, the east coast was much easier policed than the isolated parts of the west and one might have expected as a consequence less collective protest.[9]

Notes

1. The contrast between the two areas is noted by Whyte (1979), pp. 160-1.
2. Quoted in Leopold (1980), p. 13.
3. Whyte (1978).
4. Whyte (1979), pp. 141-52.
5. Dodgshon (1976), pp. 557-9.
6. Appleby (1975), p. 594, (1978), ch. 11.
7. Geddes (1979), p. 12.
8. For the enclosure of upland wastes in the Lake District, see Bouch and Jones (1961), pp. 231-9; for clearances in southern Scottish Highlands, see McNair (1973), pp. 11-13. David Jones notes the lack of protest over the 'disastrous' enclosure of the Great Forest of Brecknockshire in 1816; see Jones (1973), p. 48.
9. Richards (1974), ch. 2; Hunter (1976), ch. 6.

2.5 LOWLAND ENGLAND 1710-1860

The prominence of the disturbances on the periphery of Britain was partly a reflection of the demise of collective protests in those areas of lowland England that had been the scene of such determined resistance before 1710: the forests and fens. This was because, in the first place, the improvers of certain fens and forests and the great gentry of the forests of southern England had learnt their lesson and had retreated from their grandiose plans. In the case of agricultural improvement, the depressed state of agriculture before 1750 convinced them that they had taken the right decision. Secondly, drainage and enclosure had gone ahead and an ordered agrarian society had begun to be established, as in a number of the forests of Wiltshire, Dorset and Somerset and in the southern fenland. Thirdly, when the improvers did return in the latter half of the eighteenth century, many of the communities that had formerly resisted such changes were so changed that no protests, comparable either to those of the seventeenth and early-eighteenth centuries or to those contemporaneous ones on the periphery of Britain, could be mounted.

In the Somerset Levels, for example, there appears to have been an increasing split of interest between the poorest commoners and the small to middling farmers. The latter group now found the problems of overstocking by their more prosperous neighbours outweighed the advantage of their own right to common and wished for a small, drained allotment. Moreover, in the coastal parishes there had grown up a group of graziers and dairy farmers, increasingly wealthy, who also could see the advantage of draining the moors. Thus social and economic differentiation was fragmenting the solidarity of the community of moormen that had so unitedly opposed drainage throughout the seventeenth century. Furthermore, the poor, the 'owners of Geese' were increasingly looked on as an 'inferior class', work shy, drunken, sheep stealers, on the one hand a threat to their richer neighbours and, on the other, a potential labour force if their independence, the right to common, could be taken away from them. Drainage and enclosure could achieve that result. Such agrarian class control appealed to many above the rank of the poor in the fens as it did increasingly to many in the remaining forested areas.[1]

In the forests of Berkshire and Hampshire, for example, there were two changes to the forest community that separated the poor from the rest of society. First, the great gentry like the Duke of St Albans realised that their revival of forest law antagonised not only the 'loose idle people' but also the substantial farmers, professional men and even some of the small gentry. If the former group were to be controlled, then the latter groups must be won over to the side of the great gentry. As Thompson notes, the Duke of St Albans as Lord Warden, Constable and Governor of Windsor Forest 'allowed capital, supplemented by interest and influence, and supported where necessary by the Justices of the Peace, to work out its "natural" way'. Thus the lesser gentry and the farmers prospered and became allies of the great gentry. Secondly, the alliance was probably more firmly cemented by the aftermath of the Black Act disturbances. The campaign of covert terror and counter-terror that broke out between the keepers and the poorer commoners probably caused the gentry and farmers to feel threatened by such anarchy. The growing numbers of 'loose idle people', the bloody battles with keepers, their poaching, wood stealing and trespass, now seen as crimes by all except that group, all ensured both great and small gentry's and farmers' commitment to enclosure. The lawless foresters 'could then be brought together' from their dispersed habitations to 'collected villages, each with a constable on patrol'.[2]

The areas of lowland England that had been largely untouched by social protest since the 1550s maintained that air of tranquility as far as the issue of land was concerned throughout the eighteenth and nineteenth centuries. The yeomanry's control of village life gave way to the closed parish of the large landlord and the large tenant farmer. Agrarian change followed the same natural progression of increasing economies of scale and related advances in technology leading to increasing farm size and gradual tenant reduction. The leasing system was ideally matched for such a pattern of change.

In the pastoral areas of the west Midlands, an even more radical but equally steady transformation of the rural landscape was undertaken by landlords with little recorded clamour from their tenants. As Hey notes, in Cheshire and Shropshire in the seventeenth century the stable core of their rural communities had been prosperous peasant families with ten to 50 acres and generous common rights. The most common form of tenure by which these farms were held, was leases for three lives. In the mid- and late-eighteenth century landlords did not renew the leases as they fell in but converted them to tenancies at will. The small farms were engrossed into farm units of between 300-400 acres. In some places there was the introduction of a mixed husbandry system, whilst predominantly in Shropshire there was conversion to arable farming. The displaced peasantry were partly absorbed into the expanded labour force, for corn production and dairying continued to require a large labour input of farm servants rather than family labour.[3] Partly, as Kerridge notes, the displaced tenants moved to expanding industries in the same county.[4] 'By the nineteenth century the farming communities of Cheshire and Shropshire were [thus] divided sharply between the rich and the poor, with comparatively few of the middling peasants.'[5]

The one issue that *a priori* might have given rise to protest and opposition in lowland England was of course parliamentary enclosure of the open fields. As Turner has recently shown, in terms of density of open field parishes enclosed by this method the areas on which parliamentary enclosure was focused were the east and central Midlands.[6] As has often been noted, non-socialist historians have argued that the enclosures were carried through with little or no protest or opposition. Yet the evidence that Neeson will present below for Northamptonshire between 1760 and 1800 suggests a different picture, particularly in those communities of industrial outworkers that had developed in the open and freehold parishes of the region from the seventeenth century onwards.

This may suggest one important point on which to conclude. If direct collective action over the issue of enclosure in the countryside of lowland England, outside forest and fen areas, rested in the hands of industrial workers, then the occurrence and demise of land protests in the eighteenth and nineteenth centuries will be intimately linked to the destinies of those rural industrial communities. First, as spatial concentration of industrial capital took place, the industries of the countryside began to decline so robbing the countryside of its 'shock troops'. Secondly, if enclosure was successful and the industrial workers were robbed of that part of their independence provided by access to common, they were then more likely to turn their attention to more immediate issues of maintaining wage levels and resisting mechanisation rather than agitating for the land to be returned to them. This was particularly so as industrial change was also turning them into a wage proletariat. Mobilisation had to be to resist the onslaughts of sweated labour and drastic wage cutting as technological competition and the cyclical fluctuations of capitalism began to dominate their industries.

Thus land in England after 1800 became less of a contentious issue not just because of the power of the enclosers, that had been there earlier, but also because the communities that had opposed enclosure had been transformed into industrial and agricultural proletariats. Only in certain forest areas such as the New Forest did the communities and thus the ability to resist changes to their economy survive, as witnessed by the legal campaign against afforestation successfully waged by the New Forest commoners in the 1860s.[7]

Notes

1. Williams (1970), pp. 124, 126-7, 170-1.
2. Thompson (1975), pp. 225, 237-9.
3. Hey (1979); Hey (1974), p. 11.
4. Kerridge (1969), pp. 131-3.
5. Hey (1979).
6. Turner (1980), pp. 53-5, 58-60.
7. Tubbs (1965), pp. 23-39.

2.6 1548-52

The open conflicts of 1548-52 were popular manifestations of the underlying tensions in the economy of mid-Tudor England, brought to a head at this time by the policies of the Protector Somerset. It was those policies that were one common factor in what was otherwise a rather disparate set of revolts.[1]

The first agrarian disturbances were a scattering of enclosure riots in 1548, most of which followed in the wake of the June proclamation condemning enclosures and depopulation and appointing enclosure commissions to investigate breaches of the law about decay of tillage and conversion.[2] The protests were renewed in the spring of 1549. In April, the Privy Council had reports of peasant disturbances in the Midlands, the West Country and the south-east once more. These were minor affairs, however. The first major series of rioting began at Frome in Somerset in the second week of May. The authorities attempted to stifle the protest by appearing first to be sympathetic to the men's grievances and then arresting those chosen to present the list of grievances to Lord Stourton. This duplicity on the part of the authorities led instead to a wave of unlawful assemblies and rioting all over Somerset and Wiltshire. The disturbances had, however, already spread to Hampshire by 20 May. Kent seems to have seen rioting even earlier. Also during May, a minor series of disturbances appear to have spread through the west Midland counties of Gloucestershire, Worcestershire and Staffordshire. By the end of May, the far west of Suffolk saw the only trouble in that county during the first series of disturbances in 1549. Similarly, on 20 June there occurred an isolated incident of fence breaking at Wilby, near Attleborough in Norfolk. The troubles seemed to be coming to an end.

In the second week of July, however, rioting and assemblies erupted throughout East Anglia. July and August 1549 became known as the 'campying tyme'. Camps were set up in Kent again and for the first time in the Thames Valley in the counties of Oxfordshire and Buckinghamshire. Protests flared up again in Hampshire, but in Yorkshire for the first time. In August, rioting broke out in Leicestershire and Rutlandshire. These were short lived, owing to the actions of the counties' noblemen and the Privy Council. Similar action in the north Midlands by the Earl of Shrewsbury meant that order was maintained throughout this period.

Because of the scarcity of military resources, with troops being tied up in Scotland and in the West Country, large-scale military operations were often impractical. Thus concessions had to be granted to the rebels. These were usually presented to the camps by a privy councillor with a show of military force. In the case of the East Anglian rebels a similar procedure should have been followed, as indeed it was in Suffolk. However, at the Norwich camp the Marquis of Northampton disobeyed his orders on his arrival. Consequently, the king's pardon was never offered and a battle ensued with Northampton's troops being routed. The government were thus committed to a major military operation against the Norwich camp, once troops could be spared from elsewhere. Thus

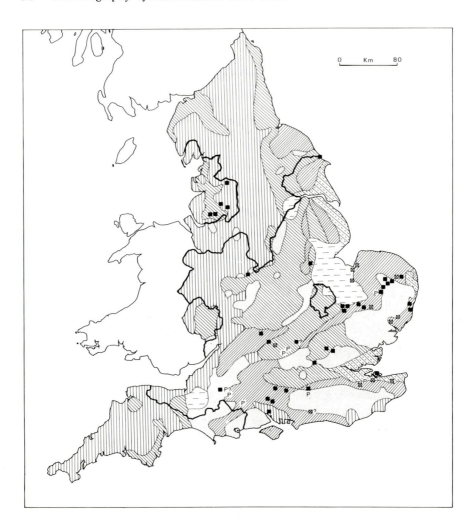

LAND PROTESTS

▲   Protests concerned with draining of fen or marsh

●   Protests concerned with forest or woodland

■   Protests concerned with enclosure or clearance

□   Villages involved in the 1596 attempted rising

◆   Protests concerned with tenure disputes

P   Attacks on deer parks or emparkments

▨   Destruction of property titles (1640-49)

⊠   Camps (1549)

■?   Approximate location, or protests known to be in
     that county but exact location unknown

FARMING REGIONS 1500-1640

⊟	Fenland
▢	Wood Pasture
▥	Open Pasture
▧	Marshland
▨	Clay Vales
▨	Downland, Wolds and Breckland

the Norwich camp lasted the longest of all the camps and the final defeat did not come until 27 August.

One other region experienced disturbances during the period 1548-52 and has so far been largely ignored by historians: the county of Lancashire. Here the disputes between tenants and landlords were over the rights of turbary and pasture,[3] and continued into the reign of Philip and Mary. Further south peasant discontent rumbled on until 1552. Thus the agrarian peasant risings of Edward's reign are much more than the events of Kett's revolt in Norfolk. It is no wonder, as Clark remarks, that they left as crucial an imprint on the consciousness of the pre-revolutionary political classes as had the events of 1381 and as the Civil War was to do.[4]

Notes

1. For the political background to the period, see Bush (1975); Cornwall (1977).
2. The description of the revolts 1548-52 is largely based on Bush (1975), ch. 4; Clark (1977), pp. 78-80; Clifford (1887), pp. 44-5; Cornwall (1977); MacCulloch (1979), pp. 36-59; Manning (1977), pp. 18-40; Gay (1904), pp. 201-9; Woodman (1957), pp. 78-84.
3. VCH *Lancashire* (2), pp. 289-91.
4. Clark (1977), p. 78.

2.7 1580-1606

The disturbances during this period can be regarded as precursors of the storms of rural protest that were to break in the following 40 years. In upland England and Wales most of the protests were a part of a series of similar disturbances that had occurred continuously at least since the reign of Henry VIII. The Lancashire disturbances have already been noted in the 1548-52 period. In Wales the protests were the result of the competitive scramble for the commons in the century after the Union of England and Wales in 1536-42; there had been a rather sudden collapse of the physical and legal controls which had governed the management of the commons for centuries past. The disturbances were mainly the result of conflicts between rival groups of freeholders, although one of the main factors behind the enclosure of the commons was probably the increasing cattle and sheep trade with England. The one series of protests that were of more recent origin were the tenurial disputes in County Durham. Since 1569 landlords had been trying to undermine the favoured tenures of tenant right but were resisted by 'combinations' of discontented peasants obstructing the holding of manorial courts and preventing the collection of fines by the lord's agent.[1]

Map 2. Land: 1548-52

Additional source: I would like to thank Professor Manning for access to his unpublished research on enclosure riots during this period. The agrarian regions on this and subsequent maps are taken from Thirsk (1967), fig. 1, amended from a personal communication from Dr Thirsk; and from Martin (1979), part III map.

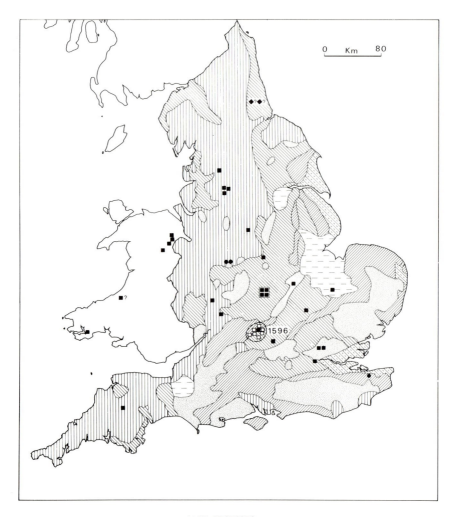

LAND PROTESTS

▲   Protests concerned with draining of fen or marsh

●   Protests concerned with forest or woodland

■   Protests concerned with enclosure or clearance

□   Villages involved in the 1596 attempted rising

◆   Protests concerned with tenure disputes

P   Attacks on deer parks or emparkments

▨   Destruction of property titles (1640-49)

▧   Camps (1549)

■? Approximate location, or protests known to be in
    that county but exact location unknown

FARMING REGIONS 1500-1640

Fenland

Wood Pasture

Open Pasture

Marshland

Clay Vales

Downland, Wolds and Breckland

Map 3. Land: 1580-1606

In lowland England those farming regions that were to be most troubled by rioting between 1608 and 1640 were already evident: the fens, the wood-pasture-forest areas and most noticeably the clay vales of the Midlands. The set of disturbances at Hillmorton led directly into the Midland Revolt of 1607, the freeholders of Hillmorton being very active in the troubles of that year.[2] The attempted rising under Bartholomew Steere in Oxfordshire in 1596 was almost a dress rehearsal of the events of 1607. Although it was planned in an area that had seen protests during 1548-52, with Steere choosing the site of the peasantry's 1549 camp as his rallying point and the park at Rycott being again one of the rioters' targets, the rebels were not now yeomen and priests but artisans. The leaders of the revolt had been particularly active in trying to persuade the cloth workers of Witney to join the rebellion. Unlike 1607 when they did respond to the call for collective action, they remained in Witney and the 1596 rising failed.[3]

Notes

1. VCH *Lancashire* (2), pp. 288-92; Wadsworth (1919-22), pp. 98-110; Emery (1967), pp. 155-6; Jones Pierce (1967), p. 380; Edwards (1929); Williams (1928); James (1974), pp. 82-4.
2. Allan (1950), ch. 4; Clark (1976), pp. 365-82; Godber (1970), pp. 147-59; Hull (1950), pp. 265-8, 462; Spufford (1974), pp. 122-5; Harrison (1979); Pam (1974), pp. 9-10; Martin (1979), part III; Pettit (1968), pp. 171-4.
3. For the most complete account of the 1596 rising, see Allan (1950), ch. 2 and *CSPD 1595-97* pp. 316-20, 323-4, 342-4.

2.8 THE MIDLAND REVOLT OF 1607   John Martin

The Midland Revolt of 1607 consisted of a co-ordinated series of enclosure riots beginning in Northamptonshire on May Eve and spreading to the adjacent counties of Warwickshire and Leicestershire by late May.[1] The peasantry by these means sought to make a political protest against the enclosing activities of local landowners so that the government would be forced to take action against such enclosure.

During the month of sustained and widespread rioting, in which the revolt threatened to spread to other counties, the authorities were spurred into action. Royal Proclamations were followed by the dispatch of lord lieutenants into the counties, attempted musters of their militia and the eventual suppression of the revolt. The decisive engagement between the rebels and the authorities occurred at Newton in Northamptonshire on 8 June, when the rebels were defeated and exemplary executions of some of their number were carried out. From then onwards the rising subsided. In spite of the defeat in Northamptonshire, the revolt in the three central Midland counties had triggered off further enclosure riots in adjoining counties such as Lincolnshire, Oxfordshire, Bedfordshire, Derbyshire and Worcestershire. In some of these counties the protests were revivals of discontent rather than new outbreaks of rioting. Lincolnshire and

Oxfordshire had experienced disturbances simultaneously with the events in the Midlands. The authorities were greatly concerned by the belated spread of the rioting; suppression, however, proved relatively easy as the rising had already collapsed at its centre. The overall geographical and temporal pattern of enclosure riots may thus best be described as analogous to the outward moving ripples on the surface of a pond after a stone has been thrown into the centre.

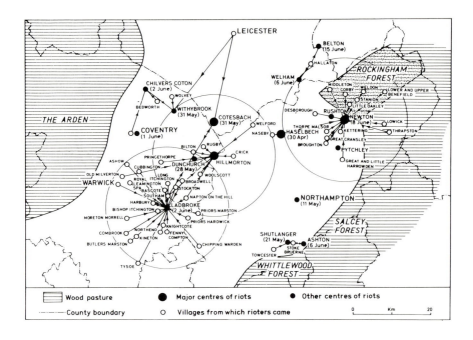

Map 4. The Midland Revolt of 1607: the Central Area

At the local scale the pattern of protest was of a convergence of peasants from surrounding villages on a chosen site of protest (see, for example, Ladbroke), supplemented by co-ordinating links established between centres of riots (for example Ladbroke and Cotesbach, and Withybrook and Chilvers Coton) (Map 4). The disturbances occurred within the felden, an area of peasant mixed-farming resting uneasily alongside large enclosed pasture farms. Participants in the riots were drawn from villages within a radius of 9-12 miles, a day's walking distance. Inhabitants of the wooded-pastoral regions on the periphery of the felden and poorer members of towns in the felden itself also played a significant role in the protests.

The reasons for the selection of sites of protest are clear. These parishes almost without exception had experienced total enclosure, considerable depopulation and the conversion of land from arable to pasture within the previous ten years. The involvement of people from the three types of area may be explained by reference to: (a) two kinds of peasant community in the felden — freehold

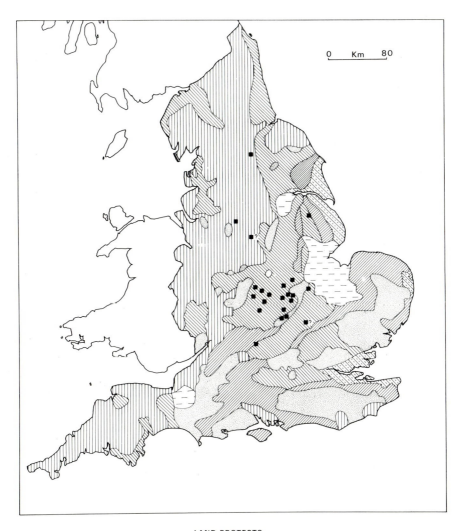

LAND PROTESTS

▲   Protests concerned with draining of fen or marsh

●   Protests concerned with forest or woodland

■   Protests concerned with enclosure or clearance

□   Villages involved in the 1596 attempted rising

◆   Protests concerned with tenure disputes

P   Attacks on deer parks or emparkments

▨   Destruction of property titles (1640-49)

▧   Camps (1549)

■?   Approximate location, or protests known to be in
     that county but exact location unknown

FARMING REGIONS 1500-1640

Fenland

Wood Pasture

Open Pasture

Marshland

Clay Vales

Downland, Wolds and Breckland

Map 5. Land: 1607

and open parishes; and (b) the dependence of the wooded-pastoral communities and the local towns on the agrarian economy of the felden. The freehold parishes were under the constant threat of enclosure of their own open arable fields by neighbouring landowners. They were prosperous communities, characterised by considerable equality in land and wealth, a factor which both caused and enabled them to resist external pressures for enclosure. By contrast, the populous open parishes were marked by great inequality and were dominated by poor cottagers and labourers. For the latter group grain supplies and labouring opportunities were threatened by the extensive conversion of arable land to pasture which accompanied enclosure in the felden Midlands. Peasant communities in the wooded-pastoral areas and the local towns were equally vulnerable. In such settlements, numerous poor were similarly dependent upon the felden for grain supplies and employment. Moreover, those in the wooded-pastoral region felt simultaneously the threat posed by the disafforestation and enclosure of forests.

At the end of the sixteenth century, the pressures caused by (a) population increase and migration; (b) the increasing shortfall in grain supplies for the poor; and (c) a rapid acceleration of the enclosure movement, combined to produce intolerable strains upon the peasantry and the poor. After the warning signs of the abortive Oxfordshire rising in 1596, these enduring trends gave rise ultimately to the revolt in 1607.

Note

1. For a fully referenced and complete account, see Martin (1979), part III.

2.9 1608-39

During this period there were five major series of protests. First, the crushing of the Midland Revolt of 1607 did not mean the end of resistance to enclosure in that region: enclosure continued and the government still appeared to be taking no effective action. The actions of the protestors in 1607 were not forgotten and seem to have encouraged others to undertake localised enclosure riots, the most noteworthy of these being the almost continuous riots at Coventry over the enclosure of the town's common fields. Secondly, in Wales, the tensions and conflicts over the upland commons still persisted and were even intensified.[1] The three other major series of disturbances have one common factor binding them together: the attempts of the Crown to increase its revenue.

On certain manors in the northern counties of Northumberland, Durham, Cumberland, Westmorland and Lancashire, tenants had gained the particularly

Map 6. Land: 1608-39

Additional source: Allan (1952), ch. 4; Kerridge (1958-9), pp. 64-6.

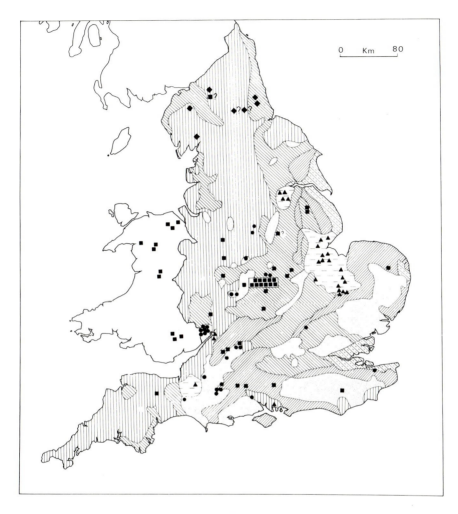

LAND PROTESTS

▲   Protests concerned with draining of fen or marsh

●   Protests concerned with forest or woodland

■   Protests concerned with enclosure or clearance

□   Villages involved in the 1596 attempted rising

◆   Protests concerned with tenure disputes

P   Attacks on deer parks or emparkments

☑   Destruction of property titles (1640-49)

☒   Camps (1549)

■?   Approximate location, or protests known to be in
that county but exact location unknown

FARMING REGIONS 1500-1640

	Fenland
	Wood Pasture
	Open Pasture
	Marshland
	Clay Vales
	Downland, Wolds and Breckland

favourable tenurial customs of tenant-right because of their reciprocal obligations to assist in repelling Scots incursions into England. With the Union of the Crowns of England and Scotland in 1603, the Crown led the way in demanding greater payments. With royal protection removed, non-Crown landlords intensified their demands on their tenantry.

In some areas such as the Lake District and Weardale in County Durham, these moves against tenant-right were met with very active resistance on the part of the tenantry. 'Tumultuous meetings' were held where the tenants entered into a 'combination', formed a 'public purse' and sought to take legal action against their landlords. The King and the House of Commons were petitioned. One mass meeting considered opposing their landlord by force. In certain areas the resistance seems to have been successful but this success often depended on whether the tenants could prove their tenements were customary estates of inheritance, irrespective of tenant-right.[2]

In the fenlands the Crown and the great landlords saw the greatest financial gains to be reaped through drainage of these large areas of wetlands. Thus in the main the protests in the fens were the direct result of such large-scale projects to drain these regions. The opposition to the Crown's attempts to claim right of ownership of reclaimed marshland was much more muted. Nevertheless with regard to both these schemes the inhabitants of the fen and marsh employed a whole range of tactics of resistance. Lawsuits to investigate the rights of commoners in the fen and marsh, appeals and petitions to the Privy Council and assemblages before the drainage commissioners, were all employed to hold up the progress of the drainage projects. If these failed, then attacks on the dikes and drains were often staged. These violent acts thus tended to increase as the completion of the project drew near.

To see how these disturbances were quelled we can examine what happened in Hatfield Chase and the Isle of Axholme. In the other areas the events of the opposition to the drainage schemes were overtaken by the growing crises in Stuart society, particularly after the outbreak of the Bishops War in 1639. A royal proclamation and the temporary stationing of troops having failed, Vermuyden, the undertaker of the scheme in Hatfield Chase and the Isle of Axholme took legal action against the people for having destroyed his crops. He then bought the commoners' consent to the scheme by waiving damages and the crippling fines the Star Chamber had imposed on them. In the other major region where drainage was proposed, the Somerset Levels, there was no such violent resistance. In King's Sedgemoor the pressure the freeholder commoners brought to bear on the justices of the peace who were acting as drainage commissioners was behind the failure of the scheme. In Aldermoor only an assemblage before the commissioners was attempted and the scheme went ahead.[3]

The fifth major series of protests was the disturbances in the royal forests between 1626 and 1639. The Crown assessed each of its forests to see how best they could be made to yield income. Except for the Forest of Dean, the forests that had protests, Gillingham, Leicester, Braydon, Chippenham, Feckenham and

Needwood, were some of those to be disafforested completely and turned into farmland rather than exploited for their timber. Those most affected by disafforestation were artisans, labourers and poor husbandmen who used the forest to provide them with essential income supplements. They were principally employed either in the cloth industry or in woodland trades that used wood, bark, hides or animal fats. In the Forest of Dean the Crown only enclosed parts of the forest. This, however, not only angered the poor cottagers but also the miners because it denied them, as it was intended to, the right to mine anywhere. The Crown wished to make the independent miners workmen of Crown grantees. Thus the Forest of Dean disturbances were somewhat different from the other forest protests. Sixteen-hundred-and-thirty-one was the year of the greatest number of forest protests. The years 1629-31were years of industrial depression and food scarcity so the similarity of social conditions and tensions was heightened in all forest areas thus aiding the rapid spread of rioting between areas.[4] Besides these major forest disturbances, there were a scattering of minor woodland disputes, as landlords sought to enclose woods as part of the general attack on wastelands during this period.

Notes

1. Martin (1979), chs. 14, 16; for Wales, see section 2.7, note 1.
2. Appleby (1975), pp. 574-94; Bouch and Jones (1961), pp. 74-6; James (1974), pp. 80-6; Watts (1971), pp. 64-87.
3. Darby (1956), ch. 2; Everitt (1967), p. 407; Harris (1953), ch. 5; Hipkin (1930), pp. 218-43; Hughes (1954), pp. 13-45; Manning (1976), pp. 112-38; Stovin (1948-51), pp. 385-91; Thirsk (1957), ch. 5; Underdown (1973), ch. 1; Williams (1970), ch. 4.
4. Sharp (1980), chs. 1, 4-7; Underdown (1973), ch. 1; Barnes (1961), p. 158.

2.10   1640-9

It has been argued by Manning that the period of political turbulence between the assembling of the Long Parliament in 1640 and the outbreak of the Civil War in 1642 marks a break in the intensity of direct collective actions on the part of common people. The rising tide of rural protests then set in motion carried on into the Civil War itself as opposition to the Crown and the landlords.[1] Yet the majority of protests that occurred between 1640 and 1649 were simply the reopening of the fierce conflicts that had broken out in the fens and forests during the late-1620s and 1630s.[2] Even in most of the areas that saw disturbances for the first time, the protests were forest and fen riots, the majority of which concerned disafforestation and drainage schemes, that had been carried out relatively peacefully in the reign of Charles I.[3] In the main, then, as Sharp notes for the forest areas, 'the riots of these two decades were in one sense expressions of the indifference felt by large numbers of common people to the great issues . . . raised by the Civil War . . .'[4] What the turmoil of the period did

LAND PROTESTS

▲   Protests concerned with draining of fen or marsh

●   Protests concerned with forest or woodland

■   Protests concerned with enclosure or clearance

□   Villages involved in the 1596 attempted rising

◆   Protests concerned with tenure disputes

P   Attacks on deer parks or emparkments

▨   Destruction of property titles (1640-49)

▨   Camps (1549)

■? Approximate location, or protests known to be in
    that county but exact location unknown

FARMING REGIONS 1500-1640

	Fenland
	Wood Pasture
	Open Pasture
	Marshland
	Clay Vales
	Downland, Wolds and Breckland

Map 7. Land: 1640-9

offer them was a golden opportunity to continue their purpose of thwarting those who had dispossessed them of their common rights to forest and fen.

Similarly, of the remainder of the protests many concerned the issue of enclosure of the commons and wastes.[5] There was no Civil War rising equivalent to the Midland Revolt of 1607; thus outside the forests and fens the greater part of England was remarkably quiet.[6] The attacks on deer parks were not, in the main, the work of a discontented tenantry but rather, as will be seen, the work of forest people, artisans and troops. The only known disturbances that had any semblance of the peasant revolts of the French Revolution were the five incidents in which property titles and records of leases, rents and dues were destroyed: Bourton in Buckinghamshire, Peterborough cathedral, Winchester where again parliamentary troops were involved, and at Stoke-by-Nayland in Suffolk and outside Colchester both probably the collective actions of cloth workers.[7]

It needs to be stressed, perhaps in this period more than any other, that only collective protests are being considered. There is evidence that copyholders in particular were taking advantage of the undermining of authority in general to make inroads into landlords' rights by tactics such as evasion or refusal to pay rents.[8]

Notes

1. Manning (1976), chs. 6, 7.
2. Sharp (1980), ch. 9; fens, see section 2.9, note 3; and Manning (1976), pp. 187-8.
3. Hill (1974), p. 195; Yarlott (1963), ch. 1; Sharp (1980), p. 243, ch. 9; Barnes (1961), p. 158; Thirsk (1957), pp. 147, 190-1; Manning (1976), pp. 124-5; Williams (1970), p. 104.
4. Sharp (1980), p. 220.
5. Coate (1928), p. 150; Holmes (1974), p. 44; Hill (1974), p. 195; Manning (1976), pp. 124-5; Yarlott (1963), ch. 1.
6. I have been unable to locate any research on similar disturbances in Wales during this period.
7. Yarlott (1963), p. 51; Manning (1975), p. 152; Holmes (1974), pp. 44-5.
8. Yarlott (1963), ch. 1.

2.11 1650-1701

Even after the ending of the Civil War, disturbances continued in the forest and fen regions mainly because the policies of the Commonwealth to these 'wastes' was no different from that of the earlier Stuart Kings. By acts in 1653 and 1654 Parliament authorised the disafforestation and sale of practically all the remaining royal forests. Moreover, with the normal institutions of law enforcement restored after the Civil War persons who had been granted land began to re-erect their enclosures. Those forests that saw disturbances because they were to be sold were Enfield Chase and Needwood Forest. The final outcomes, however, were very different. Enfield Chase was subsequently almost entirely converted to tillage, whilst in Needwood the resistance together with administrative delays saved the forest, for at the Restoration, Charles II decided not to proceed with the sale. This decision contrasted with that for Ashdown Forest in Sussex. The Lancaster Great Park was disafforested after the Restoration: destruction of enclosures ensued. The campaign of resistance culminated in a lawsuit of 1689 which let the commoners have just less than half of the forest. Similarly, the disafforestation and enclosure of the High Peak Forest in Derbyshire was proceeded with in the 1670s after lying dormant since 1640 and met with opposition and litigation. In the forests of Gillingham and Frome Selwood enclosures were erected only to be torn down again. In the Forest of Dean, Parliament proposed to enclose a third of the forest to preserve future timber growth from despoilation. This led to the inevitable riots. Indeed the next 150 years in the Forest of Dean were to be punctuated by riots if either enclosures were made or restrictions were placed on the right to common. Another forest that was to see protests well into the eighteenth century was Cannock Chase. The protest in 1690 was over the landlord's attempt to wring more revenues from the Chase and let a tenancy to a rabbit warrener.[1]

In the fenlands the ending of the Civil War meant that work was restarted. Attention was first turned to the southern fenland. In 1649 a second 'Act for the draining the Great Level of the Fens . . .' was passed. The work was completed by 1652 but throughout the whole two years of work the old hostility to the drainers had been shown. Rioting continued if on a diminished scale into the 1660s. In this area the drainers were victors against the commoners, if not against nature. In the northern fenland, on the other hand, so successful had been the disturbances of the previous fifteen years that 'both the drainers and the Crown were permanently dispossessed of their shares in the fen'.[2] At Deeping Fen, however, a new scheme was attempted but in 1699 these drainage works were destroyed by about 1,000 men. This ensured that the fen was left undrained for the time being. Similarly, a partial success on the part of the commoners in the Isle of Axholme was finally gained after a long struggle in 1691. This agreement reduced the drainers' share of the land by roughly two thirds 'for ye sake of peace'. Even this victory was not enough for some of the islanders and the enclosures were torn down later that year followed by a campaign of harrassment of the drainers' chief agent.[3]

The determination of the townsfolk of Coventry to defend their common fields had been longstanding, as has been noted. The period 1650-1700 was particularly disturbed with riots occurring in 1661, 1668, 1689, 1696 and 1699. The particular grievance stemmed from Charles II depriving the town of its commoning rights in Cheylesmore Park because of the support the town had shown for the Parliamentary cause during the Civil War.[4]

One series of incidents that requires detailed research is those in Worcestershire in 1670. These disturbances included fence breaking to allow cattle from

Map 8. Land: 1650-1701

Additional source: Beloff (1938), ch. 4.

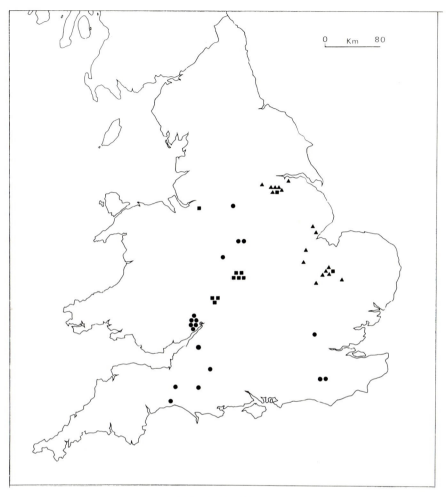

LAND PROTESTS

▲   Protests concerned with draining of fen or marsh

●   Protests concerned with forest or woodland

■   Protests concerned with enclosure or clearance

□   Villages involved in the 1596 attempted rising

◆   Protests concerned with tenure disputes

P   Attacks on deer parks or emparkments

▨   Destruction of property titles (1640-49)

⊠   Camps (1549)

■?   Approximate location, or protests known to be in
     that county but exact location unknown

FARMING REGIONS 1500-1640

Fenland
Wood Pasture
Open Pasture
Marshland
Clay Vales
Downland, Wolds and Breckland

the commons onto the enclosed land, cutting farmers' corn before it was ripe, destroying hayricks and cattle and horse maiming.[5]

Notes

1. Christian (1967), ch. 5; Hart (1951, 1953) Pam (1977); Sharp (1980), ch. 9; Somerville (1977), pp. 16-22; Thirsk (1969), pp. 1-16; Hay (1975b), pp. 221-2.
    2. Thirsk (1957), p. 126.
    3. Beloff (1938), pp. 79-80; Darby (1956), pp. 64-82; Hughes (1954); Stovin (1948-51); Summers (1976), pp. 104-14; Thirsk (1957), pp. 125-7.
    4. VCH *Warwickshire (8)*, p. 204.
    5. VCH *Worcestershire (4)*, p. 456; *CSPD 1671*, pp. 18-19.

2.12 1702-39

These years in England are the quietest so far encountered, that is, for protests linked to the development of land primarily for monetary gain. The deer park attacks that break the tranquility of the early Georgian countryside of southern England are considered separately, for those protests were concerned with the use of land primarily for social prestige.

All land and deer park protests were, however, related in that the protestors were all commoners with forest rights. In the Northamptonshire forests there was an enclosure riot and two incidents involving the denial of the right to cut wood for maypoles. In the Forest of Dean any attempts to enclose were as always vigorously opposed. This opposition was successful partly because the Crown declined to pursue a strong policy towards the management of the forest, even as regards day-to-day affairs, and partly because the forest courts were discontinued and offenders were left unpunished: the number of commoners consequently increased. On Cannock Chase the commoners continued to struggle to prevent the planting of rabbit warrens on the Chase.[1]

In Scotland, in contrast, this period witnessed a concerted series of disturbances in Galloway. This, the Levellers' Revolt of 1724, will be considered in detail in the next section.

Note

1. Beloff (1938), pp. 77-8; Pettit (1968), p. 125; Hart (1951), ch. 3, (1953), ch. 6, (1966), ch. 9; Hay (1975b), p. 222.

2.13 THE LEVELLERS' REVOLT IN GALLOWAY OF 1724
John W. Leopold

The Galloway Levellers' Revolt was a rising of tenants and sub-tenants against changes in agricultural production introduced by the lairds.[1] The revolt's name stems from the practice of destroying, or levelling, the drystone dikes used to enclose land for cattle grazing, and the levelling took place in the low lying areas of Galloway which were being converted into grazing parks. Indeed, the dikes at Palgowan were spared because they were isolated from the mainstream of developments.

The precise beginning of the levelling is difficult to date. Claims and counter-claims by the Levellers and their adversaries place the first levelling all over the Stewartry of Kirkcudbright. However, the enclosures at Netherlaw and Barcheskie were known to have been levelled on 17 March 1724. Thereafter, the revolt developed throughout April, May and June. The intervention of troops at the end of May soon quelled the revolt in the Stewartry, although sporadic incidents occurred, such as at Duchrae in October. Levelling did not develop in Wigtown-shire until the autumn of 1724. It continued until November, with a further isolated outbreak in April 1725, which was directed against the most hated laird, Basil Hamilton of Baldoon.

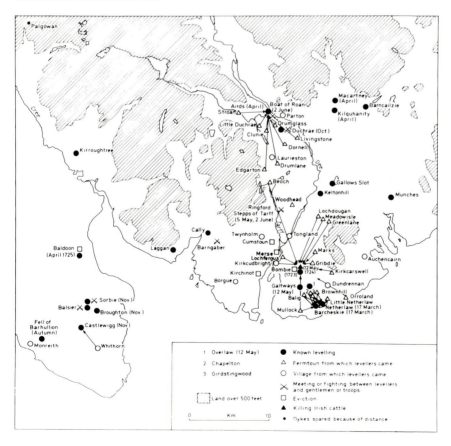

Map 9. The Levellers' Revolt of 1724

The roots of the revolt lay in the development of cattle ranching – fattening and selling cattle began in the 1680s and the 1707 Act of Union stimulated further development. In order to expand, it was necessary to enclose increasingly large areas of land as cattle parks, and to increase the size of the remaining arable farms. Eviction and rent rises became the order of the day: levelling was the response. The Levellers argued that the lairds' action disrupted and weakened traditional agricultural society. Thus they sought legitimisation of their action through traditional channels – religion and the law; and by an alternative proposal for agricultural organisation.

That they sought support through religion was not surprising; the Covenanting tradition was strong in Galloway. No part of Scotland had suffered more than Galloway in the previous 60 years of religious unheaval, and from this period came experience, which was utilised during the revolt, of both legitimate and illegitimate social and political organisation. The Levellers organised on a parish basis, calling their supporters together through messages on church doors. They gathered in large numbers – 2,000 being present at Bombie Muir on 12 May.

The Church of Scotland was divided in its attitude towards the Levelling. The General Assembly in Edinburgh condemned the revolt, and issued an Act, which although read by ministers in Wigtownshire, was read by few in the Stewartry. Some Church of Scotland ministers clearly supported the Levellers; indeed, the gentlemen had threatened the ministers with arrest. Others supported the lairds, and were consequently condemned by their more radical colleagues.

The Levellers claimed that the lairds' cattle were illegally imported from Ireland, contrary to the law; therefore, they claimed, the lairds not the Levellers were breaking the law. On the whole, the criminal courts did not deal harshly with the Levellers. However, the lairds controlled the civil courts and from March they sued captured Levellers for damages, which must have acted as a deterrent to many.

Map 10. Land: 1702-39

LAND PROTESTS

▲   Protests concerned with draining of fen or marsh

●   Protests concerned with forest or woodland

■   Protests concerned with enclosure or clearance

□   Villages involved in the 1596 attempted rising

◆   Protests concerned with tenure disputes

P   Attacks on deer parks or emparkments

▨   Destruction of property titles (1640-49)

▨   Camps (1549)

■?   Approximate location, or protests known to be in that county but exact location unknown

FARMING REGIONS 1500-1640

Fenland

Wood Pasture

Open Pasture

Marshland

Clay Vales

Downland, Wolds and Breckland

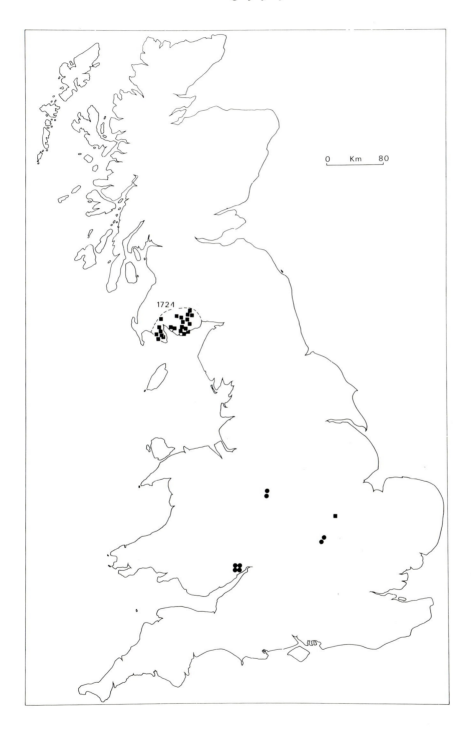

The Levellers were not against enclosure *per se*, but against its imposition by the lairds. They drew up a pamphlet outlining a system of organising agriculture in the area, which was intended to satisfy everyone: an appeal which was rejected by the lairds.

The revolt was short lived, and ultimately unsuccessful; after its demise, enclosure continued. The lairds had troops, the legal system, censorship, and the power of the pulpit on their side. Not all of these agencies fully supported the lairds, as there was unease at the disruption of an ordered society which enclosure caused. But the lairds could also incorporate some tenants into the cattle economy; thus some tenants were able to prosper by participating in cattle rearing. This led to the Levellers complaining that 'our very equals have undertaken to add fewel unto our oppression'; indeed the levelling at Balsier was directed against a tenant. A few tenants could thus become part of the successful cattle economy, but the vast majority, after the crushing of their revolt, were left defeated and demoralised.

Note

1. For a complete and fully referenced account, see Leopold (1980), pp. 4-29.

2.14 1740-79

In this period it was the latter half that was most disturbed. Indeed the 1740s were a continuation of the series of quiet decades in England that had begun in 1700. Protests commenced with the Charnwood Forest riots of 1748-51. Here the commoners successfully challenged the right of a landowner's claims to right

Map 11. Land: 1740-79

Additional source: Godber (1970), pp. 147-59; Leopold (1980), p. 4; Tate (1944), pp. 392-3; Williams (1978), p. 278; *London Gazette* (1762, 1778). (I would like to thank E.P. Thompson for the last two references.)

LAND PROTESTS

▲   Protests concerned with draining of fen or marsh

●   Protests concerned with forest or woodland

■   Protests concerned with enclosure or clearance

□   Villages involved in the 1596 attempted rising

◆   Protests concerned with tenure disputes

P   Attacks on deer parks or emparkments

▨   Destruction of property titles (1640-49)

▨   Camps (1549)

■?   Approximate location, or protests known to be in
     that county but exact location unknown

FARMING REGIONS 1500-1640

Fenland

Wood Pasture

Open Pasture

Marshland

Clay Vales

Downland, Wolds and Breckland

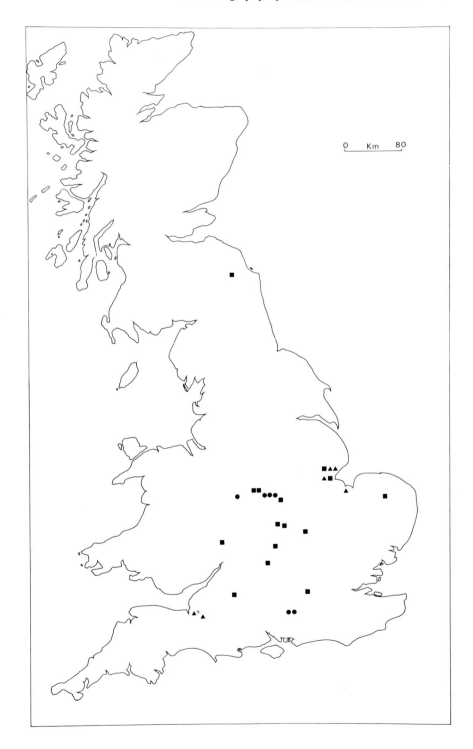

of free warren. This success helped to mobilise the men of Cannock Chase yet again in defence of their use of the common: many of those involved in the protests were industrial workers. This time they were particularly alarmed by the claim of the Earl of Uxbridge to plant the whole of the waste with warrens, and by the threat of enclosure. Other forest areas were being developed for their timber resources but the poor asserted their right to take wood as in the Hampshire villages of Frensham, Binstead, Bentley and Kingsley.[1]

The defence of wastes, either under threat of enclosure or having recently been enclosed, by industrial workers was common to many other land riots in the Midlands during this period. This is a conclusion which Neeson reaches after an exhaustive study of the Northamptonshire enclosure opposition in the period 1760-1800 (see section 2.18). The town fields of Leicester were the scene of conflict in 1754. There were enclosure riots in 1771-2 at Burton-on-Trent when again that improving landlord the Earl of Uxbridge sought to enclose the out parishes. He had already postponed his plans in 1766 because of the widespread food rioting nearby. Nor was he wholly successful this time for that part of the common belonging to Burton borough remained unenclosed until 1812. In other places men from the town came out in a body to level the enclosures; as at Shaw Hill in Wiltshire in 1757, where weavers, probably from Melksham, were involved and at North Leigh Heath in 1761 and at Warkworth in 1765, where men from Witney and Banbury respectively were the chief protestors. There were also enclosure protests at Redditch in 1772 and at Malvern in 1778.[2]

With the steady increase of agricultural prices from the mid-eighteenth century and hence greater possibilities for higher rents and returns, it was not surprising that attention turned to the fens again. Opposition to drainage and enclosure schemes in the Somerset Levels and in the fens around Boston indicated, however, that many of the fen people still saw their livelihood in danger from such plans. The Holland Fen disturbances in Lincolnshire lasted from 1768 to 1773 but even they were unsuccessful in halting the drainage and enclosure schemes permanently.[3]

Notes

1. Hay (1975b), pp. 227-8; Thompson (1975), p. 244.
2. Neeson (1977), ch. 7; VCH *Leicestershire* (4), p. 166; Hay (1975a), pp. 259-62; Wearmouth (1945), ch. 1.
3. Williams (1970), pp. 125-6; Thirsk (1957), p. 214.

2.15 1780-1831

In the Welsh uplands enclosure was needed to establish proprietary rights and to allow the commons to be developed for large-scale pastoral farming. There were regional differences in the reasons for enclosure between north Wales and south and mid Wales. In north Wales the enclosures were primarily but not exclusively to meet the needs of the developing capitalist slate industry. Landowners needed first to secure their right to the waste before development could proceed. Secondly, enclosure was to turn the 'idle and insolent', the independent cottagers, squatters or small quarrymen, into a dependent, reliable workforce for the large slate quarries. Enclosure in north Wales was thus not necessarily a question of agricultural improvement. Most of the protests to such changes occurred during the period of the Napoleonic Wars.

In south and mid Wales the opposition was mainly centred in the period 1815-20. Here enclosure was mostly for agricultural purposes and the chief opponents of enclosure were squatters and small farmers. The enclosure protests were part of a general disaffection in the west and south-west of Wales which in Cardiganshire between 1792-1813 threatened to collapse the whole system of law and order. In all three regions the landowners publicly took a stance similar to that of the Caernarvonshire squirearchy which assembled in 1808 in Caernarvon and resolved to 'oppose to the utmost of their power all manner of "encroachments" and to enforce all the different enclosure acts which have lately been obtained'. The protests were, however, at times successful particularly when they formed part of a wider campaign of legal opposition.[1]

In the northern Scottish Highlands the protests were related solely to the development of large-scale sheep farming, which on that scale required clearance of the now redundant clansmen. On the west coast and on the islands, however, large numbers of men were still needed in the kelp industry. Thus the spatial bias of the protests towards the east coast and the mainland is explained. After two protests in the 1780s, the clearance disturbances clustered at three times: the 1792 rising, the Kildonan protests of 1813 and the riots of 1820-1.

The protests of 1792 were the product of a direct clash between traditional practices of black cattle rearing and the new sheep farms, rather than the eviction of all the tenantry. The threat of eviction was there, however, through the further expansion of sheep farming. A plan was, therefore, conceived mainly by the men of Strathrusdale and Ardross to round up all the sheep and drive them out of the northern Highlands. They hoped that others would carry on their initiative and continue to drive farther south. Messages were sent out to all the parishes of Easter Ross and the Black Isle and to the neighbouring parishes in Sunderland. The authorities responded with the mobilisation of three companies of the Black Watch. There was no violent resistance: the troops arrived at Boath to find 6,000 sheep unattended.

The Kildonan protests were a response to the order for the whole strath to be cleared as part of the grand strategy for economic development on the Sutherland estate. Once again there was a call to drive out the sheep and an attempt to link different areas together, messages being sent out from 'a convention of the people'.

The incidents in the third series of disturbances at first sight seem unconnected except that they occurred during another phase of major clearances. They all occurred also, however, after the establishment of Thomas Dudgeon's Sutherlandshire Transatlantic Emigration Society in 1819. This association not only focused attention on the clearances but prominent members of the association were reported to have called for resistance to evictions. Under pressure from the authorities the leadership of the association disbanded but the rank-and-file Dudgeonites were still present in communities throughout the Highlands. Thus, whereas evictions in the early summer of 1819 had been carried out without trouble, disturbances broke out in response to similar clearances in 1820. At Unapool, in fact, the riot was caused by the ejection of a known Dudgeonite. The rebels in Culrain to the extreme east of Unapool had pledged assistance to the people of the latter community 'if they had the spirit to resist'.[2]

In England despite the fact that the enclosure movement reached its peak during this period, only certain communities were prepared to take direct collective action, and then most of these protests occurred before 1800. There were protests that harked back to the collective action of the commoners and peasantry of the seventeenth century; in the fenland and its borders in East Anglia enclosure in particular was opposed. On the borders of the Isle of Axholme a crowd destroyed fences surrounding an enclosure in 1798. In Oxford-shire from 1786 to 1831 the men of Otmoor opposed all attempts at enclosing and draining the moor. The most dramatic episode in the struggle over the moor was the '"possessioning" and demolishing every fence' on 7 September 1830 and the riot at St Giles' Fair in Oxford on the same day when the prisoners taken by the troops at Otmoor were rescued.

In the forest villagers of Frensham and Kingsley in Hampshire there was openly more mass stealing of wood. At Mere in a former forested area in Wiltshire the commoners put up stern resistance to the enclosers. The greatest disturbances in England, in terms of the numbers involved, occurred in 1831 amongst that most turbulent community, the commoners and free miners of the Forest of Dean. The free miners were yet again defending their customary right to the Forest's resources, this time against the Crown's most determined attempt to eliminate it in the interest of efficient administration and the security of property.

Map 12. Land: 1780-1831

Additional source: Leopold (1980), p. 4.

LAND PROTESTS

▲	Protests concerned with draining of fen or marsh		FARMING REGIONS 1500-1640
●	Protests concerned with forest or woodland		
■	Protests concerned with enclosure or clearance		Fenland
□	Villages involved in the 1596 attempted rising		Wood Pasture
◆	Protests concerned with tenure disputes		Open Pasture
P	Attacks on deer parks or emparkments		Marshland
▨	Destruction of property titles (1640-49)		Clay Vales
⊠	Camps (1549)		Downland, Wolds and Breckland
■?	Approximate location, or protests known to be in that county but exact location unknown		

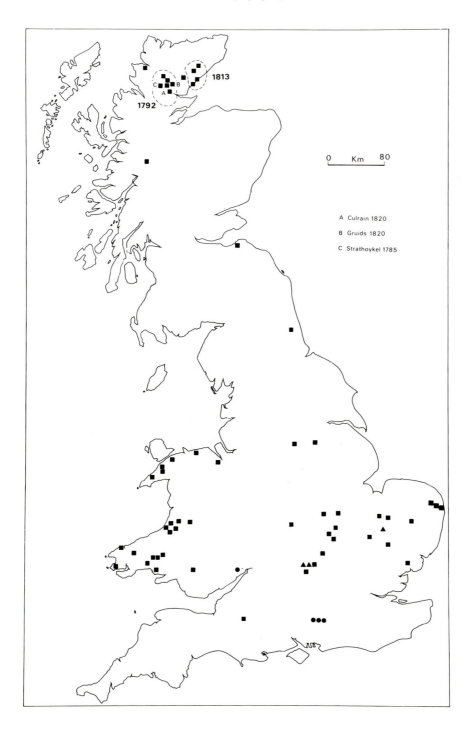

1813

1792

0   Km   80

A Culrain 1820

B Gruids 1820

C Strathoykel 1785

Many of the other communities who opposed enclosure most vigorously were occupational communities. Mention has already been made of the disturbances by industrial outworkers in Northamptonshire in the previous period; these continued during this period (see section 2.18). At Headington near Oxford the quarrymen resisted the enclosure of a traditional passageway to the village burial grounds. At Somerleyton, Blundeston and Lound in Suffolk, the fishermen were the principal rioters. On Gateshead Fell in County Durham the enclosure commissioners were attacked by the industrial labourers who were squatters on the open fell. Moreover, there were three disturbances over town fields at Sheffield, Colchester and Coventry.[3]

Notes

1. Jones (1973), part 1, ch. 2; Plume (1935), chs. 3-5; Dodd (1971), p. 76.
2. Hunter (1976), ch. 2; Richards (1974), ch. 2; Logue (1979), ch. 2.
3. Peacock (1965), p. 20, (1974), pp. 46-7; Spufford (1963), p. 54; Wearmouth (1945), ch. 1; Reaney (1970), pp. 1-47; Thompson (1975), p. 244; G.P. Maslin, personal communication; Fisher (1978), pp. 17-53; Neeson (1977), ch. 7; Samuel (1975), p. 153; Tate (1944); Hodgson (1973), p. 148; Brown (1969), p. 44; VCH *Leicestershire* (2), pp. 204-5.

2.16 1832-60

In England some of the final conflicts over land were in towns rather than the countryside. The long saga of the town fields of Coventry continued in this period – the last riot occurred in January 1859. In Oxford in the same decade there was the battle over the enclosure of the Open Magdalens. The protests at nearby Otmoor had lasted through 1832-5 'despite the frequent return of the military and the setting up, in 1832, of a special Otmoor police'. It should not be a surprise to find other enclosure protests in East Anglia with one occurring

Map 13. Land: 1832-60

LAND PROTESTS

▲   Protests concerned with draining of fen or marsh

●   Protests concerned with forest or woodland

■   Protests concerned with enclosure or clearance

□   Villages involved in the 1596 attempted rising

◆   Protests concerned with tenure disputes

P   Attacks on deer parks or emparkments

☑   Destruction of property titles (1640-49)

☒   Camps (1549)

■?   Approximate location, or protests known to be in that county but exact location unknown

FARMING REGIONS 1500-1640

Fenland

Wood Pasture

Open Pasture

Marshland

Clay Vales

Downland, Wolds and Breckland

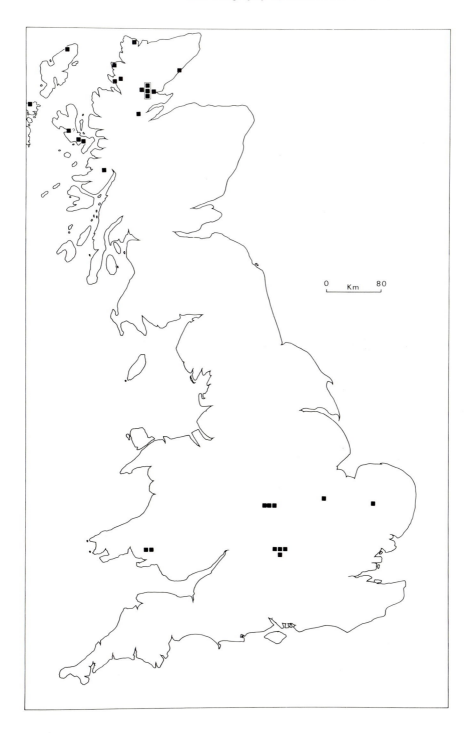

as late as 1844[1] In Wales this period was remarkably free of direct collective actions over the issue of land after the turmoil of the previous 50 years.[2]

Only in the Scottish Highlands and islands were there any protests of note. The geography of the disturbances, as in the previous period, mirrored the fortunes of the kelp industry. By 1827 kelp had ceased to be a profitable undertaking on many estates and thereafter the long but irreversible contraction of the industry began. Sheep farming came to be looked on as the main prop of estate management and this required clearances of the crofters. Thus the centre of gravity of protests was shifted during this period from the east to the west coast and the islands. With the exception of the protest in Caithness in 1835, all the riots in the east were clustered in the Strathcarron area, a region that had already seen non-violent and violent resistance to the new agrarian economy in 1792 and 1820. Indeed, in the first attempt to serve the eviction notices on the tenants of Greenyards in 1854, the officers were seized and carried down the valley to be deposited at the braes of Dounie, the scene of the Culrain riot of 1820. Here was one set of communities where folk memory stiffened resistance to further clearances. In the west, particularly on the islands, there was no such tradition of even recent resistance, except perhaps amongst the men of Assynt. The clearances in the west appear overall to have been more passively resisted. But these differences could also be because, compared to the earlier Sutherland evictions, the clearances in the west were not on such a large scale and hence involved less people. Moreover, communities on the west coast and the islands were more isolated and inaccessible than their counterparts in the east. Concerted action was thus more difficult to organise.[3]

Notes

1. VCH *Leicestershire* (2), p. 205; Samuel (1975), pp. 153-4; Reaney (1970), pp. 46-78; Peacock (1974), p. 47.
2. Williams (1955), pp. 77-85.
3. Hunter (1976), chs. 3-6; Richards (1974).

2.17 ATTACKS ON DEER PARKS 1640-1740

These have been treated separately from the general study of land protests because in the section on land protests we wished to focus on disturbances that were a response to the development of primarily agrarian but also industrial capitalism. Where forest communities opposed the presence of deer parks, they were resisting the social and economic repercussions of landscapes created for pleasure and social prestige. Indeed, deer parks were singled out for attack immediately before and during the Civil War partly because they were symbols of aristocratic power.

Thus in the first series of attacks to be considered, those between 1640 and 1649, there is more than an echo of the events of 1548-50. The major difference

LAND PROTESTS

▲   Protests concerned with draining of fen or marsh

●   Protests concerned with forest or woodland

■   Protests concerned with enclosure or clearance

□   Villages involved in the 1596 attempted rising

◆   Protests concerned with tenure disputes

P   Attacks on deer parks or emparkments

▨   Destruction of property titles (1640-49)

⊠   Camps (1549)

■?   Approximate location, or protests known to be in
     that county but exact location unknown

FARMING REGIONS 1500-1640

	Fenland
	Wood Pasture
	Open Pasture
	Marshland
	Clay Vales
	Downland, Wolds and Breckland

Map 14. Deer Park: 1640-9

is, however, as we have seen, there was no wider agrarian revolt in southern and eastern England of which the deer park attacks were but one part. The link with the protests of 1548-50 is even more direct because certain aristocratic parks were attacked on both occasions as at Arundel and Kenninghall Place, the estates of the Earl of Arundel and Surrey, and at Guildford. These form but one element of the attacks on deer parks. Secondly, there were the destruction of fences, the cutting down of trees and the killing of deer in the royal forests and private estates of the Home Counties and Hampshire, the area that was to be the scene of the Blacking protests in the 1720s. Earlier, the exploitation of the royal forests for revenue has been stressed as provoking resistance by foresters. In the forests closer to London, in contrast, James I and Charles I, like their Hanoverian descendants, intensified the game laws and their control of the royal forests for hunting, thus interfering in the forest economy. Thirdly, there were the attacks on deer parks by parliamentary troops. Although such actions occurred in the Home Counties, they account mainly for the incidents in the Midlands as the army marched north. Finally, there were the riots in Essex, chiefly in the Stour valley in 1642. As Holmes argues, the main body of rioters came from the cloth towns of the valley. The cloth industry was then in a state of economic crisis brought on by the worsening political situation.[1]

In the period 1660-1714 Beloff notes a number of attacks on deer parks that occurred in the Home Counties, Hampshire and Kent. What is missing for this period, however, is a fully researched study of the attacks on Catholics in rural areas during the Glorious Revolution of 1688. Beloff briefly refers to park-pales being torn down and deer being seized but without specific locational detail for these to be mapped.[2]

In the early 1720s there occurred the first and major outbreaks of Blacking, systematic and organised attacks on deer parks in royal deer forests and on private estates with deer parks or fisheries. These happened mainly in Windsor Forest, the Farnham area of Hampshire, Alice Holt Forest, Woolmer Forest, Waltham Chase, the Forest of Bere and, nearer to London, Enfield Chase and Richmond Park. Because of the nature of Blacking the map can only give a general impression of the numbers of incidents between areas. The whole series of incidents and its socio-economic and political context has been thoroughly and brilliantly detailed by E.P. Thompson. Control of the royal forests had been relaxed since 1649. Blacking was a response to the attempted reactivation of that forest authority for the aggrandisement of the Hanoverian monarch and, on the other hand, to the enlargement of private deer emparkments as visible evidence of the wealth and power of the new Whig elite. It thus occurred mainly in the Home Counties and Hampshire where the King and those great gentry had their hunting retreats. The deer were attacked '. . . as symbols (and as agents) of an authority which threatened' those who lived in the forests, small gentry, yeomen, artisans and labourers. It was not just that their deer poaching activities were being constrained rather what was threatened was their very livelihood: taking land from the waste, utilising the wood and timber resources of the forest, cutting turf, peat and heath, the crops standing in the fields now open to

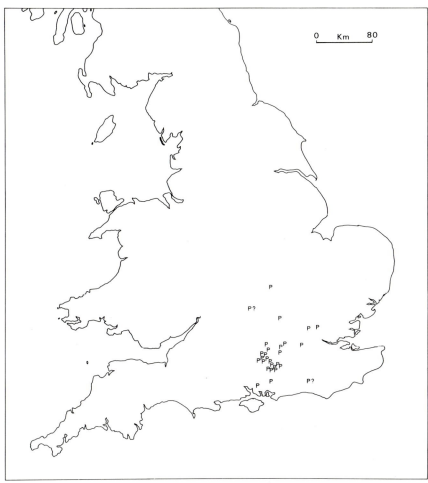

LAND PROTESTS

▲   Protests concerned with draining of fen or marsh

●   Protests concerned with forest or woodland

■   Protests concerned with enclosure or clearance

□   Villages involved in the 1596 attempted rising

◆   Protests concerned with tenure disputes

P   Attacks on deer parks or emparkments

▨   Destruction of property titles (1640-49)

▨   Camps (1549)

■?   Approximate location, or protests known to be in
       that county but exact location unknown

FARMING REGIONS 1500-1640

⊟	Fenland
☐	Wood Pasture
▥	Open Pasture
▨	Marshland
▨	Clay Vales
▨	Downland, Wolds and Breckland

Map 15. Deer Park: 1702-40

the depredations of the deer and grazing rights. Fish ponds were also attacked because when they were enlarged they probably flooded the foresters' gravel and peat pits. Landscaped parks encroached on common land itself thus extinguishing valuable common-right assets. The draconian Black Act, brought in to deal with the foresters' resistance to these changes, did not end the resistance in its heartland but channelled it from overt to covert forms: arson, maiming of beasts, gates smashed, saplings cut down, death threats to gamekeepers. In other forest areas outside those where Blacking had been prevalent, there may have been an extension of serious attacks and this accounts for those attacks away from the Home Counties, Berkshire and Hampshire.[3]

Notes

1. Yarlott (1963), ch. 1; Manning (1976), pp. 188-93; Holmes (1974), pp. 43-5.
2. Beloff (1938), pp. 42-4, 76.
3. Thompson (1975).

2.18 OPPOSITION TO ENCLOSURE IN NORTHAMPTONSHIRE c1760-1800
Jeanette M. Neeson

Gonner wrote in 1912 that the lack of protest at enclosure confirmed its general benefit and despite the weakness of his logic — injustice is not always resisted — the argument has flourished.[1] Recent findings on the high cost of enclosure and the frequent sale of small owners' lands at enclosure in Warwickshire, Buckinghamshire and Northamptonshire indicate the need for another look at the response to enclosure. Such a study of Northamptonshire parishes enclosed between 1760 and 1800 shows that enclosure was more generally unpopular and more widely resisted than Gonner or more recent historians have believed (Map 16A).

In Northamptonshire local or parliamentary counter-petitions or written protests were drawn up in 15 parishes (12 per cent of all enclosures made between 1760 and 1800); most of them were brought at least partly by small owners and cottagers. Similar men and women refused to sign the enclosure Bill in two out of every three enclosures. And the law was broken in efforts to deter or disrupt enclosing in at least 19 parishes.

All this would point to a contested transition from open field to enclosed farming in this county but arguments over the degree and significance of resistance have been bedevilled by the nature of the sources and by a misconception of what significant resistance should look like. The parliamentary evidence is opaque: many counter-petitions were only briefly noted, and surviving full copies, or locally presented counter-petitions, are few and far between. Similarly, refusals to approve the bills were weighed in terms of the amount of land, cottages and rights owned by those opposed to the bill but in a way that tells us virtually nothing about the number of commoners opposed to the enclosure. Other kinds of protest are only slightly documented: the absence of Assize records for the Midland circuit and the custom of summarily prosecuting many offences associated with opposition make it difficult to draw the boundaries of unlawful resistance other than lightly (Map 16B). Finally, historians looking forward from the rising of 1607 or back from the Last Labourers' Revolt of 1830-1 saw nothing of the same magnitude in the eighteenth century, and concluded that enclosure simply made already existing economic formations more efficient and more profitable. But the comparison misleads. Certainly there was no uprising, but then parliamentary enclosure came slowly, village by village, over a period of 60 years or more; and it came with all the force of law. Resistance is more likely to have been equally local and equally spread over time.

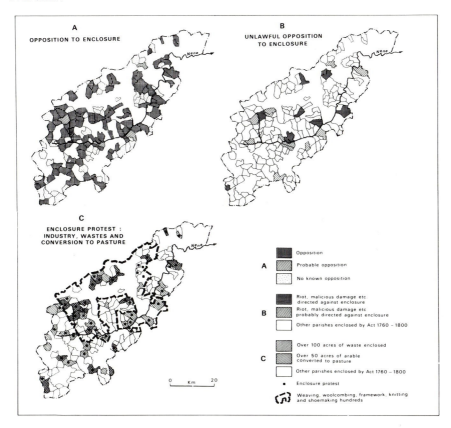

Map 16. Opposition to Enclosure in Northamptonshire, 1760-1800

Piecing together more and less valuable sources and plotting them against the incidence of enclosures of wastes and conversion to pasture — two of the most common fears of opponents of enclosure — allows a reconstruction of the probable shape of discontent to be made (Map 16C). Refusals to sign enclosure bills, the sources of counter-petitions, and the location of unlawful resistance all show a concentration of resistance in the mixed farming scarplands of middle and western Northamptonshire and in the Nene valley. We may guess that the bulk of unrecorded opposition lay here too. Why was enclosure resisted more here than elsewhere?

Almost without exception the enclosure of waste was opposed everywhere, and fears of conversion to pasture may have been almost as provocative, but both wastes and conversion were more common and met more resistance where open fields and rural industry coincided. Here small farmers, petty tradesmen and artisans won their livings from a balance of landholding, pasture rights and trades or handicrafts. Landless commoners supported themselves with fuel, pasture, browse, food and other benefits from commons, with seasonal agriculture labour and with weaving, spinning and carding, woolcombing and stocking-making, matmaking, shoemaking and lacemaking which enabled the whole family to work. More substantial wastes, more supportive rural industry and, probably, a more general absence of consolidated landowning ensured some resistance to enclosure. Elsewhere, smallholders and landless commoners shared a starker dependence on land, on less valuable common rights and on agricultural labour. Enclosure offered little to commoners in either economy, but the open fields and wastes of the Nene valley and the west (and of the still open forests and fen) supported more people; and coincident rural industry allowed commoners to escape dependence on enclosing landlords and employers — an independence expressed in counter-petitions, fence-breaking and arson.

Note

1. For a fully referenced account, see Neeson (1977).

3 THE GEOGRAPHY OF FOOD RIOTS 1585-1847

3.1 INTRODUCTION

Food riots in Britain were in the main the direct collective actions of town artisans and proto-industrial and industrial, that is non-agricultural, workers. The lists of arrested rioters read like a roll call of the trades and industries of Britain. Only in Wales did the yeoman-small farmer play any noticeable role in food rioting.[1] Even the food riots of the East Anglian fenland in 1816, the one series of riots that is cited as the exception that proves the rule were not the demonstrations of crowds composed wholly of agricultural labourers. As will be seen, the demands for decreased food prices in those protests probably came from a section of the crowd who were not full-time agricultural labourers. The reasons why agricultural labourers were rarely at the centre of food disturbances will be discussed below (see pp. 140-1). Thus there was a marked difference between the composition of the crowd in an English, Welsh or Scottish food riot and that in a French rural food riot: the latter crowd was mainly composed of peasants.[2] The fact that food rioting in Britain was mainly a strategy employed by industrial workers in defence of their living standards has certain implications for any study of the geography of food riots, particularly an explanation of regional shifts in that geography.

First it means that the task of explaining the changing regional patterns of food rioting is much more complex than was the explanation of the shift from centre to periphery of land protests. This is perhaps best illustrated by first examining an explanation of changing spatial patterns of food rioting in rural France. There rioting is seen as a response to the penetration of the peasant economy by dealers from outside. Tilly's summary of events reads:

> Actions to block the shipment of grain characteristically took place in small towns and villages ... They rose ... as an effective demand for grain to feed cities and armies extended into agricultural regions previously little involved in production for the market ... The blockage gave the village's consumers the means of coercing the sellers and the local authorities. But it could only work (and was, in fact, only likely to be tried) where there were few merchants and where the authorities were sympathetic, weak and/or divided. That means outside the areas of thorough agrarian capitalism.[3]

Moreover, the corollary to such a description would be that as those peasant economies were later completely transformed by agrarian capitalism, food rioting died out. This was because the food rioters themselves, the independent peasants, had been eliminated. This description of the advent and demise of food rioting in rural France in the eighteenth and nineteenth centuries is not unlike the descriptions we have offered to explain the advent and demise of land riots in rural Britain. The fact that in Britain industrial workers in the main led food riots rather than agricultural workers or small farmers means that a whole new set of factors have to be considered. Outbreaks of food rioting are as much related to regional patterns of industrial development and growth as to developments in internal trade or the expansion of agrarian capitalism. Industrial growth created new sources of demand for foodstuffs that cut across old established patterns of internal trade. It created new 'uncontrollable' communities from which food riots could be launched, often in regions of agrarian capitalist development. Thus simultaneously, in the same county or even the same areas, as the development of agrarian capitalism was producing tightly controlled social structures, almost cheek-by-jowl industrial communities were arising, making demands on that increasing agricultural produce, which was usually bound for out of the region, and with the ability to mobilise to claim that produce as their own if the demands were not met. In Britain, therefore, 'areas of thorough agrarian capitalism' did not escape food rioting. This will be best illustrated when the outward movement of food rioting northwards and westwards from the south and east of England is examined.

Secondly, any attempts to explain the presence or absence of food riots in a particular region must do so within the context of the evolving class relations within the particular industries that dominate the region. Only then can a full understanding be gained of the development of the solidarity of these occupational communities and of the nature of the occasions on which the moral economy of food marketing was invoked. These questions will be examined with examples from the coal industry.

Thirdly, the demise of food rioting at the end of the eighteenth century has been fitted into a 'Pilgrim's Progress' of industrial relations which has respectable trade unionists as its end point. This view tends to see as anachronistic any food riots that occurred after food rioting had ceased to be a general phenomenon of working class life and any revival of food rioting on a large scale as atavistic. This 'enormous condescension of posterity', as Thompson rightly calls it, is ever more present with the proliferation of slick theories of modernisation.[4] It is hoped to demonstrate the fallacy of such a view.

The clearest picture one can gain of the spatial shift of food rioting outwards from the south and east of England and the West Country, the main regions that had seen food disturbances before 1660, is to trace on the maps the first appearance of riots staged to halt the movement of foodstuffs in each region along the coastline of Britain. The advantage of doing this is that the appearance of the first riots can be matched against information on coastal movements of foodstuffs, for which there is much more recorded than for land or inland waterway shipments.

Many of the coastal regions of Britain had been involved in the export trade in foodstuffs at least 50 years before the first outbreaks of food rioting.[5] The presence of corn factors from either London or another large city was therefore not something novel in many regions. It was only when the normal marketing practices began to be ignored by dealers and farmers that potential problems arose. These, however, only became clashes of interest if the export trade was in direct competition with local demand and they only led to food rioting if there were communities capable of taking direct collective action to assert the supremacy of the normal marketing practices in order that local demand was met first before that of outside dealers. That was most likely to happen in areas of industrial growth. To be fully sure, however, that the arrival of outside dealers and factors were not sufficient conditions for a change in normal marketing practices to take place, one needs detailed regional knowledge of changes in marketing practices. For most of England and Wales, however, there is a dearth of such detailed evidence. The evidence is a little clearer for Scotland. Thus one has to make certain inferences about marketing practices in each of the regions examined.

Rule has discussed the changing nature of the Cornish grain trade in relation to the rise of the mining industry after the Restoration. In the seventeenth century, Cornwall had been on balance an exporter of grain. The rise of the mining industry 'created a specialised labour force dependent for its food supply on an agricultural sector whose productivity was increasing at a much slower rate than the industrial sector'. Yet the export trade continued at least until the mid-eighteenth century. As Rule notes this would not have been a problem if miners had been allowed to buy first in the markets before sales were made to corn factors and if farmers had brought to market sufficient corn to meet the needs of the miners. Rule believes that it was this preference on the part of farmers to sell in bulk to merchants and factors rather than selling corn in small quantities in local markets that was the weakest point in the Cornish system.[6] It is not clear, however, when this preference arose. It is probably most likely that it developed contemporaneously with the rise of the mining industry during the decline of interventionism in the internal trade in grain in the latter half of the seventeenth century. Before that period most exported grain would have passed through the local markets. Thus by 1700, years of either regional or more especially national food shortage were to produce conflicts for the first time between the miners and those engaged in the shipment of grain out of the county.

In the north-east of England the effects of the increased demand for foodstuffs caused by industrial growth, unlike Cornwall, did stimulate agrarian change within the region. Such agrarian change, however, undermined the local marketing practices through farmers and dealers wishing to engage in an interregional and unrestricted trade in foodstuffs. The coal industry had been established in the north-east since the sixteenth century. The demand for foodstuffs of an industrial population had meant that even by 1634 there was a large inward flow of grain into the region from East Anglia to supplement local sources of supply.[7] The growth of industry and of local markets had also led, particularly in the period 1630 to 1680, to the enclosure of many common and open field areas.[8] This has already been noted for Tyneside for the even earlier period of the 1590s. The land on newly enclosed farms was converted in many cases from arable to pasture on enclosure. As Hodgson points out, this was for two reasons: land exhausted with continued ploughing and cropping (presumably to meet the growing demands for corn locally) and to supply hay for a growing horse population for industrial uses and dairy produce for the growing towns and industrial villages. By 1731 these agrarian changes had led to Newcastle becoming a 'heavy shipper of butter' out of the region, as had Stockton-on-Tees.[9] This was capitalist, free trade comparative advantage working for the benefit of all. However, such nascent complementary interregional trade flows were fragile and could be exposed during a harvest scarcity. Then the local region could not fall back on its own grain supplies for they had been diminished to make room for the pastoral farming. Moreover, the north-east still had an export trade in grain, presumably for the same reasons as its persistence in Cornwall. In 1740 the miners took the appropriate actions, for the first time during such a scarcity, to bring to the authorities' attention such matters and to assert the values of regional self-sufficiency, one of the basic tenets of the older moral economy of food marketing.

Similarly in Scotland the northward shift of food rioting along the east coast was as much related to agrarian developments internal to the regions concerned as to industrial developments. All the areas that saw food rioting on the east coast between 1772 and 1847 had been involved in the grain trade since the seventeenth century.[10] Moreover, from Whyte's research there is a clearer picture of the practices of the grain trade in Scotland during that century than for England during the same period. On the production side it has already been noted that landowners were influential in initiating grain production for the market (see p. 23). This was also true of the marketing of grain — trade to distant markets meant shipment by sea. As Whyte notes 'the standard procedure for the sale of a consignment of grain was for the proprietor to negotiate a contract with a merchant, or group of merchants, in one of the larger burghs'.[11] Thus the shipments of grain did not pass through the local marketing system first. The practices of the grain trade are obscured in the next 150 years, again by lack of research. It can be inferred, however, from Richards' study of the 1847 food riots that the dual system of grain marketing continued and evolved with small farmers supplying local markets and large farmers contracting to sell all their produce outside the region. Over the same period, however, there were agrarian and industrial changes which on the one hand undermined the former type of marketing and on the other hand greatly expanded the local demand for staple foodstuffs.

For example, in his study of the 1847 food riots of north-eastern Scotland, Richards demonstrates how agrarian change had moved northwards and transformed this coastal region in the previous 50 years. Small holdings had been engrossed and the spread of the 'modern system' had widened productive possibilities in the region. Wheat production in particular had been greatly expanded.[12] Richards fails, however, to mention explicitly the other key change: the revolution in the herring fishing industry. The newly capitalised industry with its expanded catch and its consequent expanded shore processing demanded greater numbers of fishermen, curers and coopers, many of whom supported themselves partly on tiny plots of potato land.[13] Thus when in 1846 and 1847 there was a failure of the potato crop throughout the region and in the rest of Britain and a consequent steep rise in the demand for and price of other staple foodstuffs, the local marketing system, now bereft of many of its small suppliers, was not able to cope with the situation. There was thus the potential for a head-on clash between fishermen and their neighbours, the capitalist farmers and large merchants, with the former group appealing to the tenets of the moral economy of the now completely inadequate local marketing system and the latter group, upholding the tenets of the market economy. The crux of the problem was the undermining of local markets by agrarian and industrial change and the rigidity of the market economy in not bending to its social responsibilities during subsistence crises. Before that the two systems had co-existed together, almost as dual economies. It was not simply the spread of market principles into the region *per se* that had caused the clash between the two systems.

Thus the northward and westward shift of export rioting in the eighteenth and first half of the nineteenth centuries was more related to an underlying shift in the industrial and agricultural base of the kingdom than any simple direct change in the spatial structure of the internal trade in foodstuffs. Industrial growth placed strains on the system of local marketing whose very practices were changing and were even being undermined by developments in capitalist agriculture.

It would be wrong, however, to conclude that the growth of industrial, that is, non-agricultural, communities necessarily led to food rioting being staged as the appropriate strategy of their members in defence of their standards of living. The class relations in their industry and region were just as important as a determinant. They could even constrain industrial workers from taking any direct collective action. For example, the colliers are usually regarded as the archetypal food rioters yet not all colliers rioted in every, or even most, dearths. First, colliers were not part of a free wage proletariat in every area of Britain. In Scotland in the group of burghs on the Firth of Forth that were developing into coal and salt towns in the seventeenth century, the workforce of colliers and salters had been enserfed over the course of the first half of the seventeenth century.[14] At the same time there was a striking change in the pattern of grain sales in this region which supplied Edinburgh with the bulk of its grain. After the 1670s grain was increasingly bought in large cargoes by Edinburgh merchants. As Whyte points out, the growth of the Edinburgh grain market thus 'parallels on a smaller scale, the expansion of the London food market a century earlier'.[15] There were no food riots, however, comparable to those by the Kentish and Essex textile workers, partly because the main industrial communities of the region were not communities of free men. Moreover, the Scottish coalminers, not emancipated until 1799, were not to play any comparable role to their rebellious English and Welsh counterparts.[16]

Secondly, there was a marked difference between the industrial relations on the north-east English coalfield and those on other coalfields. In coalfields outside the north-east there were, as Stevenson notes, relatively few industrial disputes. In the north-east there were recurrent clashes between the colliers and their employers. What Stevenson fails to underline is a parallel dichotomy over the colliers' propensity to riot over the issue of food. Between 1741 and 1794 the north-east colliers were not involved in protests over food prices or food supply, whilst coalminers in other areas were either enhancing or obtaining their reputation for riotous behaviour over those very issues. Part of the answer for this regional differentiation is given by Stevenson. On the north-east coalfield 'the industry had developed to a greater degree than elsewhere through the east coast trade to London. Here the colliers appear to have been much more conscious of their bargaining power in a highly capitalised trade and were also faced by an increasingly competitive group of coal-owners'.[17] This is, however, the reverse side of the coin to the lack of food riots. They had, on the one hand, the industrial muscle successfully to take on the owners, as in the long campaign of resistance of 1765 when they defeated the owners' attempts to change the conditions of hiring.[18] On the other hand, they could see clearly that the coal-owners were their real opponents in their defence of their standard of living. This was made even clearer by the virtual absence of the 'butty' sub-contract system on the north-east coalfield.[19] By this system the only employees who received their wages direct from the employer were the few charter masters. Out of these earnings they hired and paid their own gang of assistants.[20] In the north-east coalminers worked as individuals and were employed directly by large capitalist coalowners. In other coalfield areas the lower levels of capitalisation of the coal industry, and the greater degree of paternalism in the relations between masters and men, enhanced by the butty system, meant that the dealers and middlemen could be used as a suitable target of opprobrium by the coalowners in times of dearth and so draw attention away from the level of the miners' wages. The paternalism was actively fostered for this very reason. One example of its success is from the riots of 1740 when the miners of Sir Thomas Mostyn moved about the Flintshire countryside seeking out dealers and staying the export of corn crying 'A Mostyn'.[21] Nor was it only landowners-cum-capitalists who used the tactic. In the east Shropshire coalfield in 1756, as Trinder notes, it was the new capitalist ironmasters who took steps to buy off the rioters, both colliers and ironworkers, through gifts of money, beer and bread. The local magistrate supported their actions by intervention in the marketing of food. This paternalist behaviour was to be continued for the next half century. Indeed it was so successful than on a number of occasions rioting was prevented altogether, as in 1782. Each time it was employed and indeed at each success it legitimised the men's actions and ensured they would continue that strategy as a bargaining weapon during the next dearth.[22]

Finally, there is the question of the demise of food rioting over much of

Britain in the period 1801-20 and its return in 1847 on the periphery of Britain.

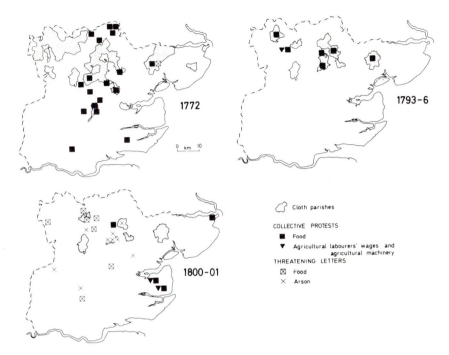

Map 17. Protests over Food in Essex, 1772-1801

Source: Cloth parishes, Brown (1969), ch. 1; protests, ibid., pp. 131-2; Amos (1971), ch. 2; Stevenson (1979), p. 36; *London Gazette* (1772, 1793-6, 1800-1). (I would like to thank E.P. Thompson for the latter material.)

In certain regions in southern England the reason for the demise of food rioting marked the decline of industrial communities themselves. The clearest example of this is the textile industry of Essex, whose workers had a record second to none for their desire to have fair marketing and a constant supply of foodstuffs in their towns and villages. In the 1750s the clothworkers of Braintree had even formed a co-operative to buy flour in bulk for sale to their members.[23] From that decade, however, the cloth industry went into decline, which turned into a dramatic collapse in the 1790s.[24] The industry's fortunes were mirrored in the changing nature of food protests. Thus one moves from the extensive food rioting in 1772, to a more limited outbreak in 1793-6, to the predominance of fires and threatening letters in 1800-1 (Map 17). The ability of workers from textile communities to intervene collectively in the marketing of food had been related to the strength of solidarity in those communities. When that ability had been cut short by the dramatic collapse of their industry, all that workers in these moribund communities could deploy in the first place against their old protagonists — the millers, the dealers, the farmers — were threatening letters and arson. In 1810-13 and 1816-18 they could not even do that. Thus the contraction of the 'war' industries after 1815 and of rural industries, particularly those associated with the clothing industry, under the impact of competition from the industries of northern and Midland England and central Scotland, left certain regions of southern England bereft of the small town artisans and rural industrial workers, who had throughout the eighteenth century, and particularly in the period 1794-1801, mounted food riots.

In the heavily capitalised growth industries such as coal, iron and textiles the decisive shift of tactics by industrial workers away from food rioting to wage bargaining came at the end of the eighteenth century. As Foster argues, the turning point was the onset of industrial cycles not related to bad harvests and stoppages due to wartime blockages of trade but to the inner transformations of capitalist development. Beginning in the 1780s, bursts of investment with unprecedently fast growth in the size of the labour force (and at times wages) were followed by falling prices, suspended investment, unemployment and wage cutting. By the end of the century also food price levels were steadily and apparently irreversibly rising. Under such circumstances workers' attention was decisively being shifted to the wages front.[25] Moreover, as Trinder concludes for the Shropshire iron and steel industries, the ancient sense of contract between ironmasters and men, by which the men refrained from damaging works in return for the masters' assuming responsibility for their relief during food crises, was broken by the start of the seven year depression of the iron trade in 1815.[26] Furthermore, the contract could only work without great expense and loss of profits for the employers if the food crises were intermittent in any case. After 1800 the employers forced through wage reductions and sent for the troops to protect their property during the strikes and disturbances that ensued. Providing cheap food would have been as costly as not carrying through wage cutting.

The stages in this final transition varied from region to region and one would need to examine in detail the class relations in the different industries of a region before an adequate explanation could be offered for the timing of the demise of food rioting in each area. Food rioting that lingered a little longer in one region should not, however, be regarded as an anachronism. Under such circumstances of industrial conflict with the workers in many industries in a fairly weak bargaining position, any tactics that seemed effective to them to protect their declining standard of living must be seen as relevant to their situation. The case for such an approach has been ably demonstrated by those historians who have sought to place food rioting in northern English industrial towns in such a context in the period 1793-1801 and in the period of the Luddite campaign of 1811-12.[27]

The demise in the urbanised industrial areas of Britain seems to have been sealed on the food marketing side by the era of low grain prices between 1819-46, the development of a rail network linking such centres to the sources of their food supply directly or via the ports, and partly consequent on this, developments in the retail and wholesale trade, which needed the fast and guaranteed transport service the railways could provide. From the 1860s there was the added and important factor of cheap food imports. On the industrial side, the continuation of successive cycles of boom and depression with the accompanying unemployment and wage cutting in the latter period kept attention focused on those issues. Yet food riots could still occur even if on rarer occasions, as at Liverpool in 1855 and London in 1860-1 and 1866-7.[28]

Why then the resurgence of food rioting on the periphery of Britain, in Cornwall and north-east Scotland, in the potato famine year 1846-7? This can best be answered by including another series of food riots for comparative purposes: the riots and boycotts that took place in Cumberland in the winter of 1916-17.[29] The common general features would appear to be: the presence of industrial communities which were still small enough, even in the case of towns, not entirely to be divorced from their rural hinterland and the continued export trade of foodstuffs to urban centres outside the region where higher prices could be gained. The rural setting gave a certain visibility to the workings of the food trade and particularly to the participants in the trade, the farmers and dealers. Moreover, class relations and attitudes between the farmers and dealers and the industrial workers meant that the former group were readily believed to be profiteering. In all the regions the industrial workers when laid off probably had experience of working for the local farmers. Furthermore, in Cornwall the paternalism of the local lords and the class memory of recent food riots continued to focus anger on dealers and farmers for high prices in years of scarcity. These are the general factors. The specific factors must await the historian of the 1847 food riots who must, as Richards notes, eventually compare areas that rioted with those that did not, say, for example, examining Cumberland in 1847 to see why that region remained quiet.

This task as well as examining food rioting in a regional and industrial context over long time perspectives should now be undertaken. It has only been possible here to sketch out some of the questions that might be asked. The maps of food rioting we have before us here cannot be given their proper interpretation without such studies. It is perhaps not surprising then that historians to date, who seem to have been more perceptive about the changing geography of food rioting than of that for any other form of social protest, have tended simply to note such spatial patterns and pass on.[30]

Notes

1. See, for example, the evidence presented in the commentaries and in the following: Jones (1973), ch. 1; Logue (1979), ch. 9; Stevenson (1979), ch. 5.
2. Rudé (1964), p. 45.
3. Tilly (1975), p. 387.
4. Thompson (1968), pp. 12-13.
5. Willan (1938), chs. 6, 8-10; Whyte (1979), pp. 228-31.
6. Rule (1971), pp. 121-5.
7. Willan (1938), p. 115.
8. Hodgson (1973), pp. 148-9.
9. Willan (1938), p. 116; Hodgson (1973), p. 149.
10. Whyte (1979), pp. 228-31.

11. Ibid., pp. 223-8.
12. Richards (1981), section II(i). I would like to thank Professor Richards for allow-ing me to see a draft of this publication.
13. Gray (1957), pp. 158-60.
14. Smout (1972), pp. 167-70.
15. Whyte (1979), p. 231.
16. Logue (1979), p. 193.
17. Stevenson (1979), p. 124.
18. Ibid., p. 125.
19. Ashton and Sykes (1929), ch. 7.
20. Dodd (1971), p. 365.
21. Ibid., p. 307.
22. Trinder (1973), pp. 376-8.
23. Brown (1969), p. 25.
24. Ibid., ch. 1.
25. Foster (1977), pp. 19-20, 38.
26. Trinder (1973), p. 382.
27. Booth (1977), pp. 99-104; Wells (1977a), pp. 38-46; Dinwiddy (1979), pp. 33-63.
28. Stevenson (1979), p. 293.
29. The account is based on: Cornwall, Rule (1971); Scotland, Richards (1981); Cumberland, Coles (1978), pp. 157-76.
30. Rose (1961), pp. 285-6; Thompson (1971), p. 110.

3.2 1585-1649   John Walter

Urbanisation, regional specialisation and market integration were the larger changes against which disorder was directed in this period.[1] Dearth, occasioned by the recurrent crisis of harvest failure and trade depression, exposed the weak points and tensions that these changes had created. The government's continued public endorsement of traditional economic suppositions and popular condem-nation of changes in marketing practice were sources of legitimation for the crowd's actions. Since the central government kept an anxious watch on out-breaks of disorder in conditions of scarcity, its records provide a reasonably accurate indication of the chronology and topography of the food riot. These records have been supplemented by and checked against a systematic search of central legal and local records. While this national survey is still in progress at a local level, and despite the difficulties of using such evidence already noted and probably at their worst in this early period, it is possible to offer a preliminary indication of the patterning of food riots between 1585 and 1649.[2]

1585-1607

In this period there were some 20 incidents of disorder recorded: three, possibly four, in 1586, five in 1595, two in 1596, five in 1597 and five in 1605. These

Map 18. Food: 1585-1607

Additional source: navigable waterways, Willan (1936), map I; wood-pasture regions, Thirsk (1967), figure 1; amended from Martin (1979), part III, map: The Midland Revolt of 1607.

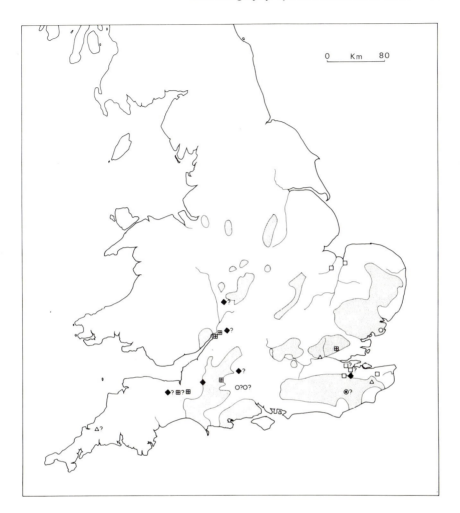

FOOD PROTESTS

⊙	Food protest: type unknown	●	Attack on mills
△	Crowd action over price of food	⊕	Attack on inns
□	Crowd action to stay transport of food	+	Attack on retailers
⊞	Seizure of foodstuffs	▼	Attack on distilleries or breweries
◇	Attack on farmers	✳	Attack on magistrates or principal inhabitants
○	Attack on storehouses, warehouses or granaries	✕	Extortions of money, food or drink
◆	Attack on dealers		

⌒ Navigable waterways   ⬭ Wood Pasture Zone 1500-1640

⊙? Approximate location , or protests known to be in that county but exact location unknown

occurred in the counties of Somerset, Gloucestershire, Wiltshire, Hampshire, Kent, Sussex, Cambridgeshire, Norfolk and Essex. In 1586 disorder was concentrated in the West Country, signalling an association that was to persist throughout the period. Crowds, 500-600 strong, in which clothworkers almost certainly predominated, twice attacked the barges moving grain down the Severn. In addition, there were otherwise unsubstantiated reports of riots in Cornwall and other western shires. Depression in the textile trade and a preceding poor harvest seem to have lain at the root of the disorder. The bad harvests of the 1590s brought more widespread disorder. In May 1595, women at Wye in Kent attacked and took grain from a yeoman, reportedly among those taking supplies to market. On consecutive days in June London apprentices enforced a policy of 'taxation populaire' on fish and butter. This policy seems also to have been the intention of the Kentish rioters. In October crowds in Wiltshire were reported to have seized grain from badgers moving it from Warminster, the region's largest grain market, and similar disorder has been recorded for Basingstoke in the same year. Despite worsening harvests and evidence of widespread discontent only two riots have been recovered for 1596: in February rioters at Canterbury stayed carts carrying grain they believed destined for export, while in November labourers' wives at Navestock in Essex took grain probably destined for the London market. In 1597 there were several riots in Norfolk aimed at preventing the shipping of grain; further disorder was reported on the Kent/ Sussex borders and in the West Country where those collecting grain for Bristol were attacked. Thereafter, the restoration of the harvest equilibrium saw a diminution in disorder. There were, however, localised riots in 1600 at Shepton Mallet, Somerset, against the activities of London merchants' deputies purchasing grain for the army in Ireland and in 1605 in Kent and possibly Wisbech, against the export of grain, which should caution against an overly deterministic model for rioting.

1608-39

In this period evidence has been recovered for some 40 or more riots, one, possibly two, in 1608, four in 1614, one in 1618, six in 1622, ten in 1629, five in 1630 and 15 in 1631. The counties of Somerset, Wiltshire, Hampshire, Berkshire, Kent, Sussex, Essex, Suffolk, Norfolk, Hertfordshire and Leicestershire were all the scene of protests. The dearth of 1608 brought only limited disorder. At Southampton a crowd of women proved over-enthusiastic allies for the town's magistracy: forcibly unloading a ship destined for London, whose cargo of grain the corporation had ordered stayed. The poor harvest may also have occasioned disorder in Somerset and Northamptonshire. An indictment of two women in the Somerset Quarter Sessions for taking grain and sacks with force may conceal evidence of crowd action, as may a reference to 'some stirring of

Map 19. Food: 1608-39

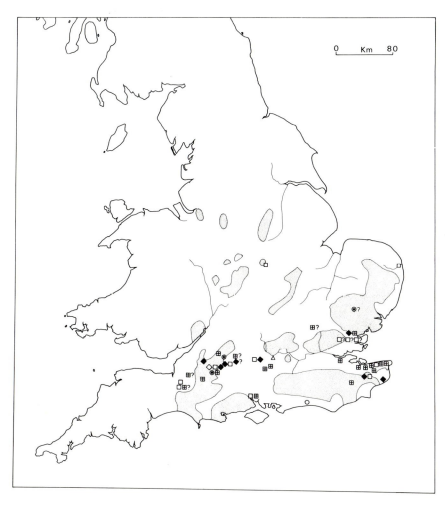

FOOD PROTESTS

⊙	Food protest: type unknown	●	Attack on mills
△	Crowd action over price of food	⊕	Attack on inns
□	Crowd action to stay transport of food	+	Attack on retailers
⊞	Seizure of foodstuffs	▼	Attack on distilleries or breweries
◇	Attack on farmers	✳	Attack on magistrates or principal inhabitants
○	Attack on storehouses, warehouses or granaries	✕	Extortions of money, food or drink
◆	Attack on dealers		

⌐ Navigable waterways   ⬭ Wood Pasture Zone 1500-1640

⊙? Approximate location, or protests known to be in that county but exact location unknown

the poor people' in Northamptonshire's markets. Disorder was similarly confined in 1614, this time to the single county of Wiltshire. The 'poor craftsmen' of that county having complained to the King of the unrestrained activities of middlemen in their markets, attempted their own reformation. Crowds, 20-60 in number, assaulted the carriers, confiscated their grain and, interestingly, deposited it with local officials. In 1622 depression in the textile industry again involved Wiltshire, but extended the disorder more generally. In Wiltshire riots took the now familiar form of crowds of unemployed clothworkers attacking those taking grain from the county's markets. Similar disorder, involving crowds up to 500 strong, was reported from the textile area of East Somerset. Protests threatened but were not realised in Gloucestershire, whilst they did take place on the Essex/Suffolk border in the area of the New Draperies. Disorder at Dover, provoked by the export of grain, provides the one exception to this series of disturbances involving textile workers.

A deadly combination of trade depression and harvest failure (1630) brought a notable increase in disorder in the period 1629-31. In 1629 there was disorder in Somerset and Essex, occasioned by a shared grievance: the export of grain. The example of Essex suggests that though disorder might be limited geographically and restricted to short periods of time, by its very nature it could appear to pose a considerable threat. In January there was a flurry of riots in south-east Essex in which bands of men and women attacked those moving grain down to the Thames for export. In March and again in May crowds, composed respectively of women and clothworkers, rioted against the shipment of grain and, in the meantime, there had been disorder at Colchester. In Somerset rioters at Langport in April and Gregorystoke in May attacked the movement of grain downstream to be shipped from Bridgwater. On the latter occasion, they returned the grain to its point of departure and informed a local justice of their suspicions that it was being exported contrary to a recent proclamation. Another group of men and women were also indicted for a riot and the taking of grain in Somerset some time before July. Some uncertainty surrounds this riot. By place, residence and date it might more correctly be related to the May riot. The disastrous harvest of 1630 initiated a period of extended disorder. In November 1630 there were riots at Newbury (Berkshire), in Somerset, Wiltshire and Kent all directed against the movement of grain out of the local, depressed economy. Rioters near Bath, for example, attacked badgers carrying grain to Bristol and publicly stated their intention to stop all such traffic in Somerset. While the West Country was quiet in 1631, there were a further series of riots with similar grievance and objective at Woodchurch, Milton and Sittingbourne, Canterbury, Whitstable, Herne, Cranbrook and Faversham in Kent; at Shoreham in Sussex; in Hertfordshire; around Basingstoke, Sherfield and Heckfield in Hampshire; and at Reading. In the latter town the collapse of the local textile industry gave the poor's complaints an added edge.

1640-9

Despite the problems of evidence during this period, what has been recovered seems to indicate a narrowing of the geographical focus of disorder. Evidence has so far been found for some 14 incidents of disorder — two in 1643, five in 1647, seven in 1648 and two in 1649. The early 1640s saw little disorder. In 1643 rioters at Harwich prevented the shipment of grain and at Melksham in Wiltshire the movement of grain to Somerset again provoked disorder. By contrast, the disastrous harvests of the late-1640s were marked by renewed disorder. For the most part, however, this appears to have been concentrated in the Wiltshire and Somerset cloth districts. In 1647-9 there were a series of riots in the area between the forest of Frome Selwood and Warminster and in the triangle between Warminster, Trowbridge and Devizes, in which crowds of clothworkers and probably artisans attacked those attempting to move grain from Wiltshire's markets to Bristol and elsewhere in Somerset. The only exceptions to this geographical narrowing were possible riots in Sussex and the North Riding of Yorkshire and the disorder at Wickham in Cambridgeshire in September 1649. In the latter settlement a crowd of 200 took grain under the notion of 'toll corn for the use of the poor'. Thereafter, the record is silent for the 1650s.

While continuing research might be expected to yield further examples and throw light on some of the dark corners of the land, it is already possible to offer a preliminary explanation for the spatial distribution of the food riot in this period. Grain riots appear to have been geographically limited in their incidence as well as confined, for the most part, to years of crisis. Despite patchy record survival, there appears to have been areas where the food riot was noticeably absent. It does not seem to have been a familiar feature in the northern uplands nor, for that matter, over much of the north and, possibly not even in the region's urban centres. There was no simple and necessary relationship between distress and disorder. Cumberland and Westmorland, for example, experienced classic crises of subsistence, but as yet no food riots have been discovered there. More local research is needed to confirm or qualify this conclusion, but evidence so far suggests that this pattern of popular quiescence may also have been found in Cheshire and southern Lancashire. In the Midlands discontent was equally marked by its absence. The region did not have either large-scale movement of grain or an extensive rural industry, and in accordance with a popular concern with enclosure, disorder took on a different form. Finally, there were the larger urban centres, which combined a sophisticated administrative structure with potential access to reserves of grain and capital, and whose wants the government took care to satisfy, even at the risk of occasioning disorder elsewhere. Only one food riot has so far been found for London in the period and that perhaps significantly, *les deurées de seconde zone*, fish and butter.

It was in settlements within or bordering upon the traditional arable regions which in normal years produced surpluses which went to feed other areas, notably the larger towns, that grain riots were most likely to occur. This was

FOOD PROTESTS

⊙	Food protest: type unknown	●	Attack on mills
△	Crowd action over price of food	⊕	Attack on inns
□	Crowd action to stay transport of food	+	Attack on retailers
⊞	Seizure of foodstuffs	▼	Attack on distilleries or breweries
◇	Attack on farmers	✳	Attack on magistrates or principal inhabitants
○	Attack on storehouses, warehouses or granaries	✕	Extortions of money, food or drink
◆	Attack on dealers		

⌐ Navigable waterways   ⬭ Wood Pasture Zone 1500-1640

⊙? Approximate location, or protests known to be in that county but exact location unknown

true above all of the area which fed London. Riots in Essex, Kent, Sussex, Hertfordshire, Hampshire, the Thames Valley and probably Norfolk can be shown to have been commonly provoked by the siphoning off of local grain supplies to meet metropolitan demand. Similarly, Bristol's voracious appetite helps to explain the other noticeable clustering of riots in the west.

Urban demand, however, provides only a partial explanation of the exact topography of the food riot. Disorder was most likely at the two weakest points in an as yet immature marketing structure. The first of these was the small market and/or industrial centre whose prime economic function in the developing market network was no longer simply to serve as a distributive centre for its immediate region, but increasingly to bulk grain from its rural hinterland, thus easing its passage to the larger urban centres. Newbury, where rioters attacked grain carts bound for Reading in 1630, was one of the few grain markets in Berkshire. Reading, the scene of disorder the following year, was an important entrepôt for the London grain trade. Canterbury acted as a funnel through which downland grain was channelled, whilst in Essex Maldon increasingly served as a clearing port for its rural hinterland. It was at this level of urban development that grain riots were most likely. Though their levels of poverty were shared by the larger towns, their narrow employment base, lack of financial resources or administrative sophistication and the central government's relative indifference to their fate meant that they were particularly vulnerable.

The other flashpoint was in the countryside, in areas of proto-industrialisation. As Professor Everitt has reminded us, the progress of commercial agriculture was by no means even in this period. Grain moving from areas of surplus to urban centres often had to pass through regions, equally dependent upon imported corn but which, in conditions of dearth or depression, could not compete with urban demand. These were the heavily populated, corn-deficient, pastoral woodland areas, all too often dependent on the vagaries of a volatile textile industry. One reason why Bristol's demand prompted so much disorder in the West Country was that grain had to be brought from the region's largest granary, Warminster, along a route traversing the densely populated, corn-deficient cloth districts of Wiltshire and East Somerset, while that brought down the Severn ran the gauntlet of the Forest of Dean on one side and the Gloucestershire cloth district on the other. Riots in Essex (1629), Somerset (1630) and Hampshire (1631) occurred in similar woodland or fen locations. Moreover, these were areas where the absence of a resident magistry may have made popular action not only easier but all the more necessary in the eyes of the poor.

It was the development of a market network, increasingly co-ordinated by metropolitan demand, and the movement of grain this necessitated to which riots were addressed. Over time, the period registered one significant change in the spatial distribution of riots. If the map for the 1640s is substantially accurate it indicates the disappearance of disorder from at least one of the capital's major provisioning areas, Kent.

Map 20. Food: 1640-9

Notes

1. The commentary is based on the author's doctoral research (forthcoming) carried out whilst he was at the University of Cambridge. Because of their number and detail, footnotes have had to be excluded.

2. Excluded from consideration in the commentary are a handful of incidents which require discussion at greater length, because the evidence only suggests the possibility of a riot, often as noted in the introduction where the only firm evidence is the indictment of single persons for assault and theft (see p. 4).

3.3 1660-1737

The years of the interregnum seem to have been marked by an absence of food rioting even though the decennial average price of grain 1653-62 was higher than that for 1623-32 and for the following decade 1663-72.[1] What may explain the quiet on the consumer front is perhaps indicated by Morrill's study of local administration in Cheshire in these years. There he found 'a comprehensive and firm handling by the Justices of the flow and price of grain', a much more effective control of the corn market than in the pre-war situation.[2] By contrast at the Restoration the policy of the government was to give as much considera-tion to the producer as the consumer. By legislation in 1663 many of the restric-tions on the activities of middlemen in the grain trade were lifted and a duty was placed on imported grain. Furthermore, an Act of Parliament of 1670 first allowed the export of grain whatever its price in the home market. Secondly, in 1672 bounties in grain exports were introduced experimentally and then established more firmly by Act of Parliament in 1689. This consolidation of the alliance between the landowning and mercantile classes was at the heart of the social structure of mercantilist England.[3] It is within this changed social and political environment that the five main periods of food rioting between 1660 and 1737 must be viewed.

The first series of protests were in 1662-3 and were concerned with the exportation of corn. They occurred in the ports of Weymouth and Wareham in Dorset and of Christchurch and Southampton in Hampshire. Their occurrence after 22 years of quiescence seems to mark the coincidence of the change in attitude of the officials of the new regime with a time of fairly high corn prices. Over the next 30 years the new policy seems to have had little effect save for a scattering of three grain riots and murmurings among the poor people after the 1670 Act. As Rose points out, this was because of the counteracting influence of a series of good harvests. The first bad harvests came in 1692 and 1693. There were 16 incidents in 1693, three in 1694 and five in 1695. Five main areas can be picked out during this series of disturbances. Again there were protests at

Map 21. Food: 1660-1737

Additional source: Willan (1936), map II.

FOOD PROTESTS

⊙	Food protest: type unknown	●	Attack on mills
△	Crowd action over price of food	⊕	Attack on inns
□	Crowd action to stay transport of food	+	Attack on retailers
⊞	Seizure of foodstuffs	▼	Attack on distilleries or breweries
◇	Attack on farmers	✳	Attack on magistrates or principal inhabitants
○	Attack on storehouses, warehouses or granaries	✕	Extortions of money, food or drink
◆	Attack on dealers		

⌐— Navigable waterways   ⬭ Wood Pasture Zone 1500-1640

⊙? Approximate location , or protests known to be in that county but exact location unknown

two south coast ports. Riots against the export of grain occurred along two major arteries of food transport: the Severn at Worcester and Shrewsbury and in the upper Thames Valley. In the county of Northamptonshire, removed from navigable waterways, there was another major series of protests, again mainly directed at movements of grain. It would seem plausible that the movement of grain out of the river basins adjacent to Northamptonshire had caused grain to move from Northamptonshire to supply towns in these regions. The fifth area was that of the cloth industry of Essex and Suffolk.

There was then a lull in food rioting more because of low prices than because of any action taken by the government. Prices rose steeply again between 1708 and 1710 and rioting broke out in 1709. One incident during the lull does deserve attention. This was the riot at Nottingham in 1701, the details of which are obscure. It was, however, the most northerly extension of food rioting in eastern England known before 1740. The seven protests in 1709 follow very much the same spatial pattern of the 1690s, with two exceptions. In the west the Kingswood colliers marched to Bristol and were appeased by a lowering of the price of grain. More importantly, in the Wrexham–Chester area the high price of corn in the local markets caused disturbances. Dealers, who were buying up grain for export to France, went in danger of their lives. This was the first appearance of food protests in the north Wales region.[4]

After 1712, there were no riots for the next 25 years and when they re-occurred in 1727-9 and 1737 they were located in Cornwall and north Wales. There had already been two incidents in Cornwall in this period in 1690 and 1700. In 1690 at Falmouth tin miners boarded a ship and seized a cargo of salt, a similar incident involving salt occurred at Falmouth in 1727. In 1700 at Truro a corn-dealer's store had been attacked. In 1727-8 rioting broke out in Penzance and Falmouth and Truro were threatened by an invasion of miners. Miners invading market towns and ports and seizing grain was the essential pattern of Cornish riots. Similar incidents occurred again in 1729 in the St Austell area and in St Ives to which tinners from Redruth had come, and in 1737 in Penryn. On this occasion the tinners were en route to Falmouth but were put to flight at Penryn. The other area which saw protests after 1712 was north Wales in 1727. The two incidents involved the export of corn from the Menai Straits region. In one case the shipment was bound for Warrington.[5]

Notes

   1. Lipson (1934), vol. ii, p. 450.
   2. Morrill (1974), pp. 249-51.
   3. Lipson (1934), pp. 431, 462; John (1976), p. 47.
   4. Beloff (1938), ch. 3. Beloff notes a disturbance at Sherborne in 1662 when in fact it occurred at Weymouth. Rose (1961), p. 281; Gruffydd (1977), p. 36; Cust (1914), p. 131.
   5. Rule (1971), pp. 121, 126-31; Isaac (1953), p. 5.

3.4 1740   Robert W. Malcolmson

The winter of 1739 was one of the coldest seasons on record, and, because of these severe conditions, the subsistence of many small consumers became conspicuously tenuous and uncertain.[1] According to William Ellis, a farmer in Buckinghamshire, 'The hard Frost that began about Christmas 1739, and ended the 23d of February following, was deemed the sharpest in the Memory of Man; for it occasioned the Death of many poor People who wanted Heat and Victuals; notwithstanding it was observed that there were never greater Acts of Charity displayed than in this Season.' William Stout, a tradesman in Lancaster, also remarked on the hardships experienced this year: 'It appered that much of the wheat sawn was killed in the ground, and it proved at most but halfe a crop. And the couldness of the spring and late seeding made a failour in oats and barley, so that in this summer corn of all sorts advanced [in price] ; . . . and [we] feared a further advance – which [fear] caused disturbances in many places, by the mob attempting to take corn by force from such as had stocks, or attempted to ship it off, or to carry it to distant markets, upon which many faire dealers were suffrers'.[2]

Several generalisations can be offered concerning the food riots of 1740 (a few extended into early 1741). First, most of these collective popular actions occurred in eastern Britain, north of the Thames; the riots in western and southern counties were less numerous, less concentrated and taken less seriously by the established authorities (north Wales is the only exception to this general pattern). Rioting, then, was found mostly in major grain-growing regions and at or around ports from which grain was being shipped. Secondly, areas to which rioting seems to have spread for the first time were the West Riding of Yorkshire, where mills were the principal targets of the rioters, Teesside and Tyneside, the Edinburgh region, thus extending the phenomenon of food rioting north of the Border, Pembrokeshire in south Wales and Staffordshire. Thirdly, most riots – and virtually all the larger ones – occurred before the harvest, in the spring or early summer (late April through July); only a handful of scattered incidents are recorded for the six months after July.

Fourthly, and perhaps most importantly, the main grievance underlying these collective actions was the exportation of grain from regions where deficiencies were either anticipated or already felt. The popular hostility to grain exports is a recurrent theme in the reports on these riots. The risings in the Dewsbury region of the West Riding, for example, were intended (so it was reported) 'to prevent the Badgers from making Wheat Meal or Flower, to send into other Countries, alledging that such Practice would cause a Scarcity in Yorkshire, and much advance the Price of Corn'. Similarly, in Colchester, Essex in mid-May 'several Hundred Persons rose in a tumultuous Manner . . . under Pretence of stopping Corn, Flower, etc. from being shipp'd for other Parts'.[3] In Northamptonshire, one of the counties most affected by rioting, several merchants and millers took the trouble to publish notices in the *Northampton Mercury*, vehemently denying that they had sent, or intended to send, grain or flour to 'foreign' parts.[4]

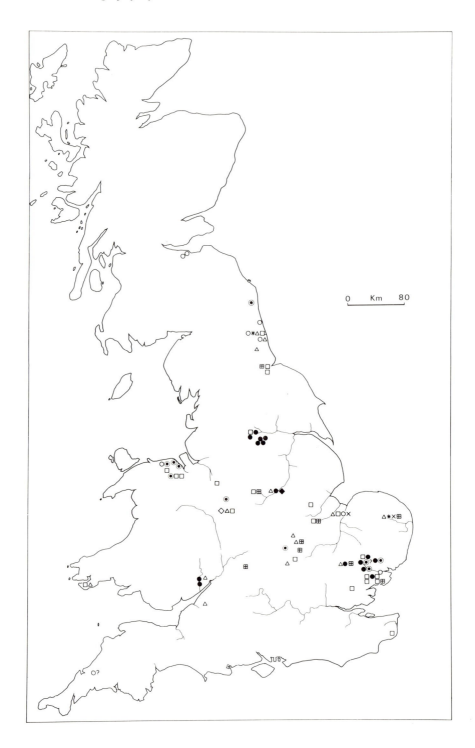

This popular preoccupation with exports (and the fear of a shortfall in local supplies) explains why most crowd actions occurred, not in the public market-place, but rather at mills, granaries and storehouses, and on the highways (when waggons loaded with grain were leaving an ill-provisioned locality), at ports and at other points of transhipment. The painful consequences of a severe winter were being exacerbated, in the opinion of many people, by the prevalence of grain exports, especially to continental markets, and the failure of the authorities to restrain these exports and properly regulate the trade. It is possible that these problems were worsened by the war preparations that were underway at this time, for there are suggestions that grain was being purchased in large quantities for military and naval consumption. Local markets, according to popular opinion, should always be adequately supplied before merchants were allowed to profit from sales abroad: exports, in their eyes, should only be permitted when there was no danger of shortages or major price increases at home. It was this attitude, then, that informed much of the collective protest during this year.

Notes

1. The commentary and map are based on the author's unpublished research on the food riots of 1740, based on the provincial press reports of such incidents with supplementary material from the State Papers Domestic. A further account of the 1740 food riots can be found in Isaac (1953), ch. 1. For Staffordshire, see Hay (1975a), ch. 5.
2. Ellis (1750), vol. VI, part iii, p. 141; Marshall (1967), p. 229. See also Jones (1964), pp. 37, 138-9.
3. *Ipswich Journal*, 17 and 24 May 1740.
4. *Northampton Mercury*, 19 May, 30 June, 7 and 14 July 1740.

Map 22. Food: 1740

FOOD PROTESTS

⊙	Food protest: type unknown	●	Attack on mills
△	Crowd action over price of food	⊕	Attack on inns
□	Crowd action to stay transport of food	+	Attack on retailers
⊞	Seizure of foodstuffs	▼	Attack on distilleries or breweries
◇	Attack on farmers	✳	Attack on magistrates or principal inhabitants
○	Attack on storehouses, warehouses or granaries	✕	Extortions of money, food or drink
◆	Attack on dealers		

╱ Navigable waterways   Wood Pasture Zone 1500-1640

⊙? Approximate location, or protests known to be in that county but exact location unknown

Additional source: Navigable waterways for this and subsequent maps taken from the appendices and maps of the following: Hadfield (1960; 1966a, b; 1967; 1969a, b; 1972/3); Hadfield and Biddle (1970); Lindsay (1968); Boyes and Russell (1977).

3.5 1756-7   Jeremy N. Caple

The food riots of 1756-7 both in their extent and intensity were amongst the most severe of the eighteenth century.[1] After the initial outbreak in the Midlands in August 1756, rioting spread rapidly to the north, to the south and south-west and to Wales. Before it ceased in December 1757 the movement encompassed 30 different counties in England and Wales with over 140 reported incidents of rioting.

In comparison with earlier years of rioting certain differences are immediately apparent; not only was there a dramatic increase in the number of riots but also crowd responses changed somewhat. Previously crowd action to prevent the export of food predominated and while still an important aspect of rioting in 1756-7 increasingly other types of riot occurred, in particular price setting riots, attacks on mills, retailers and grain dealers. Although rioting still took place at coastal and river ports, events in 1756-7 demonstrate that some of the more densely populated areas, particularly in the Midlands and the North, were subject to severe outbreaks of food rioting, as they faced increasing difficulty in feeding their growing populations. In these areas rioting tended to be centred on the market-place, as in price setting riots, or were attacks on mills, dealers and sometimes even the local magistrate. Such actions were designed to intimidate and to punish those the crowd believed responsible for excessive prices.

Riot locations relate specifically to both the immediate and long-term effects of a deficient harvest and to the proximity of transportation networks. Disastrous weather conditions in early 1756, which continued throughout the summer months, struck areas of the west Midlands, south-west England and Wales and the resulting harvest shortages pushed grain prices rapidly upwards. In the west of England and Wales coastal ports and those on the Severn were repeatedly the scene of riots as crowds attempted to prevent grain supplies from leaving the country. Initially rioting was confined to those areas most affected by the

Map 23. Food: 1756-7

FOOD PROTESTS

⊙	Food protest: type unknown	●	Attack on mills
△	Crowd action over price of food	⊕	Attack on inns
☐	Crowd action to stay transport of food	+	Attack on retailers
⊞	Seizure of foodstuffs	▼	Attack on distilleries or breweries
◇	Attack on farmers	✳	Attack on magistrates or principal inhabitants
○	Attack on storehouses, warehouses or granaries	✕	Extortions of money, food or drink
◆	Attack on dealers		

⟋ Navigable waterways   ⬭ Wood Pasture Zone 1500-1640

⊙? Approximate location , or protests known to be in that county but exact location unknown

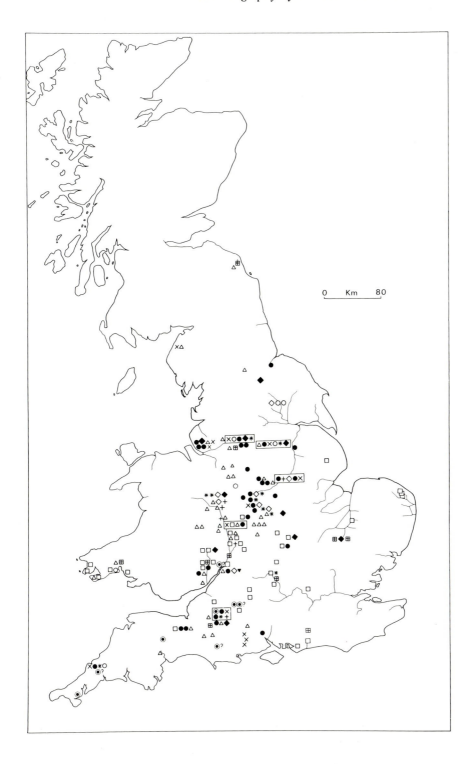

deficient harvest but by the following summer the eastern half of England, which had enjoyed a normal harvest yield in 1756, had been steadily drained of its surplus grain and was subjected to the same violent outbreaks.

Rioting began in August 1756 in Staffordshire and Warwickshire when wheat prices rose from an average 4/6 per bushel to over 8/-. Several large crowds roamed the countryside attacking boulting mills, grain dealers and retailers whilst also setting prices and seizing grain at the market place (see pp. 111-13). The following week saw outbreaks in Nottingham, Sheffield and Derby as prices rose throughout the general area. For two weeks Nottingham and vicinity were in an uproar as local colliers and the labouring poor destroyed ten mills and roamed the countryside taking money, food and drink from farmers. With prices rising rapidly in the England-Wales border region in October the lull in rioting, which had set in after the riots in Nottingham were suppressed in early September, did not last. Beginning in Gloucestershire in October rioting spread to Shropshire and Worcestershire in November and to Herefordshire and Monmouthshire in December. By January 1757 the price of wheat reached 9/- per bushel in south Wales and colliers from Pembrokeshire rioted, seizing grain from ships at Haverfordwest and Laugharne. Rioting had also spread to Cornwall, Devon and Somerset by this time while isolated outbreaks occurred in the north at Berwick-on-Tweed and in Cumberland. April, May and June saw the most widespread rioting of the entire 17 months. Wheat prices reached their peak in early June in most markets in England; at Mark Lane, in London, the price of a quarter of wheat was 70/- while at Devizes it was nearly 80/-. Areas hitherto unaffected now experienced three months of almost continuous rioting which began in Dorset and spread to Hampshire, Oxford, Cambridge, Norfolk and also to the Manchester area. July and August were quiet months but when prices failed to return to acceptable levels in September, fresh incidents occurred and continued until December.

Although prices did not decline significantly for some time no rioting is reported after December. The opening of ports for grain importation, supplies of grain provided through subscriptions, by individuals and by city corporations and a government ban on the use of grain for distilling purposes all helped to mitigate the effects of shortages on the poor.

Note

1. For a complete and fully referenced account of the riots see Caple (1978).

3.6 1766   Dale E. Williams

In 1766 England was in the midst of a major economic slump.[1] The export manufacturing districts of the nation, having during the Seven Years' War experienced a period of prosperity and full employment, felt the change severely.

The transport system which had grown apace with prosperity had enabled those districts to become even more economically specialised — to export more manufactured goods and to import more provisions. A combination of circumstances in 1766 which included cattle murrain, crop failure, extraordinary foreign demand and government inactivity ensured that the commodities which comprised the provision trade were expensive and/or in short supply.

Left to itself, the situation in 1766 was bound to be troublesome. It would not have been so disorderly had not the governments of the Marquess of Rockingham and of the Earl of Chatham unwittingly set the stage for the crisis. Rockingham allowed to lapse in August 1765 parliamentary provisions which admitted corn duty-free; the usual bounty of 5/- per quarter on exported wheat automatically went into effect. Corn merchants who had previously imported corn without paying duty were then enabled to export the same corn for a profit. Corn dealers all over the country took advantage of this and began shipping out as much as possible. This situation led to disturbances in Hampshire and at Lyme in Dorset in January 1766. Parliament acted to re-establish the embargo as soon as it reassembled in January, but that measure was set automatically to expire in August of 1766.

In the spring and early summer of 1766, a southward displacement of usual weather patterns meant fair weather and a good wheat crop for Scandinavia, Scotland, northern England and for part of Prussia, and the opposite for southern England, France, Spain and the Mediterranean areas. The corn harvests in Scotland and northern England were outstandingly good. Fair harvest weather obscured the bad news in the south: the crop *looked* good, but proved to be light in weight and diseased once it was harvested. The unexpected news became known in England at about the same time enormous purchase orders, unrestricted as to price, arrived from Italy, Spain and France. England's embargo expired on 26 August, at the worst possible time. By mid-September the trickle of corn bound for southern Europe increased to a torrent. The spot price for available wheat soared.

Timely measures taken by the Chatham government would have prevented further export of the old crop, prevented the export of the new crop and probably would have prevented the riots. But Chatham's government in August was preoccupied with political manoeuvrings. On 10 September the government issued a rather confusing proclamation which reiterated the Tudor and Stuart laws concerning forestalling, regrating and engrossing. On the same day another proclamation prorogued Parliament from 16 September to 11 November. Together these documents amounted to a public statement that (1) the government had no legal authority to prohibit exportation without parliamentary sanction; and that (2) parliamentary sanction could not be forthcoming for over seven weeks.

Most of the rioting in 1766 came in response to the situation which developed after the government's proclamation of 10 September (graph, Map 24). Every farmer within economic reach of a good road, a navigable river or a port was encouraged to thresh out his wheat as soon as possible for export or, alternatively, to withold his crop in expectation of high prices resulting from domestic scarcity. Additionally, high prices greatly extended the territory from which corn could be exported, so that areas which had not ordinarily exported might then have begun to do so. High prices and the prospect of scarcity tended further to increase prices for staples such as cheese, butter and other varieties of corn; it offered greater temptations to adulterate wheaten flour. Temporarily high transport costs caused difficulties for manufacturers and interfered with the transport and mining of coal. In Britain's economy a temporary demand of such extraordinary magnitude greatly tended to distort complex economic relationships in a number of ways.

Disorder in 1766 did not 'spread'; rather, it would be truer to say that it was brought about by a process akin to spontaneous combustion. It is also misleading to speak of 'waves' of disturbances, for that term implies the progression of a regular pattern of disorder across the countryside. This could not have been the case in 1766, at least initially. Almost all the disorder occurred within a period of about five weeks, from the second week of September to the third week of October (graph, Map 24). What is more, regional disorder reached peak levels almost instantaneously. In East Anglia, the Upper Thames and the Midlands, the levels rose simultaneously from almost zero to their peak in the same space of time, just a week later.

The type of activity which comprised the disorders in 1766 varied with locality, but the practical question of obtaining sufficient provisions was always the common factor of greatest importance. Most frequently it was the corn factor on his way to market in the Midlands, it was mills and millers' houses in East Anglia, warehouses and shops in the West Country and retail markets on the Upper Thames. Forcing artificially low prices by indirect means – threatening letters, physical intimidation, non-violent 'visitations' – was prevalent in all disorderly districts to about the same degree. The evidence suggests that on the whole the crowds were remarkably successful in satisfying their aims, although this is not to say that hunger was entirely escaped.

Map 24. Food: 1766

FOOD PROTESTS

◉	Food protest: type unknown	●	Attack on mills
△	Crowd action over price of food	⊕	Attack on inns
□	Crowd action to stay transport of food	+	Attack on retailers
⊞	Seizure of foodstuffs	▼	Attack on distilleries or breweries
◇	Attack on farmers	✳	Attack on magistrates or principal inhabitants
○	Attack on storehouses, warehouses or granaries	✕	Extortions of money, food or drink
◆	Attack on dealers		

⌐ Navigable waterways   ⬭ Wood Pasture Zone 1500-1640

◉? Approximate location , or protests known to be in that county but exact location unknown

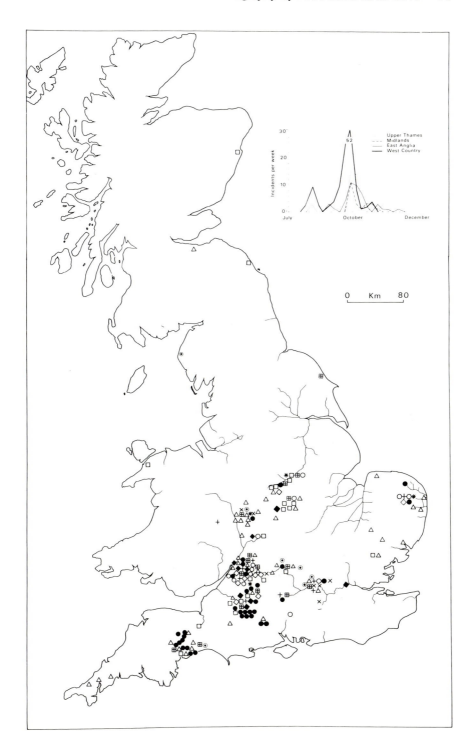

The rioting was contained by the concessions and exertions of local magistrates and townsmen, and perhaps more importantly by their vigorous programmes of relief. Where frequent large-scale disturbances overmatched the abilities of the magistrates the government sent in troops. Only twelve peacetime regiments in all were available for this task, and the King, on the advice of Secretary at War Barrington, wisely concentrated them on the centres of disorder — the clothing district of Wiltshire and, to a lesser extent, on the Midlands. Once the populace in these places were overawed and defeated they were administered a carefully calculated measure of judicial terror. Order was restored in other areas without the intervention of troops. Altogether seven men were executed and 57 others were convicted of felonies but suffered lesser penalties. The most important action the government took was to reimpose the embargo, which it did on 26 September. Order returned when economic equilibrium was restored.

Note

1. For a complete and fully referenced account of the riots see Williams (1978).

3.7 1771-3

After the normal harvests of 1768 and 1769 there followed a succession of five poor harvests from 1770 to 1774. In the middle of this period there occurred major series of food protests in five regions of Britain.[1]

The most striking feature was the first major series of disturbances in a Scottish region: the Tayside protests of the winter of 1772-3. Here there was a conjuncture of circumstances: industrial depression in Scotland, causing

Map 25. Food: 1771-3

FOOD PROTESTS

⊙	Food protest: type unknown	●	Attack on mills
△	Crowd action over price of food	⊕	Attack on inns
□	Crowd action to stay transport of food	+	Attack on retailers
⊞	Seizure of foodstuffs	▼	Attack on distilleries or breweries
◇	Attack on farmers	✳	Attack on magistrates or principal inhabitants
○	Attack on storehouses, warehouses or granaries	✕	Extortions of money, food or drink
◆	Attack on dealers		

⌐ Navigable waterways   Wood Pasture Zone 1500-1640

⊙? Approximate location, or protests known to be in that county but exact location unknown

Additional source: Wearmouth (1945), p. 39; Logue (1979), p. 7.

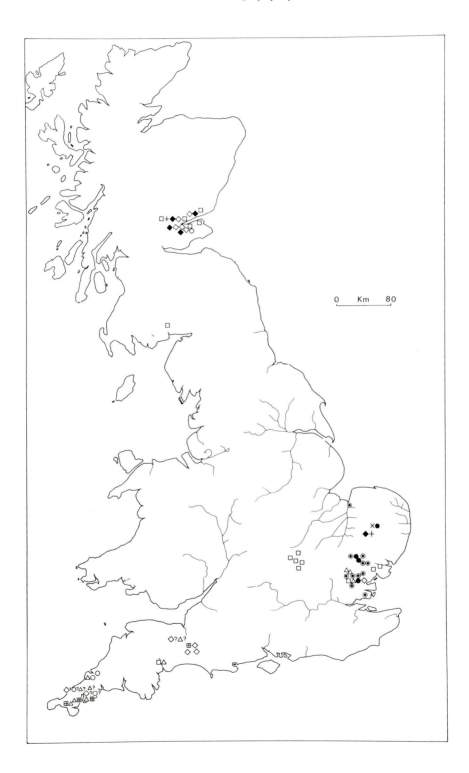

unemployment and wage cutting in the major local industry, linen. At the same time there was a sharp rise in grain prices. Merchants, however, continued to ship grain out of the region because the price differential between Tayside and central Scotland and England was still maintained. Thus the industrial workers took matters into their own hands. They marched out of their towns and villages and into the countryside to visit farmers and dealers to take corn from their stores and marched to the ports to stop the export of grain.[2]

Even more widespread were the direct collective actions of the cloth workers of Essex and Suffolk who protested in a series of villages and towns in 1772. Again there was probably more to these riots than mere food shortage. The cloth industry was in general decline in this region: in 1772 in Essex several firms were on the point of closure. The food riots consisted of, in the first place, attacks on millers and attempts to pull down mills. Farmers and dealers and shopkeepers were compelled to lower their prices and not only on wheat. At Chelmsford and Witham meat was included as one of the items to be 'regulated'. At Bury St Edmunds and Barnston cheese and butter were lowered in price.[3]

There are two regions where little research has been undertaken to establish who were the main participants in the riots: the protests in Devon and Somerset and those in Bedfordshire and Buckinghamshire. The former disturbances in the south-west occurred in 1772. At Exeter in April flour intended for transport to Wellington was seized. In June at Ilminster, Crewkerne and Chard seizures of butter and cheese took place; farmers were also threatened, as they were near Taunton where they were obliged to sell their wheat to the rioters at a price stipulated by them. The latter protests in 1773 were in market towns mainly on major roads from the Midlands to London. The rioters had cut open sacks of wheat and strewn the wheat about the streets, ' "declaring it should not be sent to London" '.[4] The fifth major series of protests broke out in Cornwall in 1773. Again the tinners were the initiators of the protests.[5]

Notes

1. Ashton and Sykes (1956), p. 126.
2. Lythe (1967), pp. 26-36.
3. Amos (1971), pp. 10-11; Brown (1969), pp. 14, 131.
4. Wearmouth (1945), pp. 38-9.
5. Rule (1971), pp. 135-7.

3.8 1776-93

This period was relatively quiet compared to that which preceded it, 1756-73, and to that which followed, 1795-1801. In southern and eastern England there were only three food riots, one of which was linked to a strike of agricultural labourers for higher wages. In the rest of Britain serious rioting only occurred in 1782-4, 1789 and 1792-3 and then there were never more than nine incidents in any one year. For the period was marked, except for these years, by reasonably good harvests. The protests took place in a number of distinct regions.[1]

First, there were the protests on the east coast of Scotland, north from Edinburgh. The riots occurred in the Edinburgh area; Fifeshire, Perthshire and Angus, the region essentially that had seen its first major protests in 1772-3, and at Inverness. The Inverness riot in 1793 is noteworthy because it marks the spatial extension of food rioting northwards of Aberdeen for the first time. Two other features worthy of note are, first, the attacks on the distilleries in Edinburgh and near Dalkeith in 1784. These seemed to have stemmed from the fact that the distillery at Edinburgh, large and of recent construction, had had an adverse impact on the price of meal. Secondly, at Dundee in 1792 the crowd took the unusual step of demanding the unloading of a ship that had been prohibited from doing so by the Corn Laws.[2]

Secondly, there were three series of riots down the west coast of Britain. In 1783 two ports in south-west Scotland saw outbreaks of rioting. In 1778 rioters stopped the transport of grain from Flint in north Wales. In 1789 in the same region, there was a major series of protests between Holywell and Oswestry with thousands of colliers scouring the area in search of food. In 1793 at Liverpool it was soldiers who had seized butter and paid the farmers at their own fixed price. Also in the same year the first food riot in south Wales took place. Here the townspeople of Swansea sought corn in the houses of maltsters, merchants and farmers. Two days later an army of copper workers marched to Swansea raiding farmhouses on the way and similarly threatening farmers and a maltster. In 1789 and 1793 the Cornish miners took action over the price and the export of grain. There was only one incident in 1789; the major rioting occurred in 1793.[3]

The majority of the remaining food disturbances took place inland and involved the two industrial regions of the west Midlands and the West Riding of Yorkshire in 1782 and 1783. In the former region riots had occurred at or near Walsall in 1776 and 1780. In 1782 there were a series of price regulations throughout the Black Country mainly the work of colliers marching around the area. In 1783 pottery workers at Etruria halted a boat-load of flour bound for Manchester. In the West Riding the disturbances took the form of stopping waggons on the roads, attacks on mills and warehouses and price 'regulations'.[4]

Notes

1. Ashton and Sykes (1956), p. 127; Brown (1969), pp. 131-2.
2. Logue (1979), ch. 1.
3. Ibid.; Dodd (1971), p. 400; Ashton and Sykes (1956), pp. 127-8; Wearmouth (1945), p. 45; Jones (1973), p. 20; Rule (1971), pp. 137-9. Rule notes that the presence of the military prevented any rioting in 1789. Jenkin and Rowe, however, both cite one incident. Jenkin (1962), p. 156; Rowe (1953), p. 104.
4. Barnsby (1977), p. 2; Hay (1975a), ch. 5; Trinder (1973), p. 378; Wearmouth (1945), pp. 41-2.

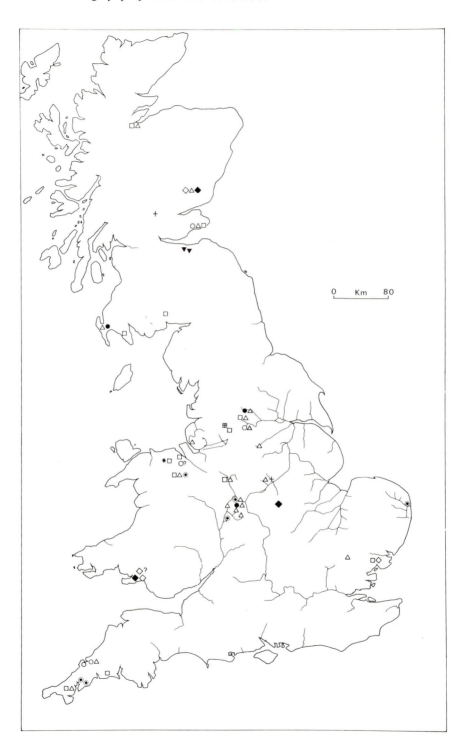

3.9 1794-6

Thompson has called 1795 the 'climatic' year for food riots in England, with no region being exempt from protests. A combination of circumstances brought this about. The wheat harvest of 1794 was about 25 per cent below that of 1793; as a result wheat stocks in 1795 fell to a dangerous level. Moreover, many industrial workers were either laid off or taking wage cuts in 1795, trade also being sensitive to the price of wheat. Thirdly, the war with France had disrupted grain imports. Fourthly, the authorities seem to have been taken unawares by the scale of the crisis; 1795 taught them a lesson they did not forget in 1796 and in the food crisis of 1799-1801. The map of the food riots of 1794-6 is a composition of the various stages of the *crises de subsistence* of those years. The patterning of the development of the crisis in England has been most skillfully documented by Wells.[1]

In 1794 and the first two months of 1795 there was but a scattering of riots in England and Wales. The first major series of riots began in March. In Wales, particularly north Wales, and in Cornwall there were mainly crowd actions to stay the export of grain. The colliers and the tinners of these two regions were ever vigilant to stop a rundown of their region's stocks. The Welsh colliers' main aim was to stop the export of grain; the Cornish tinners often went further, and having found the grain for export, had it sold it at their stipulated price. The staying of foodstuffs at this time was unusual; in the other regions the main direct collective action of the rioters was price 'regulation'. In Cornwall the movement of grain was probably in response to the food supply problems in neighbouring Devon, where price fixing disturbances were already beginning to be staged.

In Devon and southern England the presence of the military to meet the threat of invasion had a profound effect on the food market. First, they placed

Map 26. Food: 1776-93

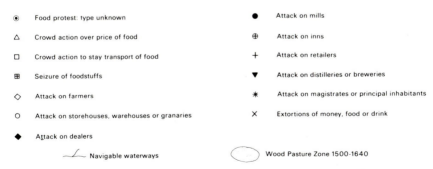

FOOD PROTESTS

⊚	Food protest: type unknown	●	Attack on mills
△	Crowd action over price of food	⊕	Attack on inns
☐	Crowd action to stay transport of food	+	Attack on retailers
⊞	Seizure of foodstuffs	▼	Attack on distilleries or breweries
◇	Attack on farmers	✳	Attack on magistrates or principal inhabitants
○	Attack on storehouses, warehouses or granaries	✕	Extortions of money, food or drink
◆	Attack on dealers		

⌒ Navigable waterways   ⬭ Wood Pasture Zone 1500-1640

⊚? Approximate location, or protests known to be in that county but exact location unknown

Additional source: Wearmouth (1945), pp. 39-46.

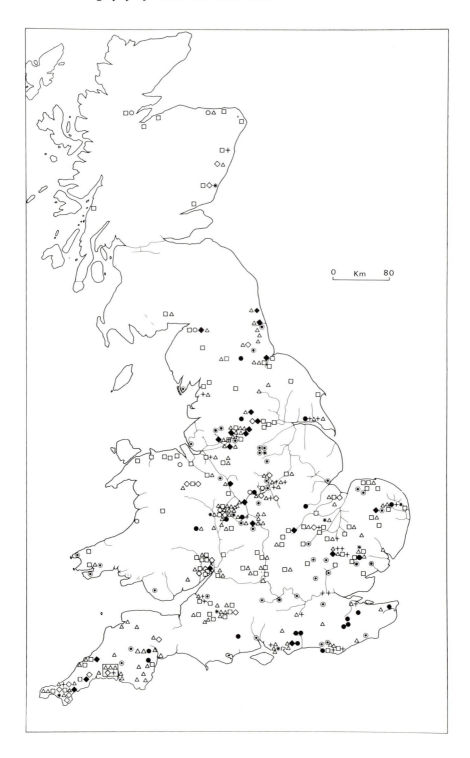

an extra burden of demand on the food supply and so caused increases in the price of grain and other foodstuffs. Second, they themselves became active in food rioting. The militia in particular became notorious on the south coast.[2]

The price of foodstuffs continued to rise, particularly in the chief centres of demand. In both areas that had seen food rioting and in areas where warning was taken from riots elsewhere, the authorities took action to ensure future supplies of food. Large quantities of food began to be moved from the producing to the consuming regions. A panic gripped many of the former regions and crowds began to halt the movement of foodstuffs. This was especially noticeable in East Anglia and in a belt of country across the south Midlands from Bristol to Peterborough. This staying of food movements had obvious consequences for the consuming regions; as the supply diminished, the price increased. Rioting took place again in the Midland industrial areas and towns and broke out for the first time in Lancashire and the West Riding of Yorkshire. The protests were mainly price 'regulations'. The situation became so bad that even movements of food, internal to these regions, became targets for the crowd's protests. One group, however, employed this tactic throughout the whole of the 1794-6 crisis: the miners of the Forest of Dean.[3]

By the autumn of 1795 it was clear to the authorities, gentry and employers that they must take action, given the poor harvest crop of 1795, to avert further disastrous food shortages in 1796. Actions to increase the supply of food and to lower the price of food both by the authorities and private individuals were undertaken. The coming of the harvest itself had brought some relief and protests declined in the autumn, the north and the north-east being the only areas to experience anything more than sporadic outbreaks of protests. In towns in Cheshire and north Wales crowds were halting the transport of foodstuffs.[4]

Map 27. Food 1794-6

FOOD PROTESTS

⊙	Food protest: type unknown	●	Attack on mills
△	Crowd action over price of food	⊕	Attack on inns
☐	Crowd action to stay transport of food	+	Attack on retailers
⊞	Seizure of foodstuffs	▼	Attack on distilleries or breweries
◇	Attack on farmers	*	Attack on magistrates or principal inhabitants
○	Attack on storehouses, warehouses or granaries	X	Extortions of money, food or drink
◆	Attack on dealers		

⟋ Navigable waterways   ⬭ Wood Pasture Zone 1500-1640

⊙? Approximate location, or protests known to be in that county but exact location unknown

Additional source: Amos (1971), p. 11; Bohstedt (1972); Jones (1973), pp. 22-3; Richardson (1977), pp. 176-368; Stevenson (1974), pp. 33-74; Thomas (1975), pp. 37-47; Thompson (1971), pp. 76-136.

The one new area that saw major rioting in 1796 was Scotland. Save for a protest over the export of grain at Dundee in August of the previous year, Scotland was untroubled by food disturbances during that year. This was because the oat crop, the staple diet of Scotland, had neither failed in 1794 nor in 1795. There were no protests in the urban centres and industrial areas of the Central Lowlands in the 1794-6 period. What caused the disturbances was the impact of the scarcity of grain and staple foodstuffs in England on Scottish food supplies. Staying the export of barley and potatoes by sea was thus the rioters' main preoccupation. The actions of the dealers it would seem were mainly felt along the east coast. The first protests occurred there in January 1796. In the west only two riots took place and these not until March.[5] In England during the same period, although these were three of the four peak months for prices in the 1794-6 crisis, the rate of increase in prices in January and February continued to slow down. March, however, saw a sharp upward push to food prices before heavy imports of foreign grain broke the price spiral. During this period and in April, however, there were only sporadic outbreaks of protests that is until the first two weeks of April, when farmers in Cornwall became the target of protestors, being compelled to sell grain at the miners' prices. Rule suggests a certain complacency on the part of the authorities when faced with the ubiquitous miners' protests. They had perhaps not felt the need for the elaborate relief systems adopted in other areas.[6]

Notes

1. Dodd (1965), pp. 89-107; Wells (1978b), pp. 101, 193-235. Dr Wells' study is the definitive account of the English crises at the national level; the appendices on location, type and date of food riots were indispensable, and this summary and map of the events of 1794-6 draw heavily on them. It is to be regretted that Dr Wells' work has not yet been published.
2. Jones (1973), pp. 20-1; Stevenson (1974), pp. 47-8.
3. Wells (1978b), p. 193-235; Booth (1977), pp. 84-99; Wells (1977a), pp. 25-7.
4. Wells (1978b), p. 193; Booth (1977).
5. Logue (1979), ch. 1.
6. Stevenson (1974), pp. 35, 52; Rule (1971), pp. 142, 174; Wells (1978b), p. 193.

3.10 1799-1801

The harvest of 1799 was poor, and over the whole of Britain prices of grain rose steeply between December 1799 and May 1800. Moreover, the industrial areas of the country were experiencing the start of a trade depression. Thus it is not surprising that the first crisis of disturbances came in some of the main industrial areas of Britain during this period. In Lancashire there were disturbances over prices in October and November 1799 but the main period was in January and February 1800. Price riots began in Yorkshire in April 1800, though earlier there had been a riot over the price of potatoes in Huddersfield. There was also some halting of grain in transit. In the Midlands protests occurred in February, April and May, prices, particularly those set by retailers, being the major complaints of the crowd. An additional and significant feature were protests against farmers. Unlike 1794-6, the main urban centres of the Central Lowlands of Scotland saw food rioting. In February 1800 there were attacks on grocers' and mealsellers' shops in Glasgow. Similar attacks took place in Leith and Edinburgh on 29 April and 1 May. Edinburgh was to be one of the most persistently riotous places during the whole of the 1799-1801 period. Another industrial region to see food protests was the industrial belt of South Wales.[1]

In south-east England there were a number of protests where the crowds mobbed the authorities. Elsewhere in other more rural areas there were but sporadic and scattered outbreaks of disturbance mainly connected with the movement of foodstuffs. This type of protest was seen in west Wales, the Lake District and south-west and north-east Scotland. Once again throughout 1799-1801 this was the main form of protest in the Forest of Dean. In western and south-western Scotland there were attempts to prevent the transport of food-stuffs across land in the period from December 1799 to January 1801. The reason for this new type of protest is related to the high prices in urban centres during this period which made it economic to transport food long distances overland.[2]

The first crisis of 1799-1801 was ended by the government's active encourage-ment of imports. They wanted no repetition of the mid-summer panic of 1795. The hot summer also relieved the tension because it seemed to presage a good wheat crop, and prices plummeted in anticipation of such a harvest during August. However, events of late August changed all this; the crops were too wet to be threshed, and thus many urban centres were left without supplies and prices rose dramatically. What Wells calls the 'hyper-crisis' of September 1800 began. Although September had the second lowest monthly average price for wheat, what so angered the consumers was the shattering of their perception that prices would be lowered by a good harvest. Moreover, they believed that the harvest was good and that the price rise was due to farmers, dealers, merchants and retailers speculating in the grain market and withholding stocks until prices rose. These men became the main targets of the crowd in their actions to lower the prices. Major incidents occurred in London, a highly unusual event because the government always tried to maintain the food supply of the capital, along the coasts of north Kent, Hampshire and Dorset, through the south Midlands and in the Black Country, Nottinghamshire, Derbyshire and south Yorkshire and Lancashire outside the Manchester region. In industrial south Wales shopkeepers in particular were singled out.[3]

In Scotland in contrast September was quiet. There were several instances of carts being stopped in central Ayrshire in October and in November riots occurred in Glasgow and in nearby Pollockshaws. Sporadic rioting was to continue in Scotland until December 1801. In England the high prices of grain persisted through the winter of 1800-1 and in industrial areas the recession was now at its height. The government had ordered magistrates to deal swiftly with any signs

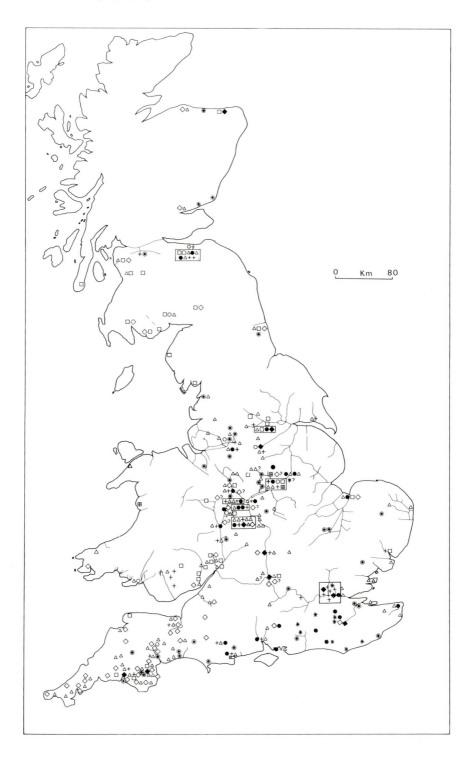

of trouble again fearing that riots would exacerbate the situation by halting the movement of food to urban centres. Thus levels of rioting did not match the continuing high prices.[4]

The major exception to this trend was the south-west. So far, save for sporadic outbreaks of rioting in July, August, September and notably December 1800, the south-west had no major protests. One important factor to account partially for this was that the south-west had a relatively good harvest in 1800. Thus the south-west did not experience the sharp rise in grain prices in late August-September as did the rest of the country. This, however, attracted buyers from outside the region and by November the price of grain began to increase dramatically. By spring they were at a record high and a massive series of protests swept through the region. The size of the harvest also explains why the farmer became such an object of opprobrium during these riots. They had tended to sit back, hold on to their stocks of corn and wait for the best prices.[5]

Notes

1. Dodd (1965), p. 102; Rose (1961), p. 284; Booth (1977), pp. 90, 91; Wells (1977a), pp. 27-8, (1978b), appendix 'Early Phase 1799-1800'; Logue (1979), ch. 1; Jones (1973), p. 23. Again, the enormous debt to Wells' research in particular must be gratefully acknowledged.
2. Wells (1978b), appendices 'Early Phase 1799-1801' and 'West Gloucestershire and Monmouthshire'; Jones (1973), p. 23; Booth (1977), p. 90; Logue (1979), ch. 1.
3. Wells (1977a), pp. 5-6, 28-9, (1978b), 91, ch. 8; Stevenson (1974), p. 53; Thomas (1975); Booth (1977), p. 90; Jones (1973), pp. 23-34.
4. Logue (1979), p. 31; Wells (1977a), pp. 6, 10, 38; Stevenson (1974), p. 37; Booth (1977), pp. 102-3.
5. Bohstedt (1972), particularly pp. 137-40.

Map 28. Food: 1799-1801

FOOD PROTESTS

⊚	Food protest: type unknown	●	Attack on mills
△	Crowd action over price of food	⊕	Attack on inns
□	Crowd action to stay transport of food	+	Attack on retailers
⊞	Seizure of foodstuffs	▼	Attack on distilleries or breweries
◇	Attack on farmers	✳	Attack on magistrates or principal inhabitants
○	Attack on storehouses, warehouses or granaries	✕	Extortions of money, food or drink
◆	Attack on dealers		

⌒ Navigable waterways   ⬭ Wood Pasture Zone 1500-1640

⊚? Approximate location, or protests known to be in that county but exact location unknown

Additional source: see Map 27; and Wells (1977b), pp. 713-44.

3.11 1810-18

Between 1802 and 1818, two periods of food rioting can be picked out: 1810-13 and 1816-18, both of which were clearly related to food shortage and high prices. Both the corn and potato harvests of 1811 had been deficient and in the spring of 1812 there was a rapid rise in the prices of these particular foodstuffs. Once again it was the tinners of Cornwall who were the first to take action, in the last week of March and the disturbances lasted into the first week of April. Again their protests took the usual form of searching for corn in store-houses and at farms, although something more unusual was the search of the Redruth brewery for malting barley. There was also a disturbance during April in Plymouth and Barnstaple, and by then trouble had spread north to the city of Bristol. There had been a price 'regulation' of butter in March 1811 by 'colliers and workmen'. In 1812 there was again price fixing, this time of potatoes, by the crowd, unidentified by occupation in the *Annual Register*, as well as an attack on dealers in the marketplaces. At roughly the same time protests broke out in Carlisle; Liverpool dealers were thought to have cornered the market in corn and potatoes. Movement of these was halted and stocks sold at reduced prices. The crowd then moved into the countryside to search warehouses and corn mills.[1]

The authorities' attention was quickly shifted, however, to the industrial areas of Lancashire, north-east Cheshire and the West Riding of Yorkshire. Or rather that is what we are led to believe by those historians who wish to differentiate between the events of the violent food riots of April in these counties and the industrial Luddism and political agitation of the months prior to and during April 1812. There does, however, seem to be evidence for the intertwining of these three elements of popular protest in these counties (the geography of Luddism has unfortunately not yet been described in detail). The main targets of the food rioters were shopkeepers. One of the most energetic incidents involved the men of Stockport who after attacking steam looms and

Map 29. Food: 1810-13

FOOD PROTESTS

⊚	Food protest: type unknown	●	Attack on mills
△	Crowd action over price of food	⊕	Attack on inns
□	Crowd action to stay transport of food	+	Attack on retailers
⊞	Seizure of foodstuffs	▼	Attack on distilleries or breweries
◇	Attack on farmers	✳	Attack on magistrates or principal inhabitants
○	Attack on storehouses, warehouses or granaries	✕	Extortions of money, food or drink
◆	Attack on dealers		

⟋ Navigable waterways   ⬭ Wood Pasture Zone 1500-1640

⊚? Approximate location, or protests known to be in that county but exact location unknown

the houses of their owners on 14 April split into two parties the next day. One party marched to Macclesfield to aid the men of that town in a food riot and in an attempted attack on a factory, while the other party marched through Bredbury to Gee Cross in Hyde breaking into a granary and attacking a corn mill. Chester also saw disturbances during April. There were further food riots in the West Riding in June and August. In another centre of Luddism, Nottinghamshire, food rioting was much more sporadic.[2] In Scotland protests were on a much smaller scale than in England, whilst there were no such incidents in Wales.[3]

In a period that had seen the highest bread prices, the scale of the food riots compared to 1799-1801 was much diminished. This trend was continued into the next period, 1816-18. In May and June 1816 there occurred one of the sharpest price rises in the whole period 1790-1831, but nothing comparable to the September hypercrisis of 1800 took place. In 1810-13 the spatial pattern that had begun to emerge in 1799-1801, increasing concentration of food rioting in large towns and industrial areas completely divorced from the countryside, was also continued and emphasised. In 1816-18, although towns and industrial areas were the locus for food protests in most regions, in one, the fenland of East Anglia, there was one sharp reversal of the urbanisation of the food riot. Yet even there, as will be seen below, it is not so simple to describe the protests in the fenland as the work of agricultural labourers. Elsewhere the pattern of disturbances was familiar, if now somewhat muted: protests over the exportation of foodstuffs along the west coast and disturbances over food prices in industrial areas, often related to other industrial disputes.[4]

Notes

1. Richardson (1977), p. 368; Logue (1979), p. 26; Rule (1971), pp. 144-6; Stevenson (1974), pp. 36, 53; *Gentleman's Magazine*, March 1811; Darvall (1969), p. 95; *Annual Register*, April 1812.

Map 30. Food: 1816-18

FOOD PROTESTS

⊙	Food protest: type unknown	●	Attack on mills
△	Crowd action over price of food	⊕	Attack on inns
□	Crowd action to stay transport of food	+	Attack on retailers
⊞	Seizure of foodstuffs	▼	Attack on distilleries or breweries
◇	Attack on farmers	✳	Attack on magistrates or principal inhabitants
○	Attack on storehouses, warehouses or granaries	✕	Extortions of money, food or drink
◆	Attack on dealers		

⌐ Navigable waterways   ⬭ Wood Pasture Zone 1500-1640

⊙? Approximate location, or protests known to be in that county but exact location unknown

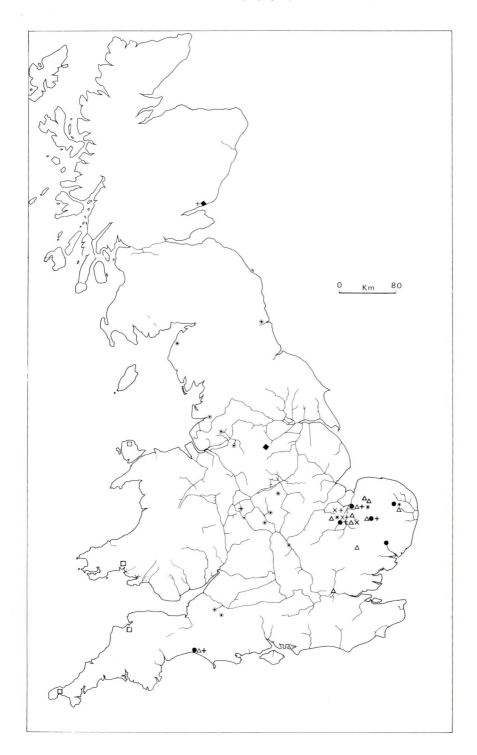

2. Thomis (1970), pp. 20-3, appendix; Darvall (1969), pp. 95-100; Dinwiddy (1979), pp. 33-63; *Gentleman's Magazine*, 1811-12; *Annual Register*, 1812.
   3. Logue (1979), ch. 1.
   4. Stevenson (1974), pp. 33-74; Peacock (1965), pp. 12, 148; Jones (1965), ch. 3; Rule (1971), p. 146.

3.12 1847   Eric Richards

In Britain food prices rose steeply throughout the country at the beginning of January, developed to a peak in March, to a still higher level in mid June and then declined rapidly as the new harvest demonstrated its promise by late July. The major outbreaks of food rioting, however, were confined to three districts.[1]

In England the food riots were limited to the south-west and affected many centres including St Austell, Callington, Redruth, Helston, Padstow and Wade-bridge. Prices rose abruptly at the end of May and potato and corn dealers were mobbed, and butchers and bakers were compelled to sell at 'the mob's own prices'. Although employment in the quarrying and china-clay trades was buoyant, the lateness of the spring had held back food supplies, and poor weather had reduced greatly the fishing catches. Women and miners were particularly prominent in the crowd actions which frequently were well disciplined and closely directed at specific targets such as beershops, warehouses and certain retailers. There was very little looting. These riots were good examples of popular price fixing in the traditional mode.[2] There were concurrent disturbances at St Helier in Jersey in the Channel Islands, which were marked by an effort to organise a general strike of the working population to protest against the price of food. The rioters attempted to induce all workmen to join a strike and support an attack on flour mills and stores in the town. The tumult was soon put down by a military force which captured about 80 of the crowd. The St Helier events were notable for a mixture of spontaneity and improvised organisation which required a minimal degree of determination and leadership.

Map 31. Food: 1847

FOOD PROTESTS

⊙	Food protest: type unknown	●	Attack on mills
△	Crowd action over price of food	⊕	Attack on inns
□	Crowd action to stay transport of food	+	Attack on retailers
⊞	Seizure of foodstuffs	▼	Attack on distilleries or breweries
◇	Attack on farmers	✳	Attack on magistrates or principal inhabitants
○	Attack on storehouses, warehouses or granaries	✕	Extortions of money, food or drink
◆	Attack on dealers		

⌐ Navigable waterways   ⬭ Wood Pasture Zone 1500-1640

⊙? Approximate location, or protests known to be in that county but exact location unknown

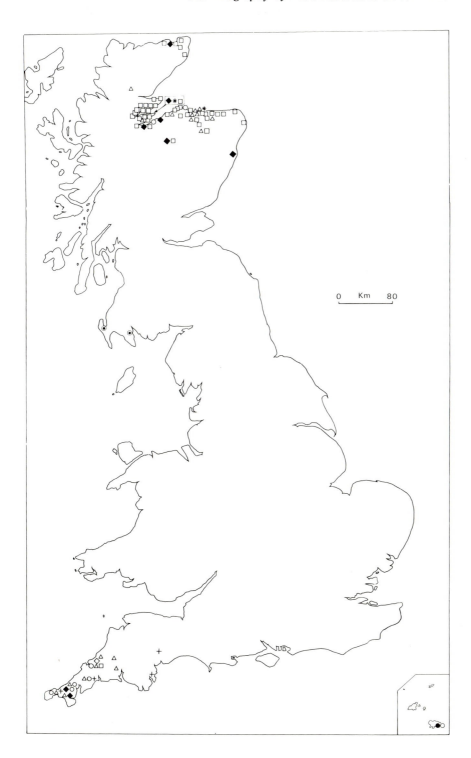

By far the most extensive and most sustained round of food riots occurred in the north-east of Scotland in the first three months of 1847 and, therefore, somewhat before the greatest peak of food prices. There were about 40 locations of riot along the eastern lowlands from Aberdeen to Thurso, a coastline of about 200 miles where, for two months, the weakness of the local authority was clearly exposed. The riots were directed against grain exports from the region and the forms of crowd behaviour were strikingly similar to the well-established patterns of the eighteenth-century food riot. Marked features included: the coalescence of a collective will among the common people; the relatively specific demands concerning exports and prices; the demonstration effect of rioting between one village and another; and the element of self-discipline and rationality within the crowds. Mostly these events were blunt demonstrations of popular demands which, for their effect, depended almost entirely upon a unanimity of spirit among the common people. The composition of the crowds suggests a high level of participation among the local population, little co-ordinating leadership and a prominence of women and fishermen.

The region had exported food for decades and the grain harvest had been good; many farmers believed that there was no danger of famine. Nevertheless, there is vivid evidence of extreme poverty and want amidst general plenty: the herring fishing was in acute depression, most of the potato crop had been diseased and the common people were compelled to buy oatmeal in a very poorly serviced retail market in which prices doubled within a week. Real and prospective distress caused people to oppose the very large outflows of grain. The riots were successful in that they delayed shipments, reduced pressure on local prices and induced proprietors to subsidise the retail market and pledge the retention of adequate supplies in the region. These were gains achieved by riot and by the appeal to the social conscience of the community at large. An unstated assumption in all the agitation was the notion that there was some morally tolerable prices for food, a price above which no seller could properly ask. The impact of the riots was strongly reinforced by the widespread sympathy for the rioters in the community, and the extreme reluctance of the citizens to act as police to combat the disorder. The availability of military force in the region was derisory, and the local authorities were generally impotent for the period of the riots.

The response to the riots exposed widespread weaknesses in social leadership in the affected districts. Symptoms included the virtual abdication of the lords lieutenant, the absence of middling groups of landholders, the alienation of the fishing and crofting populations and the growing role of Free Church ministers. Despite recent and radical changes in social structure, traditional expectations of paternalistic intervention remained strong among the people. In the aftermath, legal action against some of the rioters produced severe sentences. Local protests against the punishments were ignored. At least one landlord took private retribution against his rioting tenants. The termination of the riots occurred before the decline in prices, but coincided with improved prospects in weather, employment and fishing, and a strengthening of the law.

Notes

1. For a fully referenced and more complete account, see Richards (1981).
2. For details of the Cornish food riots, see Rowe (1942), pp. 51-67, Rule (1971), pp. 147-51.

3.13 NORTH MIDLANDS: AUGUST AND SEPTEMBER 1756
Jeremy N. Caple

The Midland counties suffered the earliest outbreaks of rioting in 1756 and in particular the area between Birmingham and Nottingham saw a great deal of crowd activity in August and September.[1] The immediate cause of rioting was the rapid and substantial increase in wheat prices from 4/6 per bushel in early August to over 8/- by the middle of the month. Price increases alone however do not explain subsequent events. Food rioting was a process, an interaction between the food rioters and the authorities in which each party played a specific role. Rioters reminded and pressured the authorities by their actions; reminded them of their responsibilities and sought to pressure them into reducing the price of food and providing sufficient supplies at the market place. Riots were directed against individuals deemed responsible for high prices and by thus exposing and disciplining them the crowd sought to exert pressure on the authorities. In the area concerned, Quakers, some of whom were grain dealers, were suspected of exporting grain causing high prices and shortages. Quakers in general therefore bore the brunt of the crowd's displeasure as meeting houses were sacked, grain seized and money, food and drink extorted.

Rioting began on 16 August when a group of colliers from Dudley led a crowd 500-strong in destroying a boulting mill at Werrybridge, near Walsall. That same day another band of colliers, on this occasion from Bedworth, leading a large crowd marched into Nuneaton where they stoned the house of a 'known engrosser of corn . . . and broke all his windows'; the man was then forced to take his grain to market to be sold at a price set by the rioters. The following day saw the rioters return to Nuneaton where they ransacked a Quaker meeting house before marching off toward Hartshill. Moving in a northwesterly direction and unhindered by either magistrates or constables, the rioters attacked and destroyed more Quaker meeting houses in Hartshill, Atherstone and Baddesley; farmers were also visited and relieved of money, food and drink. At Grendon and Polesworth two mills were pulled down before the excited crowd marched into Tamworth at about noon on the 17th. Their presence overawed the mayor and the local magistrates, those individuals being unable to either resist the demands of rioters or effect arrests. Having ransacked a mill and carried away the grain the rioters returned to gut yet another Quaker meeting house. Meeting no resistance, the crowd terrorised the local inhabitants securing money and drink by threatening to pull down the houses of the reluctant donors. After staying overnight they left Tamworth in the direction of Burton-on-Trent.

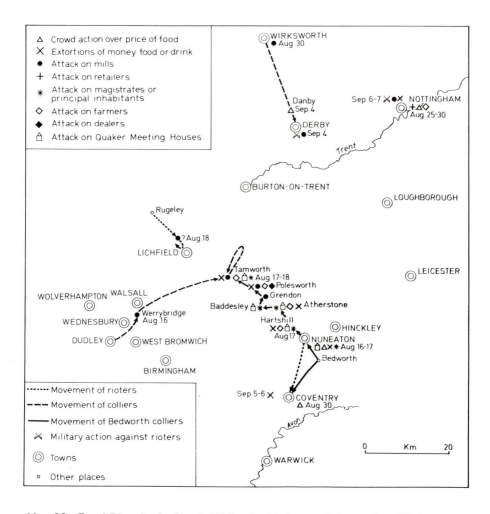

Map 32. Food Riots in the North Midlands, 16 August-7 September 1756

This initial outbreak of rioting was followed by three weeks of sporadic incidents in Coventry, Derby and in and around Nottingham. Local authorities reacted slowly to the incidents and, apart from reading the proclamation against rioting, were too intimidated to pursue their duty. Their nerve steeled by the arrival of Lord Chief Justice Willes, magistrates began their search for the ringleaders. Four were arrested almost immediately, promptly tried and two of them hanged two days later. This sanguinary warning served its purpose in Warwickshire but failed to deter rioters in Derby or Nottingham. In fact rioting increased and it was only by military force that order was restored. Even so a series of punitive raids into the country around Nottingham were required to subdue completely the vestiges of disquiet.

Repressive tactics were the ultimate response to rioting but by no means the only method utilised in suppressing disorder. Both the local authorities and those in London were aware of the specific complaints held by the rioters and acted accordingly. The moribund statutes against forestalling, regrating and engrossing were invoked by Lord Brooke, Lord Lieutenant of Warwickshire, while at both Coventry and Nottingham enquiries into the cause of high prices were promised by the magistrates. Copies of the old statutes proscribing various forms of grain speculation were posted in strategic locations throughout the area and efforts made to encourage grain dealers to bring their supplies into the marketplace.

The rioters thus achieved some measure of success; grain dealers who, according to the rioters, caused shortages and consequent high prices, were punished by the actions of the crowd. Some rioters were themselves punished severely but those in authority were forced to acknowledge the problem of high food prices and to take measures to mitigate their impact. By invoking the old statutes against market abuse and by providing grain at subsidised prices, disorder was effectively arrested and further outbreaks of rioting were avoided.

Note

1. For a fully referenced account, see Caple (1978).

3.14 GLOUCESTERSHIRE – WILTSHIRE 1766   Dale E. Williams

Heavy July rains and outbreaks of cattle murrain resulted in speculation in local corn markets and higher provision prices.[1] These occasioned price-fixing disturbances in several villages on the Exe and Culm rivers north of Exeter. The return of fair weather in August reassured most people about harvest prospects: 'Our Fields are so clothed with Grass, and our Hills stand so thick with Corn, that they laugh and sing . . .' Many thought that farmers, who had held back their stocks of old corn on the basis of the July rains, had miscalculated. Unhappily, the optimists turned out to have been wrong. The revelations about the poor local corn crop came just as the prohibition on corn exports expired on 26 August. By 10 September the public knew that imposition of the embargo was not legally possible until Parliament convened in November. It was obvious that the huge orders placed for British corn at very high prices threatened to denude the country not only of the remaining stocks of old wheat, but also of the new crop, as soon as it could be threshed and dried. No other area in the country was more vulnerable, economically, than the West Country clothing districts: work was scarce, wages depressed, the economy specialised – no alternate form of employment was widely available; the diet of the people there was dependent on the regular supply of corn to an extraordinary degree; the forces of authority which were usually associated with rural areas – parson and squire – were largely absent.

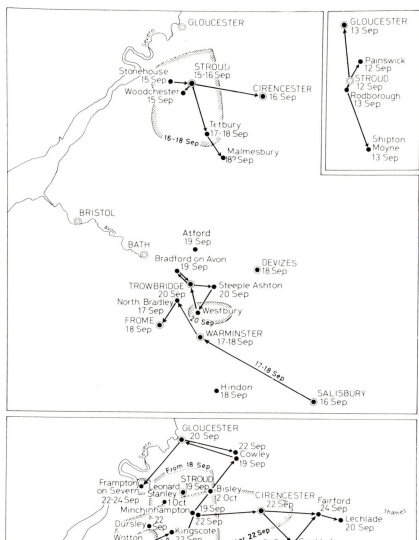

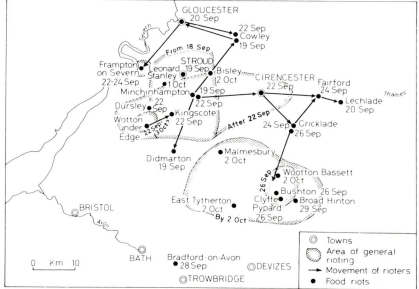

Rioting in England began in the west as soon as news of the government's proclamations of 10 September were known. The disorder began in the Gloucester clothing district on 12 September, and then in Wiltshire five days later (Map 33:1, 2). There was little or no interaction between the crowds in these two areas at first. In the vicinity of Stroud in Gloucestershire the initial disturbances concerned local bakers, millers and dealers in provisions; women and boys played an important part here. The pattern suggests that the crowd's object was to secure local supplies at reasonable cost. As local supplies were consumed, or as local provision dealers withdrew their supplies from the neighbourhood, crowds went increasingly further afield, and their composition changed with the addition of a larger number of men. By the 17th crowds had marched as far east as Cirencester and as far south as Malmesbury.

The same sort of thing was happening in Wiltshire, the centre of the disturbances being the clothing town of Bradford. From 16 to 20 September, increasingly large crowds confronted local provision dealers. Crowds in Wiltshire were exceptionally large and disciplined; their targets seemed to be local provision dealers of considerable size.

The government initially concentrated available military forces in Wiltshire. By 21 September four companies of horse had been brought forward from Salisbury to Devizes, and except for an incident at Bradford on the 28th, there were no further major disturbances in the clothing districts of Wiltshire (Map 33:3). But the disorders were not yet over; they were transferred outside the clothing districts to the north and to the south of Stroud, further to the east on the upper reaches of the Thames, and along the Gloucester–Wiltshire border in a swath from East Tytherton to Wootton Basset. Most of the available provisions in the clothing districts had been taken, and the combined actions of the crowds and of magistrates anxious to appease the crowds had completely disrupted the activities of corn factors and middlemen in the provision trade. In this situation the populace simply went further afield in search of food. The concentration of troops in the clothing district of Bradford in Wiltshire prevented further disorder there; disturbances to the north of the Wiltshire clothing district were mostly the work of crowds from Gloucestershire. The most extraordinary instance of coherent, long-range crowd action was the march on 22 September from the vicinity of Minchinhampton through Cirencester, Fairford, to Lechlade on the upper Thames. The disturbances which closely followed at Cricklade and Fairford should also probably be associated with the Gloucester crowd, as should several incidents which occurred further to the south in the vicinity of Wootton Basset. The timing of a series of disturbances on the upper Thames from Oxford (24 September) to Maidenhead (1 October) suggests that here the impetus might originally have come from the Gloucestershire cloth workers as well.

The cessation of disorder in the west can be attributed to the government's readoption of the embargo on 26 September, to the effectiveness of the troops in Wiltshire under the unified command of Lieutenant-Colonel Ward and to

Map 33. Gloucestershire – Wiltshire, September 1766

effective relief measures promoted by farmers, traders and gentlemen. The prohibition of exports meant that the price of London wheat suddenly became lower than the price in local markets. The restoration of order made it possible for corn factors to begin bringing back supplies of corn to the west with the same efficiency with which they took them out.

Note

1. For a complete and fully referenced account, see Williams (1978), ch. 3.

3.15 DEVON 1795 AND 1800-1   John Bohstedt

Two waves of food rioting swept across Devon in 1795 and 1800-1.[1] Some 43 riots were touched off by soaring grain prices, occasioned by harvest shortages, aggravated by the wartime demands of offshore fleets and the booming dock-yard at Plymouth. These riots clustered in two of Devon's sub-regions: south Devon and east Devon each had two and three times as many riots as north Devon in 1795 and 1800-1. That contrast cannot be explained by economic hardship, for grain prices in the north were actually higher than in the south and east. Rather that contrast reflected significant differences in social geography.

Upland north and west Devon was primarily devoted to stock-raising. The pastoral north was thinly populated. Outside its few sizeable towns, mostly clustered around Barnstaple, villages were 'few and small', and cottages and farmsteads scattered. Both south and east Devon were twice as densely populated as north Devon, and contained more sizeable and more nucleated towns. The South Hams was a fertile crescent of rich red loam, the bread basket of Devon. East Devon, also 'strong loam', was the centre of Devon's decaying woollen industry, and also of a thriving dairy district.

Riots were most likely to occur where communities were most sharply set off from their rural hinterland. First, the larger the town, the more likely was riot. Only ten per cent of Devon's 450 parishes contained more than 1,500 people. But 90 per cent of the 43 riots occurred in 23 towns of 1,500 or more. Secondly, riots occurred primarily in towns which were economically differentiated from the countryside rather than in rural villages. Farm labourers typically got grain direct from their employers, by sale or pilferage. Non-agricultural consumers depended on the market place, and so dearth precipitated their sense of collective interest and antagonism towards farmers and middle-men.

Hence riots took place in the woollen centres of east Devon, like Crediton, Tiverton and Exeter. Riotous Modbury was full of 'decayed manufacturers', and Ashburton's weavers were thought to require 'some control'. Likewise, eight of Devon's ten seaports had food riots, as did the inland trading town of

Map 34. Food Riots in Devon, 1795 and 1800-1

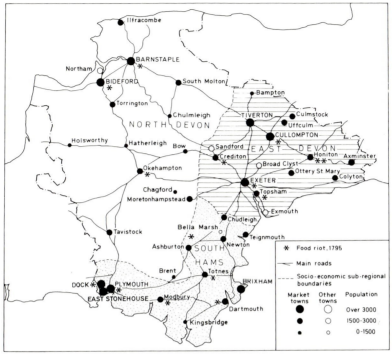

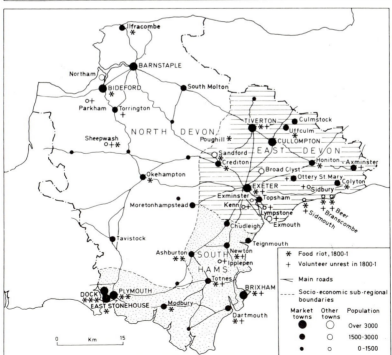

Oakhampton on the road to Cornwall. Besides consumer consciousness, some of Devon's workers had militant traditions of collective action, in particular the weavers, combers and fullers of Tiverton and Exeter. The combers' and weavers' societies at Cullompton and Tiverton were repeatedly blamed for the riots in that neighbourhood. The powerfully organised dockyard workers at Plymouth also furnished nucleii for food mobs. The riots of 1801 coincided with their industry-wide campaign for higher wages.

Moreover, five-sixths of Devon's food riots took place in market towns. Obviously, markets brought consumers and suppliers into immediate confrontation, but they were also nodes of social intercourse. The weekly market ritual established a centripetal camaraderie among townspeople, and markets also relayed riot news and example. By comparison with these dense communal and regional networks in the south and east, north Devon was infertile ground for riot. Large towns, market towns and non-agrarian towns were few and far between except around Barnstaple, where riots did indeed occur.

Finally, the most important organised nucleii for bread riots in Devon were the Volunteer Corps. In late 1800 and early 1801, unrest spread along the Volunteer network of east Devon. At Axminster, Sidbury and Exeter, volunteers declared their unwillingness to protect the 'Damnation Farmers' and millers. At Branscombe, Exeter, Newton, Totnes, Dartmouth and Brixham, volunteers actually led mobs, often in full uniform. Volunteer leadership was crucial, not only because it dashed the gentry's hope for a bargain-rate peace-keeping force. The Volunteers were equipped with both the habit of collective action and a highly visible, officially sanctioned status in their communities. Once again, the sub-regions contrast. The riotous Volunteers of south and east Devon were artisans and labourers of the towns, like their fellow rioters. The 'reliable' Volunteer Corps of quieter north Devon contained much higher proportions of 'husbandmen'.

Note

1. For a complete and fully referenced account of the food riots in Devon in 1795 and 1800-1, see Bohstedt (1972).

4 TURNPIKE DISTURBANCES IN THE EIGHTEENTH AND EARLY-NINETEENTH CENTURIES

A further series of disturbances related to the transformation of eighteenth-century economy were those protests against the spread of a transport innovation — the turnpike. Despite the ubiquity of turnpikes by 1800, protests only occurred in four main areas.

The colliers of Kingswood near Bristol were 'a set of ungovernable people' *par excellence*. Thus in 1727 on the first day when tolls were levied on coal movements on a number of roads on the Kingswood side of the city, the colliers together with miners from another community nearby demolished the tollgates. These protests did achieve a toll exemption on coal movement. In 1731 and 1732 a new turnpike act and new legal powers against turnpike rioters respectively led to the creation of gates to the east and north-east of Kingswood which probably again did not exempt coal traffic. Once again the colliers levelled the gates in 1731 being joined by some of 'the country people'. There were renewed disturbances in 1735. Fourteen years later a new initiative was taken to improve the roads leading into Bristol. The carriage of coal continued to be exempt and most of the new gates appear to have been this time on the west side of Bristol. This angered the farmers of Somerset who with their labourers destroyed the gates. The colliers of Kingswood were called on to give assistance as well; but as the Kingswood men had no real cause this time their collective actions were less enthusiastically undertaken. This was not, however, the last disturbance over tollgates in the Bristol area. In 1793 there were riots near the centre of the city itself over the issue of tolls.[1]

The second area of turnpike riots was just to the north of the Bristol region and followed on from the first series of Kingswood disturbances. This time, however, the rioters were mainly the 'country people', the small farmers. In 1734 they entered the city of Gloucester and rioted over the issue of payment of tolls, whilst a tollgate nearby was destroyed. In the same month as the latter incident, the attacks on gates in the Ledbury region to the west began, although the gates there had been erected in 1722. Further disturbances followed in 1735. In 1736 the protests spread to Wilton near Ross, where a final incident occurred in 1738.[2]

Both the Bristol, Gloucester and Ledbury areas had seen the multiplication of turnpikes in their small regions before 1740, the next major region of rioting, the West Riding of Yorkshire, had seen the proliferation of turnpikes between 1740 and 1751. The trouble seems to have stemmed from the erection of new gates. The riots began in 1752, the major rioting occurring in 1753, and the

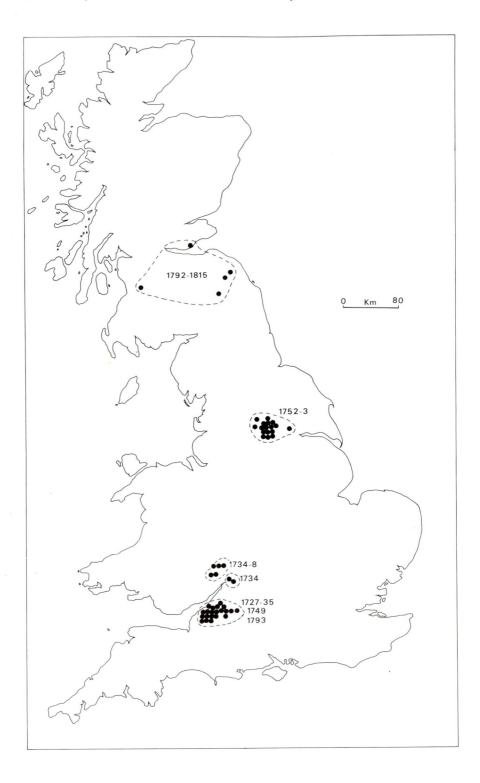

crowd's main objection being the high toll on coal, a commodity necessary for cloth production. Thus given this end, and location of the protests, it is clear that small independent clothiers would have been at the centre of the disturbances.[3]

The final region affected by protests in the eighteenth century was the southern part of Scotland, where the end of the century saw the consolidation of the turnpike network. Four of the disturbances were the result of new local acts of 1792, the fifth was in response to the setting up of a new toll-bar or gate. Three of the protests were linked to the same turnpike trust in Berwickshire. The trustees decided to set up the toll-bars on 3 July 1792; over the next two days townspeople from Duns and small farmers and labourers destroyed the gates. As in the Bristol region, two of the Scottish protests involved an alliance of small farmers and colliers.[4]

The question remains why were the disturbances against turnpikes relatively few in number. The turnpike was promoted by the large industrialist, the large landowner and the large capitalist farmer. They all benefited from the innovation, since payment for good roads through tolls was more than equally rewarded in lower transport costs, fewer delays and access to new markets. Thus it was perhaps not surprising that turnpike riots did not occur in areas of advanced agrarian and industrial capitalism but occurred in areas where communities of small farmers, independent colliers and clothiers and small town artisans still existed.

To these small men, the turnpike was not an indirect source of profit but simply a tax on his already small income. But why rioting only occured in these few areas, when communities of small men still existed in other areas, is difficult to say. One reason may be the density of turnpikes in all of the English regions that saw protests; each of the regions was crisscrossed by a whole series of turnpikes which meant that even short journeys were liable to encounter a number of gates and hence the payment of a toll at each gate.[5] A similar complaint over the multiplication of turnpike trusts arose in south-west Wales in the period before Rebecca destroyed the tollgates there.[6]

Notes

1. Malcolmson (1980), pp. 85-114; Stevenson (1979), p. 329.
2. Isaac (1953), ch. 5.
3. Ibid., Pawson (1977), figures 24, 26; Heaton (1920), pp. 289-301.
4. Logue (1979), pp. 177-83.
5. Pawson (1977), figures 26, 27.
6. Williams (1955), pp. 177-8.

Map 35. Turnpikes: 1727-1815

5 THE CLUBMEN AND MILITIA PROTESTS

The state made a number of demands of rural communities. From time to time communities in the countryside would be asked to provide quarters and provisions for troops, whilst at other times the state would require men to serve in the militia. In times of war the countryside could become a source of plunder for troops. The disturbances examined here will concern protests over such demands being made.

5.1 THE RISINGS OF THE CLUBMEN IN 1644-5   Garry Lynch

The initial spark for the risings wherever they occurred would invariably appear to have been provided by the presence of plundering troops or some exhorbitant demand from a local garrison.[1] The risings were largely confined to western and southern England and south Wales, predominantly 'Royalist' areas, and to be the scene of much fighting during 1645. In early 1645, however, there was also intense popular dissatisfaction with the war in several 'Parliamentarian' counties, highlighting that the popular basis to the risings lay in a wariness of military exactions and disorders.

Some idea of the extent and strength of the anti-war feeling may be gauged from the geographical spread of the revolt and from the numbers participating in the risings (Map 36 indicates the main places involved in the risings of 1645). Places of origin of prosecuted Clubmen are not shown, unless they appear in some other connection. The spread of the movement was therefore even wider than the map indicates.[2]

The risings began in late 1644 in south Shropshire and soon spread to north-west and central Worcestershire and to north-east and central Herefordshire, culminating in a massive siege of Hereford in which some 12,000-16,000 people are reported to have taken part. Considerable embarrassment was caused to the Royalist cause in the area until the risings were suppressed in April 1645. By this time, however, the unrest had spread to the west of England. As the seat of war moved towards this region, particularly after the Royalist defeat at Naseby, large parts of Dorset, Wiltshire and Somerset took up arms for their self-defence. There was considerable co-operation between the Clubmen of this region — as the protestors were beginning to be called from the nature of their rustic weaponry. Salisbury was a major centre of unrest, and the Clubmen there

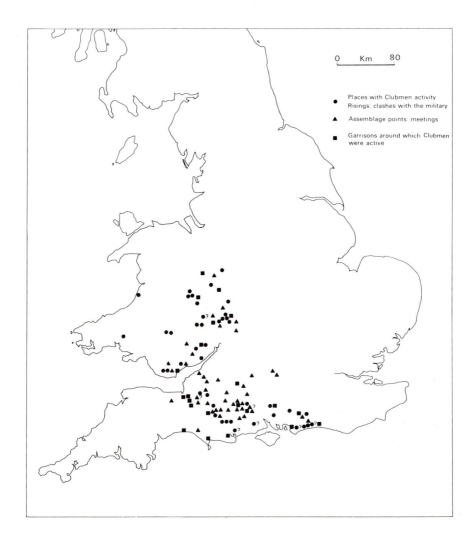

Map 36. The Clubman Rising of 1644-5

boasted that they could raise 20,000 men at 24 hours' notice.[3] Peace petitions were drawn up to King and Parliament, but the hopes of such third-party men were crushed on Hambledon Hill by Cromwell and the New Model Army in August 1645. Thereafter the Clubmen of this region acquiesced in the Parliamentarian drive against the remaining Royalist forces. Royalists were briefly successful in fomenting unrest in parts of Berkshire, Hampshire and Sussex, again involving several thousand inhabitants. The attempt by the King to raise a further army from Wales about this time, however, served only to provoke a massive rising there against the war, which Parliament was swift to exploit to bring about the final demise of the Royalist cause.

It ultimately proved impossible to keep the movement aloof from the issues dividing King and Parliament, particularly as the local gentry and clergy began to assert influence over the movement. Under such influence, as Morrill points out, the public demands of the Clubmen, whenever the movement arose, came to be highly coloured by the ' "pure" Country constitutionalism of the 1630's', i.e. by a rigorous assertion of the right of the local community to control its own affairs.[4]

The risings were far from being a composite, unified movement, however. The timing and nature of the risings were in large part determined by varying local circumstance. Analysis of the differing agrarian regions from which the Clubmen came has recently led Underdown to put forward the interesting hypothesis that in areas where arable farming predominated the Clubmen were more inclined to support the King, whereas in pastoral areas they tended to favour Parliament.[5] Certainly this highlights a need for a more thorough investigation of the agrarian basis of early modern English society. What is most impressive about the risings, however, is that the Clubmen wherever they arose were able for so long to resist the blandishments and coercion of either side, and stand fast to their first principles of remaining neutral.

Notes

1. The fullest treatment of the Clubmen Risings to date is Lynch (1973). See also, Morrill (1976), pp. 98-111, 196-200 and Underdown (1980), pp. 25-48.
2. See, for example, Underdown (1980), p. 31.
3. *Lords' Journals (VII)*, p. 485.
4. Morrill (1976), p. 106.
5. Underdown (1980).

5.2 THE MILITIA RIOTS OF 1757   Jeremy N. Caple

While the authorities attempted to cope with the food riots which disturbed a large part of the country, the new Militia Act of 1757 provoked disturbances in other areas. For the most part, such disturbances were confined to the eastern half of the country and were particularly concentrated in Yorkshire, Lincolnshire and Bedfordshire.[1]

Map 37. Militia: 1757

Additional source: see Map 22.

Passage of a new Act reorganising the militia was necessitated by the strains of fighting a far-flung colonial war in several different theatres. Pitt wished to replace badly needed troops by a more efficient system of raising men for home defence but his methods were not well received. Under the old Act, any man with an income of £50 or more from land or possessed of an estate worth over £500 was charged with equipping an infantry man. The new Act, however, provided for a ballot to which every man in England between 18 and 50 years of age was subject, with the exception of peers, officers of the militia and regular forces, clergy, dissenting ministers, peace and parish officers, articled clerks, apprentices and seamen. Substitutes were allowed, but in general this was an option which only the rich were able to exercise. The poorer classes perceived the Act as an attempt by the wealthy landowners to engage the poor in defence of their property. Lincolnshire rioters declared: 'We will not fight for what does not concern us, and belongs to our landlords; let the worst happen; we can but be tenants and labourers as we are at present.'[2] It was not, however, only the poorer classes who expressed displeasure with the Act. More frightening to the gentry were the activities of tenant farmers who in many cases led the rioters, threatening to 'raise an army of them and beat, pull down and destroy, all the gentlemen's seats in the county'.[3] Moreover, it was not only resentment against defending the gentry's property that incensed those who rioted. Rumours to the effect that militia service meant service abroad circulated rapidly, while the question of pay further exacerbated tensions between the central government and the country at large. In fact, the 1757 Act made no provision for payment and this led to further rumours that men were to be paid 6d per day for service away from home.

The method of raising men, the absence of any provision for payment and the ambiguity surrounding the location of service created an intense feeling of outrage and resentment which was ultimately directed at those charged with carrying out the balloting. Beginning on 23 August at Washingborough, Lincolnshire, rioting spread rapidly to other parts of the county and to Bedfordshire and Nottinghamshire. By the middle of September outbreaks had occurred in Yorkshire, Lancashire, Kent, Cambridgeshire, Middlesex, Essex and Northamptonshire and by early October Surrey, Derbyshire, Gloucestershire and Norfolk had also experienced rioting. Following a year of widespread food rioting the appearance of substantial crowds, sometimes 2,000-3,000 strong, and led, often, by middle class farmers, caused serious concern in London. The army was already hard pressed in providing troops in areas affected by food rioting and these new and somewhat more portentious disturbances, which tended to occur almost simultaneously, strained resources at the War Office.[4]

The pattern of rioting was quite similar in all cases; the primary object of the rioters being confiscation of ballot lists to prevent any names going forward for service. In Stockport, on 13 September, a crowd of over 300 marched to the White Lion where the local justices were meeting to ballot for the Act. They demanded and took the lists, along with one crown from each justice of the peace, informing them that they wanted 1s 6d per day and that they could not serve for 6d per day.[5] Similarly, in Bakewell over 1,000 men protesting the Militia Act, including a number of 'men of repute', forced their way into the constable's home and seized the lists.[6]

Rioters, however, were not merely content with confiscating lists and very often set out to intimidate the gentry by invading their isolated homes. At Biggleswade the crowd even invaded the races and attacked and burned a nobleman's booth. Rockingham at his Wentworth Woodhouse estate was led to expect an attack by a large crowd from Sheffield and Sir George Saville was roughed up at Mansfield. In Bedfordshire a large crowd of rioters threatened the Duke of Bedford, claiming they would go to 'Woburn Abbey to murder him and pull down his house'.[7] Large crowds roaming the countryside threatening both gentry and officers of the law met little resistance. The gentry were isolated and too dispersed to act collectively and constables were generally too afraid to enforce law and order. In most areas it required either a determined defence of property or the introduction of military force to quell rioting.[8]

Ultimately the Act was accepted; but acceptance required meetings held to explain the Act both in areas where rioting had occurred and where it had not. And to dispel any further doubts the following year a bill was passed to better explain the 1757 Act.

Notes

1. Neave (1976), pp. 21-7; Godber (1970), pp. 147-59; Western (1965), pp. 290-8.
2. Neave (1976), p. 21.
3. Ibid., p. 26.
4. PRO WO. 1/974 ff. 40-3, ff. 547-8; see also Hayter (1978), pp. 98-103.
5. *Manchester Mercury*, 15 September 1757.
6. *Derby Mercury*, 20 September 1757.
7. PRO WO 1/974 fo. 43.
8. Western (1965), pp. 290-303; *Derby Mercury*, 27 September 1757 and PRO WO 1/974 ff. 41-3.

5.3 MILITIA RIOTS 1795-8

The next major episodes of protests over the recruitment of the militia occurred between 1795 and 1798. There had, however, been sporadic rioting over this issue since 1757, the most serious being in the north-east of England in 1761 at Gateshead, Morpeth and Hexham when at the latter place at least 20 had been killed in clashes with the mobilised militia itself.[1] The pressure on military resources posed by the French wars, particularly the threat of invasion and the fear of a revolutionary situation arising in Britain, led the government to strengthen the home defence forces under its command. Its first consideration was England and Wales.

By an Act of 1786 each county was required to draw up an annual list of men eligible for service which would then be returned to the central government. This was implemented for the first time in 1795, and it is likely that it was this first move that began to stir the populace, particularly taken at a time of high prices and anger over army and navy recruitment and increasing taxation. As Neave points out, the direct collective actions of the men of Lincolnshire and the fear of such actions made the magistrates in 1795 in that county suspend the drawing up of lists on a number of occasions. After a riot at Denbigh in north

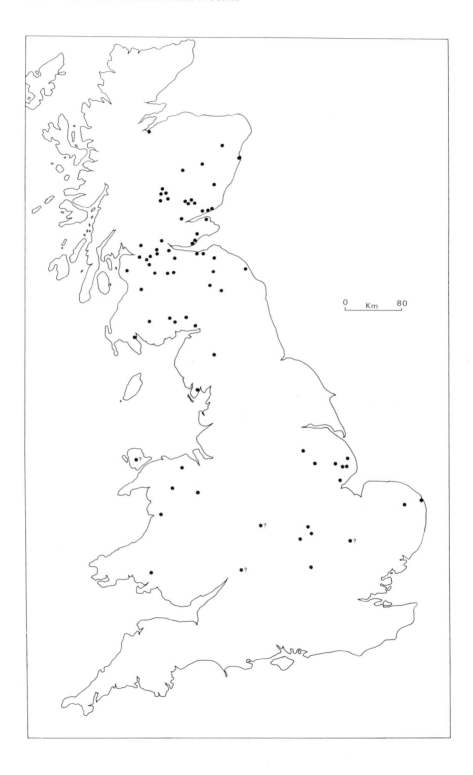

Wales the magistrates there similarly backed down. This simmering discontent, probably more widespread across the country, was brought to a head when Parliament passed an Act in November 1796 augmenting the militia. News of the presentation of the bill itself was enough to cause renewed disturbances in Lincolnshire. The next two months saw further rioting particularly in Norfolk, Northamptonshire, north and mid-Wales and the Lake District. The riots took very much the same form as in 1757: attacks on officials and the destruction of the militia lists. In 1796 the repression of the disturbances was much more vigorous and speedy than in 1757, even though, as Neave notes for Lincolnshire, there were more signs of organisation and planning behind the protests than in 1757.[2]

In Scotland pressure against a Militia Act in 1757 had been so strong that no such institution had been set up. Thus the Act of 1797 was the first of its kind to be implemented in Scotland, and hence the more massive reaction can be partly explained. The rioting spread through the countryside in a sequence largely determined by the authorities. Protests only took place after a district meeting to draw up lists of those eligible for the ballot was in active preparation and so the order in which the authorities decided to implement the Act in different districts explains the pattern of spread. Once again one of the major problems was the lack of explanation by the authorities of the meaning of the Act and thus allowing the terms of the Act to be misrepresented.[3]

The militia riots of the 1790s, as those of 1757, can be seen in some areas as the small farmers' collective protests not just against the government's demands but also against their economic plight in a time of high prices. The disturbances can almost be regarded in some areas as equivalent to the food riots of the industrial workers, for what is striking about the spatial distribution of both the 1757 and the 1790s militia riots, particularly in England, is the fact the riots occurred in regions free from food protests. In Lincolnshire the communities involved in the disturbances were either bordering the fenland or in the fen and marshland. In north Wales, the Lake District and Scotland the small farmer was dependent on family labour and was thus particularly hard hit by the removal of sons to serve in the militia. The widespread reaction in Scotland was partly because those eligible for recruitment were restricted to those between 18 and 23 years old, those most able to do farm work and those most economically active. Underlying the protests also was an antipathy of the rich who could buy themselves out of the militia leaving the poor to defend their property. The weavers, prominent among the rioters in Scotland, were a group noted for their radicalism. In Lincolnshire in 1796 the militia protests were accompanied by other acts of violence and threats against the rich.[4] The issue of militia recruitment, like so many other of the issues that we have looked at, opened up underlying divisions within rural society.

Map 38. Militia: 1795-8

Notes

1. Western (1965), p. 298; Stevenson (1979), pp. 38, 167-9.
2. Neave (1976); Western (1965), pp. 290-8; Jones (1973), pp. 52-3.
3. Logue (1979), ch. 3.
4. Holderness (1968), p. 286.

6 THE GEOGRAPHY OF PROTESTS BY AGRICULTURAL LABOURERS 1790-1850

6.1 THE RISE OF AN AGRICULTURAL PROLETARIAT[1]

It should be clear by now that the major agrarian disturbances of the seventeenth and eighteenth centuries rarely saw agricultural labourers at the centre of such protests. Moreover, as Dobson has made clear, what labour disturbances there were amongst agricultural workers before 1790 were almost all concerned with haymakers in the London area, once again not a group likely to be drawn from a purely agricultural background.[2] Before 1790, therefore, agricultural labourers appear to have played a very small role in overt class conflict. It is thus necessary to examine why this was so and what structural changes and conjunctural circumstances led to the very different picture we have of agricultural labourers from 1790 onwards. Even before the first concerted series of disturbances against agricultural machinery and low wages in East Anglia in 1816, there had been a scattering of protests primarily over the issue of wages throughout southern and eastern England between 1793 and 1805 (Map 39). The timing of the onset of such disturbances is, however, not all that needs to be considered. It is also necessary to inquire why the protests by farmworkers were in the main confined to southern and eastern England during this period (Maps 39-42).

Any explanation of the timing of the outbreaks and the geography of farmworkers' protests must begin with a consideration of the differing fates of the landless class in southern and eastern England and their equally landless counterparts in the rest of lowland Britain. In particular it will clarify the explanation if the comparison is restricted to the history of the farmworkers of southern and eastern England and that of their equivalent class in that premier region of capitalist mixed farming, the lowlands of central Scotland. The latter region was, as regards labour troubles, with one or two exceptions, superficially tranquil during the period 1790-1832, yet it had seen some of the most rapid and far-reaching advances in the development of agrarian capitalism.

During the latter half of the eighteenth century agrarian change differentially affected the lot of the farmworkers in these two regions of lowland Britain. At the beginning of the eighteenth century in both regions a system of mixed farming predominated. Stone probably gives the best and most succinct account of the work regimes and recruitment systems of such mixed farms in southern England, before they were transformed by the new husbandry, in his description of the common field farm in the 1780s:

The occupations of a common-field farm is generally managed by servants hired into a farmer's house; and the necessity of this, is that the labour attendant on the farm is early and late . . . As there are no quick sets to plash, weed or mould up, trees to preserve, wheat peas or beans to drill, or in many situations no considerable quantity of turnips or beans to hoe, *labourers on these accounts are unnecessary* and the chief employment of the labourers in the common field situations (except only in time of harvest) is to thresh out the farmer's grain; which business being accomplished, as the summer advances, and until harvest returns, they have but little or no employment . . . and if the farmers in the most enclosed counties in England, where there are no manufactories, could get no further assistance during their harvest than from their own inhabitants, their grain would frequently be spoiled in their fields before they could get it home: they are, therefore, dependent upon both the friendly aid of our brethren of a sister kingdom, and the manufacturers of this for assistance to get in their harvest.[3]   (author's emphasis)

Map 39. Labour: 1793-1805

Map 40. Labour 1815-16

In the eastern lowland of central Scotland at the beginning of the eighteenth century the working population of landless servants was complemented by a substantially larger population of cottagers and subtenants than that found in southern Britain. These people worked for their superior tenant, in return for land and grazing rights. Moreover, the system of servants living in with their masters was varied, as in the Lothians and Berwick, to the provision of cottages for married men.[4]

Population growth in such societies was still subject to the 'traditional social controls that maintained a demographic equilibrium in which each generation replaced its predecessor'.[5] In so far as economic independence was a necessary precondition to marriage, age of marriage — the lynchpin of that demographic equilibrium — was kept high, on the one hand, by the inelastic demand for labour in early modern agriculture. As Stone noted there were few employment opportunities for large numbers of labourers in the mixed-farming system and that is why open field parishes were less populous.[6] On the other hand, where gaining one's independence by obtaining access to land was still possible, as in some areas of southern Britain but more particularly in northern Britain, one waited to get married until one's father died or retired before assuming control over the family farm.

Map 41. Labour: 1822 (see Map 40 for key)

From about 1760 onwards, just as the landholding structures of lowland central Scotland and southern and eastern England were becoming very similar, this relatively common system of agrarian economy was differentially transformed. In southern and eastern England, the one region most suited climatically to the production of large outputs of barley and especially of wheat, farmers began to take advantage of the steadily rising corn prices by adopting the labour-intensive innovations of the new husbandry and by gearing such techniques increasingly to the production of wheat.[7] To do this farmers needed cheap labour in large numbers. The supply of labour thus had to be increased. As Levine has shown, this demand for labour, particularly for unskilled labour, meant that there was no longer a need to postpone marriage since one reached prime earning capacity at an early age. Moreover, further enclosure and engross- ment robbed the wage earner of any chance of gaining independence as a cottager or small farmer and thus further hastened earlier marriages. Thus the demo- graphic equilibrium was disturbed. The population of labourers grew to fill the gaps in the expanding agricultural workforce but in consequence forced wages down and kept labour cheap for the farmer.[8]

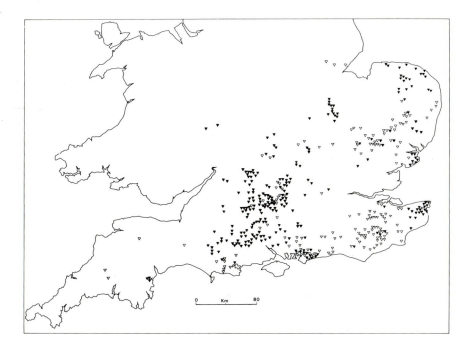

Map 42. Labour: 1829-31 (see Map 40 for key)

The new husbandry of southern Britain not only required larger numbers of labourers than previous systems of agriculture it also required 'men who have no other means of support than their daily labour, men whom they [the farmers] can depend on' at all times.[9] That is, farmers wanted an elastic supply of labour necessary to meet the highly fluctuating demands of a complex and overlapping range of farm tasks, of which the most important were those noted by Stone. This new labour-intensive husbandry could, therefore, not depend on casual labour from cottagers and domestic workers. Indeed, farmers were increasingly hostile to such groups in society because they threatened the elasticity of labour supply. Enclosure, engrossment and the decline of rural industries ensured the removal of that threat for the farmer.

The decline of the supply of seasonal casual labour meant, however, that farmers required a large pool of resident workers in reserve to cope with the vagaries of the corn harvest, which was not only the absolute peak of labour demand in the year but also highly susceptible to fluctuations in the weather.[10] As Stone noted the areas 'most cultivated in corn, and most enclosed, are so very populous, that the harvest can be got in without any extraordinary aid'.[11] Yet this situation only accentuated the difference between the summer rush and the winter slack: in winter threshing was still the only major source of regular employment. The problems of keeping a reserve army of labourers was not, however, felt until the post-1815 agricultural depression. This was because between 1760 and 1815 the expansion of capitalist agriculture in southern and eastern England required large amounts of labour to transform the landscape through either enclosure, engrossment or land reclamation. All these required new farm and field layouts, whilst the latter where it required paring and burning was especially heavy in its labour requirements.

One other major change for the farmworker of southern and eastern England was the steady decline in the number of long-hired farm servants.[12] The principle of long-hire was ill-suited to the marked fluctuations in demand for labour over the farming year. Moreover, the ample supply of men always at hand and the lack of competition in the labour market from alternative employment meant that farmers did not need to use long-hirings to ensure a supply of workers.

In the eastern lowlands of central Scotland, as Gray notes, 'the progress of improvement was tending, at least from 1750 onwards, to narrow the opportunities to acquire land'.[13] At the same time employment opportunities for the landless were expanded. As with that group in southern and eastern England, this upsetting of the old equilibrium of society was accompanied by an accelerating natural increase of population. The impact of all this on the landless class there differed from that of their fellows in southern Britain for two major reasons: the nature of the agrarian economy and the presence of alternative sources of non-agricultural employment.

The climate dictated that farmers could only achieve maximum levels of output, and hence profit, by adopting the new husbandry as part of a mixed-farming system. As Devine has shown, this encouraged an extension in the working year, rather than a concentration of intense work loads in the summer months. Spreading work more evenly throughout the year was also important because of the farmer's need to use his work horses, expensive items of capital, economically. These animals, plus cattle, were vital to the mixed-farm economy. Therefore, a permanent, specialist team of farmworkers to work with and care for such animals was required. 'In Scotland a particularly high proportion of the farm work would be done by the steady toil of such full-time employees'.[14] Thus there was no elimination of long-hiring. There still remained, however, a problem of meeting the seasonal variations in employment, hay and corn harvests being the most demanding in terms of extra labour. As in southern Britain, the dispossession of cottagers and sub-tenants following enclosure and engrossment had caused part of the supply of casual labour to dry up. These fluctuations in labour demand could, however, be met either from the families of the permanent servants, as in the Lothians, or from workers in manufacturing and domestic industries, as in other areas of the eastern lowlands, or, at corn harvest especially in all of the eastern lowlands, Irish and Highlander seasonal migrants.

The presence of alternative sources of employment nearby was the other major difference that affected the lot of the farmworkers of northern Britain. The competition in labour market from local industries and, in the case of Lothians, from the labour demands of Edinburgh, ensured that farmers paid their workers relatively good wages either in money or kind, and that they responded promptly with increases in those payments when a labour shortage threatened. Moreover, this proximate demand for labour meant that whenever a surplus of labour arose in agriculture through either population increase, agricultural depression or agricultural innovation, those labourers who found themselves redundant could move to or, in the case of casual workers, fall back on industrial or urban employment. It is not surprising then that the threshing machine, effectively invented in 1787, was rapidly and widely adopted in such a region with a self-regulating, tight labour market. Thus although agrarian change was more rapid and, as far as landholding was concerned, more far-reaching here than in southern Britain, in some ways the new agrarian economy was the old system writ large.

The social consequences of agrarian change for the agricultural workers in southern and eastern England were that they were gradually becoming a group apart from their employers. The rise of larger work teams, irregularly employed, and the increasing tendency of large farmers to be entrepreneurs and super-visors of the work-day rather than working side by side with their men, made the masters more remote figures. When the men were banished from the farmer's table or when the farmer built a new farmhouse on his newly laid out farm, away from the village, he was seen to want a different lifestyle from his workers. This growing segregation of the two classes was further compounded in the latter half of the eighteenth century by the clearer emergence of 'open' and 'close' parishes.[15] In close parishes the number of labouring families living there was controlled by landlords and the parish vestry so as to limit the number of such families gaining settlements, and hence being eligible for poor relief. During a period of rapid population growth this meant that many of the day labourers employed by farmers in close parishes were forced to live in neighbouring open parishes. Thus there began to develop in many villages, but in particular in the more populous open villages, a separate community of labourers, all experiencing a higher degree of insecurity in employment and increasingly antipathetic to their masters.

At the same time the processes of social and spatial segregation meant that labourers were increasingly freed from the patriarchal web of control of the farmhouse and the close village.[16] Moreover, with the growth in size of the labouring community, specific institutions centred on the labourer developed, both formally and informally: meeting houses, chapels, pubs, friendly societies and benefit clubs, poaching gangs, football teams, drinking parties.[17] Thus the labourers had the freedom and the opportunities to discuss together their grievances and hence to identify common points of antagonistic interest between themselves and their employers. Contemporaries reached similar conclusions but were more flamboyant in their language. Beershops, for example, were described in 1834 as places 'where the dissolute may meet unperceived', with 'facilities for union and combination', but the attributes could have been just as well ascribed to the labourers' pub or the drinking party at the village shoe-maker's in earlier days.[18] It was thus from these emergent communities of labourers, relatively free from social control, and with the necessary groupings of men for mobilising for collective action, that the protests of the agricultural labourers sprang.

The social consequences of agrarian change in the eastern lowlands of central Scotland offer a marked contrast. There the material conditions of farmworkers were not adversely affected by agrarian change, since there was secure and relatively well paid employment, that is, by agricultural standards. This was, however, a very unequal society and the Lothian farmer was as rich as his southern counterpart. The gulf between the farmer and his men would probably be perceived even more sharply than in southern England by that group, now landless, who either had been or had had fathers who had been cottagers and sub-tenants. That these underlying tensions did not break through to the surface was possibly for three reasons. First, no separate community of farmworkers emerged: on the new farms the considerable labour force gathered around the farmhouse, sometimes in the shape of married men with their families in cottages, sometimes of unmarried lads who would eat in the farm kitchen.[19] The work-force was thus constantly under the eye of their master. Discipline and social control were also built into the hiring system; once a servant was hired for a year he was utterly dependent on his master for that period.[20] Similarly the cottages where the married farmworkers lived were tied cottages.[21] The importance of these limitations on the freedom of action of the farm servants is stressed when it is remembered that only overt labour discontent in Scotland in the period 1790-1832 occurred in the Carse of Gowrie, a region where the bothy system predominated. Here a separate grouping of workers could form, as the men were housed and prepared their food together in the bothy away from the farmhouse.[22]

Thirdly, the subservience of hired servants can, however, be overemphasized. As Dunbabin and Carter have indicated, the hiring fairs or feeing markets pro-vided 'an institutional alternative to strikes ... wages had to be re-negotiated each year'.[23] In central and southern England it was very difficult for farm-workers to get their employer to consider a wage claim before the establishment of trade unions. Moreover, as Carter has shown for north-east Scotland, farm servants had a number of strategies to protect themselves against the farmer. The mobility of farm servants was seen, for example, as limiting the hold a farmer could get over his men. If the farmer wished to keep good servants, he needed to maintain a 'good reputation' in his treatment of his workers.[24] These were tactics that were not open to a proletarianised workforce save perhaps at harvest time (and then only in areas of labour scarcity).[25]

Notes

1. Parts of this essay have already appeared in Charlesworth (1980), pp. 101-11.
2. Dobson (1980), pp. 23-4, appendix.
3. Stone (1787), pp. 29-31.
4. Gray (1973), pp. 108, 143.
5. Levine (1977), p. 11.
6. Stone (1787), p. 31.
7. This account is based on Collins (1970), ch. 1; Samuel (1975), pp. 1-26 and Devine (1978), pp. 331-40.
8. Levine (1977), p. 11.
9. William Marshall quoted in Collins (1970), p. 9.
10. Digby (1978), p. 101.
11. Stone (1787), p. 31.
12. Kussmaul (1978), ch. 7. (I would like to thank Professor E.A. Wrigley for drawing my attention to this thesis.)
13. Gray (1973), p. 132. The following account of the agrarian economy of the eastern lowlands of central Scotland is based on Gray (1973) and Devine (1978).
14. Gray (1973), p. 141.
15. Holderness (1972), pp. 126-39; Samuel (1975), pp. 14-16; Digby (1978), pp. 89-97; Walton (1976), pp. 143-6.
16. Walton (1976), p. 146; Samuel (1975), p. 16.
17. Peacock (1965), chs. 2, 3; Hobsbawm and Rudé (1973), chs. 3, 10.
18. PP, *Reports of the Commissioners of Poor Laws 1834 (9)*, XXVII, appendices vol. B5, question 53. Sussex: Isfield, Ticehurst, Brede.
19. Gray (1973), pp. 133-4.
20. Devine (1978), p. 336.
21. Carter (1977), p. 108.
22. Devine (1978), p. 337.
23. Dunbabin (1974), p. 132; Carter (1977), pp. 110-13.
24. Carter (1977), pp. 113-18.
25. See below, p. 141.

6.2 THE FRENCH WARS 1793-1815 AND THE FIRST OUTBREAK OF LABOURERS' PROTESTS

Up until 1793 change in the countryside for the agricultural labourer of southern and eastern England had been gradual in comparison with the conjuncture of rapidly changing circumstances that occurred during the next 30 years. The French wars from 1793-1815, with the attendant boom in economic activity and the dramatic onset of the post-war agricultural depression, were to be all important in shaping the southern and eastern labourers' consciousness of their new position in the social order. The fate of those labourers during this period was again to differ sharply from that of their northern fellows. For in the lowlands of northern Britain the war, with its drain on manpower resources, merely meant even fiercer competition in the labour market and that the well-tried strategies of maintaining long-hires, increasing wages and further adoption of farm machinery were continued by farmers.

In southern and eastern England the wartime boom and its attendant inflation rapidly brought into fruition many of the underlying structural changes in rural society and agrarian economy that have been outlined above. The steep rise in wheat prices turned the region unequivocally into the bread basket of Britain. To complete this transformation there was a 'hectic scramble to enclose and to expand cultivation' and 'a widened enthusiasm for improved methods of farming'.[1] For the labourer this meant an upsurge in temporary work associated with 'reshaping the physical capital of farming', an increase in piecework and a 'reinforcement of the natural periodicity of arable farming'.[2] Wheat was notorious for accentuating the difference between winter and summer labour requirement. Under these conditions most farmers could see little point in keeping living-in servants.[3] The rise in food prices contributed to this decision but, more importantly, was the fact that the increased profits allowed the farmer to afford more easily the trappings of the opulent 'stock jobber' culture. Farmhouses equipped with pianos, with dining rooms containing elegant plate and where farmers were served port wine, were no places for the boarding and feeding of farmworkers.[4] The social distance between farmer and labourer decidedly widened between 1790 and 1815.

The agricultural boom combined with the demands of war industries, which was felt most in the coastal counties of southern and eastern England, led to a relative scarcity of labourers.[5] This induced farmers there to adopt machinery – especially threshing machines – for the first time on a wide scale.[6] It did not, however, lead to a substantial change in the real wages of agricultural labourers; they did not share in the booming farm profits. Wage rates rose but not sufficiently to prevent real wages from declining. Moreover, poor relief may not have fully made up the difference.[7] It was against this background that the first scattering of labour protests broke out throughout southern and eastern England (Map 39). All the protests concerned the issue of wages. A few also included demands for decreases in food prices but in some of these the demands referred to perquisites, as at Pegwell Bay in Kent, and in others, other groups of men were involved, as at Steeple and Southminster where the marshmen played an active role in the demonstration.[8] These demands for decreases in food prices were exceptional. Indeed the agricultural labourers of north-west Norfolk in 1795 wanted an end made to a subsidy to keep wheat prices low, and wanted instead a subsistence wage 'proportioned to the price of wheat'.[9] Why were labourers' collective actions directed to the issue of wages whilst many other workers still directed their attention to food prices?

Farmers wanted to ensure that their crops got to market and to do this they had to make sure their labourers had adequate food. How they ensured this was the reverse side of the coin to how they coped with demands for higher wages. Farmers preferred to give the labourers perquisites, charitable doles or, through the parish vestries, poor law allowances, or to increase employment. They did this because they feared that if they increased wage rates they would not be able to lower them quickly enough when prices dropped.[10] This was a well-grounded fear in the period 1793-1815, when food prices were subject to such violent fluctuations. Perquisites and charitable doles, on the other hand, could be removed at once when the threat of a dearth had passed. Labourers could, therefore, see the advantage of gaining a wage increase. Moreover, supplementation of the men's income could be viewed as an attempt to revive the paternalistic bond between master and men. The insistence of wage increases and, in the case of the Norfolk labourers, the rejection of such supplementation methods would seem to indicate that the gulf between farmers and their labourers had become so wide that labourers resented such attempts. They now saw such paternalism as 'degrading dependence on the caprice' of their employers.[11] This, as we shall see, was an attitude carried over into the very different economic conditions of the post-war depression.

These overt protests were one of the first signs of the growing strength of the emergent community of agricultural labourers in the face of farmers trying to hold back wages in a period of unprecedented rises in food prices. Other signs of labourers' collective action during this period of relative labour shortage were the successful attempts at collective bargaining by threat of either moving on or absenteeism particularly at the critical times of hay and corn harvest.[12] This was something new for labourers in southern and eastern England. In the tighter labour markets north of the border, as we have noted, this type of collective bargaining was part and parcel of conflict between farm servants and farmer. The labourers were thus testing their strength at times and in places when the farmers were most likely to have to give way to their demands. The location of many protests in coastal areas, areas where labour shortage would be most acute, and in lightland areas where capitalist arable farming made the greatest demands on labour supplies, confirms this. It was, moreover, the experience of these early overt struggles that finally began to cement the solidarity of the labouring community, and thus helped to sustain the labourers' resolve to protest openly against the changed conditions of the period 1815-31, when the advantage of labour shortage except at harvest was gone completely in many regions of southern and eastern England.

Notes

1. Chambers and Mingay (1966), pp. 108-18; John (1967), ch. 2.
2. Jones (1965), pp. 323, 325; Richardson (1977), p. 70.
3. Kussmaul (1978), ch. 7.
4. Chambers and Mingay (1966), p. 112.
5. Richardson (1977), pp. 150, 398.
6. Jones (1965), p. 324; Richardson (1977), p. 398.
7. Baugh (1975), pp. 61-2; Richardson (1977), p. 457, table 34.
8. Dobson (1980), p. 117, appendix; Amos (1971), p. 18. Additional details of these early farmworkers' protests: Bohstedt (1972), p. 348; Emsley (1979), p. 31; Hobsbawm and Rudé (1973), p. 58; Wells (1979), p. 127; Holderness (1968), p. 285.
9. Quoted in Digby (1972), p. 180.
10. Dobson (1980), p. 116; Digby (1972), pp. 135, 156.

11. Quoted in Digby (1972), p. 180.
12. Jones (1965), p. 324; Brown (1969), p. 131.

6.3 THE POST-WAR AGRICULTURAL DEPRESSION AND THE PROTESTS OF THE 1815-31 PERIOD

The wartime boom was abruptly swept away in 1815. 400,000 men from the armed forces and another considerable body from the war industries were thrown onto the labour market.[1] Grain prices slumped whilst rents, fixed during the wartime inflation, held with the consequence that farmers' profits shrank. The farmers of southern and eastern England were faced with more acute problems than their northern rivals now that their wartime farming decisions had almost transformed their region into one dominated by wheat monoculture. To ensure their profits were held at a level to keep themselves in the manner to which they had become accustomed during the war, they had to cut costs and so they directed their energies to labour economies. Wages had to be lowered and men laid off. At the same time, however, they still had to have a reserve labour force ready to meet the peak demands of haytime but especially of the corn harvest. They devised strategies therefore to keep underemployed men in the parish.[2] On the one hand they attempted during the winter to give 'them odd jobs at the lowest wage that would induce them to remain',[3] on the other hand they continued the poor relief allowance system to supplement such low wages. Employment schemes under the auspices of poor law officials were also extended to share the burden of the costs of unemployment. For farmers as ratepayers bore the cost, though not always proportionately, whether men were employed by them or unemployed and on poor relief.

Yet in these changed circumstances farm machinery was not immediately scrapped. In the first instance farmers believed at first that the low prices were only temporary. In the case of the threshing machine, the logic of capitalist technological innovation took hold. The advantage of possessing a threshing machine was that it allowed you to get your grain to market quicker.[4] This was all important as grain prices began to fall immediately after each harvest. No wonder the threshing machine still continued to spread after 1815, despite the increase in the poor rates it caused through its ending of the traditional mainstay of winter employment for labourers. It was more important to get the threshed corn to market and realise one's profit. In a depressed price situation if one was late, it might mean the farmer suffered a loss. Moreover, the very large farmer, who also genuinely enjoyed the economies of scale that the machine yielded, did not bear proportionately his share of the cost of the displaced labour, unless a labour rate system operated. In Norfolk, however, Digby notes that these were only becoming established in the period 1824-30.[5]

Nor was there a fear that the supply of recruits for the agricultural reserve army would dry up: population growth continued throughout the depression. Because of the changes in demographic structure noted earlier, 'each new cohort now entering the marriage market would be significantly larger than its predecessor. In this way population growth developed a self-sustaining impetus'.[6] Furthermore, the allowance system was based on allocation according to size of family so labourers were cushioned from the most dire effects of continued expansion of their numbers.[7] Nor did agricultural labourers migrate. The further decline of the industrial base of the rural south and the contraction of the war industries led to a decrease of mobility compared to the wartime period.[8] There were not enough nearby alternative centres of employment to sustain large-scale migration from the countryside, a very different case from the central lowlands of Scotland.[9] It should, however, be emphasised that many farmers would not have wished for such a migration. They did not believe that there was a surplus of labour for the requirements of capitalist arable agriculture.[10]

In the years after 1814, therefore, to cope with the high unemployment levels amongst the agricultural workforces of southern and eastern England, there was instituted a new set of daily groupings of men that the labourers were to take part in. Men on poor relief were increasingly to be found in road gangs,quarrying parties and parish gangs for general farmwork.[11] These insitutions not only emphasised for the men their common experience of exploitation but also gave them further opportunities to 'corrupt one another' and to listen 'to every bad advice', there being no one to 'look after them'.[12] Peacock even quotes a report of unemployed labourers drilling in a gravel pit.[13]

The farmers of the central lowlands of Scotland were not so affected by the sudden and continued collapse of grain prices. As Devine notes, because of the range of crops grown, the relative unimportance of wheat and the importance of animal rearing and fattening, farmers there had more alternative strategies open to them. Under such conditions, economic pressure, rather than causing stagnation, reinforced the drive towards improvement. Productivity was raised in an attempt to counteract the low prices. This was particularly evident once costs reciprocally declined. Mixed farming became even more predominant amongst the region's farming systems. This all meant an expansion of employment opportunities rather than a contraction as land reclamation and drainage schemes were undertaken and turnip husbandry was extended. Moreover, any surplus of labour that did develop could readily migrate to the nearby towns or expanding centres of the textile industry.[14]

It would seem that once again circumstances worked in favour of the farmer and the ruling classes in the central lowlands of Scotland. The class nature of their society was never exposed for what it was by the remorseless pauperisation of its lowest classes. Those who might have become a pauperised community — the old, the infirm, the seasonal migratory workers — were driven from the parish when they were no longer able to work or needed for work.[15] Thus the whole landscape had the air of a giant close parish. In southern Britain farmers might make a close parish of their own parish but the needs of capitalist arable farming were such that they must of necessity have an open parish adjacent. It was from these 'uncontrollable' parishes that renewed direct collective actions sprang in the post-war period.

During this period wages were not the only major source of conflict. Indeed between 1815 and 1831 the use of agricultural machinery was to become the central issue around which conflict between the labourer and the farmer centred (Maps 40-42). The first protests against threshing machines occurred in East Suffolk as early as March 1815. To the labourers now robbed of their traditional winter employment by the spread of threshing machines, these machines seemed to be at the root of their troubles and they were the most frequently singled out targets. In 1816 in the strong loam belt of Suffolk and the heavy clay region of Essex the mole plough, which economised on the use of labour for drainage operations on heavy clay and loam lands, was similarly resented.[16] There is, however, a degree of controversy over why the threshing machine was so singled out. Digby and Macdonald have suggested that the machine was not so widespread to have caused major displacement of labour during the winter slack.[17] The labourers should therefore be seen as protesting both against a *potential* threat to their livelihood and the attitudes of employers which had produced it. The threshing machine was a focal point of their resentment, a symbol of their deteriorating condition after 1814, and of their new position in rural society.

Similarly, the issue of wages was not just a bread and butter issue. As we have seen, the way in which the labourer obtained his income was all important to him. The ending of the paternalistic farming community during the latter half of the eighteenth century figured largely in the minds of the labourers. They might appeal to farmers in threatening letters to remember their duties to their men, but there they were only using the language of paternalism so beloved of farmers to show up the hypocrisy of their masters and to shame them into acting as they professed to behave. The labourer knew differently, and he wished that his daily dealings with his employer were not encumbered with the veneer of false values. This is why they rejected the entanglement of subsidies from the poor relief with the wages the farmer paid.

This was demonstrated most forcibly during two of the major demonstrations of the 1816 protests. At Downham the turning point in the escalation of the rioting there was when the magistrates angered the labourers by only offering them an increased allowance and subsidised flour. They refused to grant the labourers' demand of a wage of 2s a day because 'the Farmers and others could not afford to grant what they wished'.[18] At Ely, however, three days later the magistrates agreed to the demand that the labourer should be 'paid his full wages by the farmer who hires him'.[19] Moreover, as in the period 1793-1805, this determination to have a subsistence wage paid by their employer was shown by the numerous incidents that focused on wages alone.

It would be wrong to draw the conclusion from this that the labourer wanted an end to the allowance system. What they wanted was a clear separation of wage payments and poor relief, to match the reality and values of the society they now found themselves in. The demands for allowances in 1816 were demands for the allowance system, set up to cope with short periods of high prices and dearths, to be continued to meet the new situation of unemployment engendered by low prices. This was a struggle that was to continue up until the

1834 New Poor Law. It was to be continued, however, not on the streets but through the magistrates meetings.[20] The poor had the right to 'appeal to the bench against the relief decisions of the overseers and the ratepayers in the vestries'. The fact that the poor were able to extract more generous relief by exercising this right of appeal may help to explain the relatively small number of collective protests over poor law issues during the years 1815 to 1831. Moreover, as Huzel states, their success on this matter together with the friction surrounding the administration of the poor law added to the labourers' resolve to protest over the issues of wages and machinery.[21]

In the 40 years between 1790 and 1830 agricultural labourers had moved from relative quiescence to the staging of open demonstrations in village streets and market places across most of southern and eastern England. The arguments presented here to explain that change have stressed the collective strength of the farmworkers, once an occupational community of labourers had emerged. The overt collective protests of the agricultural labourers between 1793 and 1831 can be matched against many of the series of food riots by rural domestic workers in the eighteenth and early nineteenth centuries. As Raymond Williams reflects:

> For all the talk of the degeneration of the labourer . . . what I notice from this terrible period, is a development of spirit and of skill.[22]

Notes

1. Jones (1965), p. 325.
2. Collins (1970), p. 18.
3. Quoted in ibid.
4. Hobsbawm and Rudé (1973), appendix iv.
5. Digby (1978), p. 115.
6. Levine (1977), p. 65.
7. Ibid., p. 124.
8. Hobsbawm and Rudé (1973), p. 23.
9. Devine (1978).
10. Digby (1978), p. 101.
11. Peacock (1965), chs. 2, 3; Hobsbawm and Rudé (1973), ch. 3.
12. PP *Reports* (9), vol. B.5 question 53 Sussex: Slaugham; Berkshire: Bradfield.
13. Peacock (1965), p. 54.
14. Devine (1978), pp. 339-42.
15. Ibid., pp. 343-4.
16. Peacock (1965), p. 73.
17. Macdonald (1975), p. 74; Digby (1972), pp. 177-8.
18. Quoted in Peacock (1965), p. 89.
19. Ibid., p. 102.
20. Dunkley (1979), p. 378.
21. Huzel (1976), p. 31.
22. Williams (1975), p. 224. For a contrary view, see Wells (1979). For a detailed rebuttal of Wells' case, see Charlesworth (1980).

6.4 THE EAST ANGLIAN PROTESTS OF 1816

The disturbances in East Anglia in 1816 have been regarded by historians as the first concerted series of collective protests by agricultural labourers acting alone.[1] Yet, the more important aspect of 1816 was that men from many different occupations over the whole of a rural area made common cause by each responding to the protests and demonstrations of their fellow workers. In a way that was only rarely seen in the large waves of protest in 1830, townsmen, industrial workers, cottagers, fenmen and agricultural labourers were linked together in 1816.

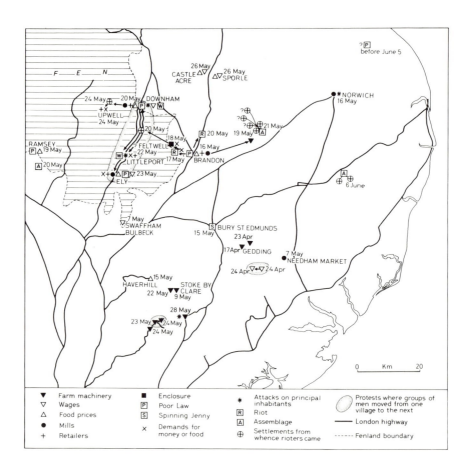

Map 43. East Anglia: Collective Protests, 1816

The disturbances can be classified into three types, depending upon their location: the town and market town incidents, the protests in the strong loam and clay lands of Essex, Suffolk and Norfolk and those in the fenland. The first group of protests were all food riots except for the attack on the spinning jenny at Bury St Edmunds. The protests were a continuation of the long tradition of the bread riots and of collective protest by textile workers in the towns and market towns of East Anglia (see Maps 18-28). As in previous such demonstrations agricultural labourers would play a very minor, if any, role. In direct contrast in the second group of disturbances it would appear that agricultural labourers were at the centre of the protests over the use of mole ploughs and threshing machines and over the demand for higher wages. In the latter all that was demanded was a subsistence wage; there was no mention of poor law allowances. Thus these protests followed on from the demands made by farmworkers in the previous period 1793-1805.

In the fenland, the variety of the disturbances and the diversity of the crowd's demands reflects the heterogeneity of the society that existed in the fens before the effective drainage and enclosure of the fens in the 1820s and 1830s. The crowds of protestors were not composed entirely of full-time farmworkers. In the Littleport and Ely protests one in three of those arrested were not agricultural labourers. A good number of these were small tradesmen and artisans from the towns and large villages of the fens. Just over one in seven of the rioters had some land. Those who had access to land or who earned some money from the cultivation of hemp and flax and the cutting of turf, sedge, reed and osier were all part of the pre-drainage, peasant economy of the fenland. Onto this peasant society had been grafted a new group of workers attached to the drainage of the fens and the maintenance of the drainage schemes, the 'bankers'.

It would have been the same men who would have been involved in the enclosure protest at Feltwell and in the riot at Hockwold. Enclosure had accelerated in the fenland, as it had throughout Britain, during the wartime agricultural boom. Drainage and enclosure meant the end of their independent way of life.

The authorities at the local level had limited means for taking effective action to stop the spread of rioting. After a riot occurred they would either make arrests, swear in special constables, organise night patrols or ask for military assistance. They might issue a proclamation threatening the protestors with arrest if they persisted in taking collective action to try to halt the spread of the disturbances. In the case of the towns, where workers had greater ability to take direct collective action, more than one strategy was tried. At Bury St Edmunds all four tactics were employed by the magistrates. In addition a further safeguard for civil peace was attempted in Bury St Edmunds when the magistrates announced concessions over poor law allowances and proposed a flour subsidy. Concessions were used to buy time to allow the authorities to marshall their forces. This happened at Brandon where the magistrates granted the crowd's demands. Thus riots took place; the authorities acted in some way to prevent a recurrence in their locality and were usually successful as regards collective protests. They were, however, unsuccessful in preventing the spread of the disturbances to other places.

The spread of the disturbances after a certain point in time, however, could not be allowed to continue. In 1816 this point was reached once the men of the fenland decided to take collective action. The repeated outbreaks of collective violence in the Downham, Littleport and Ely incidents were probably the result of the lack of gentry in the fens. If there had been more men of authority to organise effective action against the demonstrations, such a dramatic breakdown of law and order probably would have been avoided. Be that as it may, such a breakdown in law and order could not be tolerated by the central authorities. Sidmouth, the Home Secretary, ordered the military to be deployed in force throughout Norfolk and Suffolk, not just in the fenland. He took to task magistrates who had bought time by making concessions. These actions, together with the severity of the sentences passed on the fen rioters, ensured that the rioting spread no further (Figure 1).

Note

1. The information on the East Anglian disturbances of 1816 is largely drawn from Peacock (1965) with supplementary material from H.O. 41/1 and 42/150-1 and the national and local press.

6.5 THE AGRICULTURAL LABOURERS' PROTESTS OF 1822

The protests of agricultural labourers acting alone in 1816 had been rather tentative. Only when they had joined with their fellow workers had they been involved in large disturbances over a fairly extensive area. In comparison the series of protests in 1822, which were all protests by agricultural labourers alone, were much more assertive.[1]

The first collective protests occurred in the third week of February in the Diss and Eye areas. All three involved the destruction of threshing machines by parties of agricultural labourers. Unlike 1816, when the magistrates acted quickly and stopped any recurrences of protest in the Gedding area, in 1822 the arrests of the first machine breakers seems to have heightened the tension rather than reasserted order. In Diss on 16 February there had been a demonstration staged in an attempt to prevent those arrested at one of the incidents being brought before the magistrates. The labourers seemed to gain rapidly in confidence. During the following week there was only one day that was without an attack on a threshing machine by a group of labourers (Figure 1). After the customary 'day of rest' on Sunday 3 March, Monday and Tuesday saw a surge of activity with parties of labourers parading round their villages either attempting to persuade farmers to put aside their threshing machines or when this failed actually destroying the machines themselves. In contrast in 1816 the attacks on mole ploughs and threshing machines had seemed more symbolic, designed more to draw attention to the farmworkers' plight. The disturbances of 1822 had become a campaign to sweep away all threshing machines.

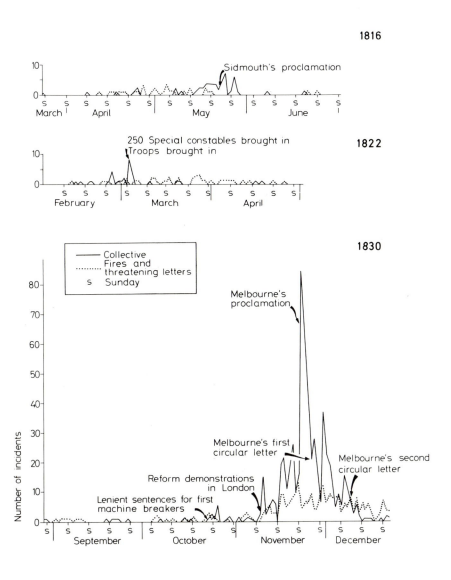

Figure 1. Time Series of the Agricultural Labourers' Protests

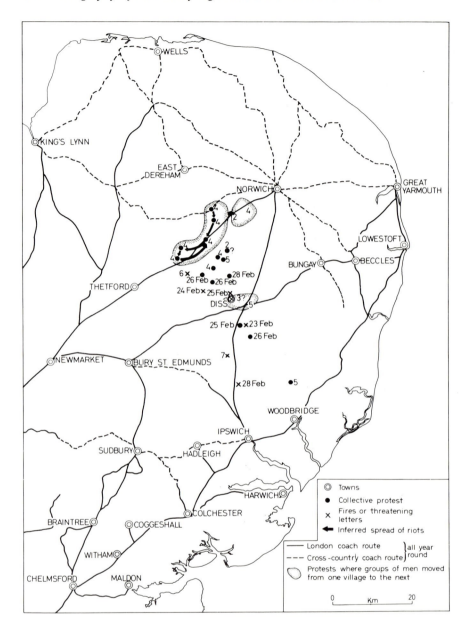

Map 44. The Main Period of the 1822 Disturbances: 23 February-7 March

Yet again, as in the fenland in 1816, once such a dangerous and seemingly insurrectionary movement had developed the county and central authorities acted swiftly to repress the revolt. Already on Monday 5 March in the area to the east of the riotous zone between Diss and Wymondham, the magistrates there decided to take action against these neighbouring parishes before the troubles spread to their area. All persons with horses were requested to meet at Harling on the Tuesday morning. There, 250 'respectable people' were sworn in as special constables. They were joined by the Eye troop of horses and together they moved against the labourers of Buckenham, Burnham, Attleborough and New Buckenham. No more collective protests occurred in that area. Similarly in the Diss area troops were sent for from Ipswich on 5 March and order was reasserted. This was the pattern of events from then on. Wherever demonstrations threatened either the military or yeomanry were put 'in readiness to aid the Civil Power' and 'no attempts at violence were made' by the labourers. The main rising by agricultural labourers in 1822 had been driven underground and a series of arson attacks followed (Figure 1).

Note

1. This account is based on information derived from the national and local press; *Annual Register* February-April 1822; and H.O. 40/17 and 41/6.

6.6 THE CAPTAIN SWING PROTESTS OF 1830-1

The direct collective actions of the agricultural labourers in 1830 commenced in east Kent in late August with two night attacks on threshing machines.[1] The collective disturbances lasted until well into December with a recurrence of activity again in east and mid Kent in late July and August 1831. The protests took many forms. In some areas there were demands for higher wages; in others tithe reductions were demanded (Map 45); in certain places poor law officials or workhouses were the crowd's targets (Map 46); and in central southern England forced levies of money, food and beer by the protestors were common (Map 47). Most widespread of all was the destruction of threshing machines (Map 42). As a background to the collective protests there was the firing of barns and ricks and the receipt of threatening letters often signed by the mythical 'Captain Swing'. Unlike 1816 but like 1822, the protests were with a few exceptions the work of agricultural labourers.

What marks off the 1830 revolt from the earlier risings of 1816 and 1822 is the massive scale of the Swing protests. They were not confined to the region where the first protests began but spread across the whole of southern and eastern England. The explanation of this does not appear to lie with any differential worsening of the economic and social conditions of the labourers in different regions in the years preceding 1830. An understanding of the massive mobilisation of labourers in the autumn of 1830 must lie with the historical events of that period.

The start of the revolt of 1830 was much more tentative even than the events of 1816 (Figure 1). There was much more the feel to these protests of testing the reaction of the authorities than there had been in 1816 and 1822.

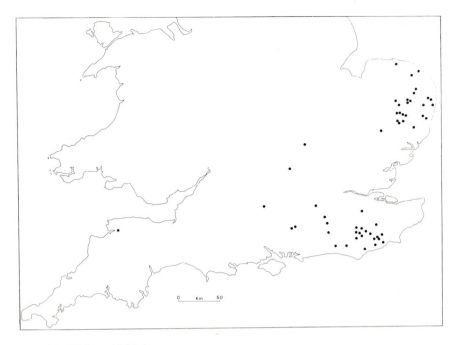

Map 45. Tithes: 1830-1

Map 46. Poor Law: 1830-1

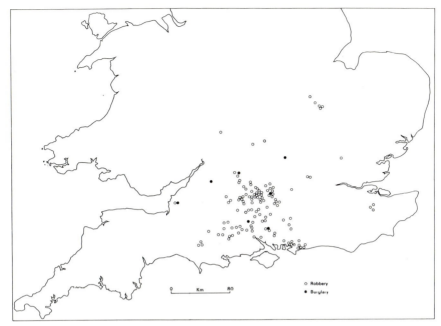

Map 47. Robbery and Burglary: 1830-1

The first indication that the authorities' attitude to the protestors in 1830 was to differ from that of the authorities in 1816 and 1822 came with the very lenient sentences passed on the first machine breakers. Immediately the labourers interpreted the light sentences as approval of their action and of the justice of their grievances: a new phase of revolt had commenced (Figure 1).

The labourers' cause went from strength to strength. By 8 November the first of a series of major waves of protest that were to sweep across southern and eastern England commenced in east Sussex. Space only permits us to show the major waves in central southern England (Map 48). The protests had by then lasted ten weeks and were seemingly gaining in momentum. Vacillation on the part of the authorities and the feeling of the middle classes of having a common cause with the labourers of Kent and east Sussex over the issue of reform had allowed the protests to last so long and to spread so far across south-eastern England. The labourers themselves were not unaware of the mounting demands for reform. This awareness owed much to the presence of grassroots radicals within rural villages. The clearest indication of the link between rural radicals and the reform agitation in London came with the turning point of the revolt in the second week of November.

This is not to argue that labourers were completely isolated from political events before 1830. Rather it is to emphasise the special conjuncture of circumstances in 1830: the growing numbers of radicals in the countryside by that date, the outbreak of agitation for parliamentary reform and its culmination in the reform crisis of early November and the effects of such agitation and crises on both the rural middle and working classes. This is what sets the protests of 1830 off from those of 1816 and 1822, not any greater degree of misery on the part of the labourers.

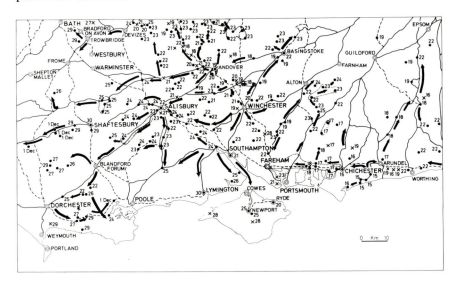

Map 48. The Waves of Rioting in Central Southern England: November-December 1830

The suppression of the revolt came finally with the accession of the new Whig administration on 22 November. It was politically expedient for them to take a more determined stance against the rioters. The putting down of the disturbances and the containment of the spread of the riots were one of the new government's first priorities. As the administration was pledged to bring in parliamentary reform, the middle classes were no longer alienated from the central government and co-operated with the government's measures to quash the revolt. 'Military officers were sent into the counties to supervise the disposal of troops and to advise magistrates on the levying of local volunteers.' Moreover, the government were aided at a crucial stage in the revolt by the fact that the gentry of Wiltshire and Hampshire put down the protests in their counties with extreme vigour. The revolt had, however, spread to so many counties that it took time for order to be reasserted completely. Moreover, in Norfolk the sympathetic attitude of the magistracy aided the labourers' cause during this very period. They received a sharp rebuke from Lord Melbourne, the Home Secretary, for their trouble and troops and officers were redeployed from the West Country to put down the revolt in East Anglia.

Note

1. For a more detailed account, see Hobsbawm and Rudé (1973) and Charlesworth (1979).

6.7 AFTER SWING

The rapid and fairly easy suppression of Swing and the draconian sentences meted out to the protestors have led some historians to believe that after Swing the labourers' will to resist was destroyed and did not revive until the agricultural union movement of the 1870s. Even Hobsbawm and Rudé, who attempted to counter such a pessimistic view, still conclude that after 1830 'on the whole . . . organized and public activity was uncommon, and after 1834-5 insignificant'.[1] The next two sections show that their conclusion was wrong, at least for the 1830s. It is not, however, surprising that they did misinterpret the events in rural England after 1830 because as they point out:

> Of all the many gaps in our knowledge of the farm-labourers' world in the nineteenth century none is more shocking than our total ignorance of the forms of agrarian discontent between the rising of 1830 and the emergence of agricultural trade unionism in the early 1870s . . . The only exception to this is the Tolpuddle incident of 1834 . . . (but) it has never been studied in relation to contemporary rural movements.[2]

The two studies that follow are the work of a number of scholars who are slowly piecing together what happened in those years.

Notes

1. Hobsbawm and Rudé (1973), p. 244.
2. Ibid., p. 242.

6.8 ANTI POOR LAW MOVEMENTS AND RURAL TRADE UNIONISM IN THE SOUTH-EAST 1835   John Lowerson

The anti poor law movements and the rural trade unionism in the south-east in 1835 show both the potent influence of 'modernisation' grafted onto traditional rural protest after the Napoleonic Wars and the possibilities of a continuum of organised agrarian radicalism. The 1834 Poor Law Amendment Act was designed specifically to cope with the severe problems of rural England and to prevent, by deterrence, a repetition of the 1830 incidents in the epicentres of Kent and Sussex, where it was implemented first in 1835. There, complex soil patterns, small-scale farming and low investment rates combined with a rapid population surge to produce an average dependence on permanent relief of some 25 per cent of the population.[1] An additional urgency was generated by claimed links between Swing, local crime and organised smuggling and decaying social relationships which appeared intractable for the extant combination of paternalism, 'shovelling out paupers' and encouraging spade husbandry, with overstrained parochial agencies.

In April 1835 the assistant commissioners began to form poor law unions with an arrogant, impatient zeal which alienated most levels of local society. After mild protests from farmers and tradesmen, the sharpest response shook authority's illusions of rural backwardness and temporarily revived fears of a new Swing. In Kent and Sussex there were at least 93 recorded incidents involving direct protest against the new measures in the second half of 1835; 30 of these were arson against the property of local overseers or guardians, made easier by the relaxation of stringent Swing precautions.

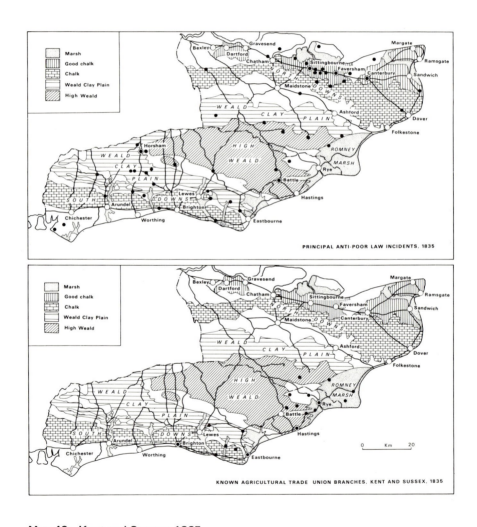

Map 49. Kent and Sussex: 1835

Additional source: Richardson (1977), p. 167.

The continuum of arson was punctuated by blocks of overt protest in areas surrounding particular market towns, often substantially isolated from other centres of trouble. Between 30 April and 7 May groups of labourers carrying clubs, with flags and blackened faces, demonstrated in the villages round Sitting-bourne, where they finally besieged local magistrates in the workhouse, until troops dispersed them; 37 labourers were imprisoned for terms up to two years.[2] The Sussex demonstrations were more scattered in time and place, but with three main centres. Late April and early May saw mass open-air meetings near Eastbourne, where the Swing practice of 'carting' unpopular officials across parish boundaries, unhurt save in dignity, was revived until special constables and armed coastguards intervened. On 22 May at Ringmer, 30 men invaded the overseer's office, demanding 'money or blood' but dispersed when paid in cash rather than kind; three were subsequently convicted. In May, 'carting' appeared in the Battle area, succeeding orderly marches and petitions which attacked with quiet dignity the prospect of family breakup which would follow the end of outdoor relief. Dragoons were eventually introduced to keep order, staying until 1838.[3]

After the summer and harvest intervals the only 'riot' took place in Steyning on 14 September, prompted by rumours of treadmills in workhouses and an attempt to move some paupers to a neighbouring parish. After four hours the angry mob which had besieged magistrates in the workhouse was cleared by troops. The bulk of those caught were bound over at the assizes — clearly there was a local attempt to play down the severity of this and other covert protests.[4] Thereafter, trouble was concentrated within the workhouses and the autumn saw a resurgence of arson in both counties.

This 'traditional' pattern masks a powerful and inseparable accompaniment of rural trade unionism. Scattered evidence suggests that the short-lived wage rises won in 1830 were underpinned by a readiness to demand further changes, for which an organisational nucleus existed in the Battle area.[5] In the north Sussex Weald small branches of the political unions provided regular meetings and group readings of the *Poor Man's Guardian* for local craftsmen with a strong Paineite tradition. From February 1835 they were linked further in the weekly pages of the *Brighton Patriot*.[6] In late April of that year farm labourers in the Rye area, bordering Kent and Sussex brought union activity into the open, undeterred by the suppression at Tolpuddle. Known alternatively as 'The United Brothers of Industry' or 'The Agricultural Labourers' Conjunction Union Friendly Society' they were involved in the Eastbourne demonstrations and individuals were reported at other incidents. Thomas Maule of Westfield and John Goddard of Guestling, 'a little schoolmaster', founded branches with zeal; at one point, they claimed a network from Seaford to Dover, with the nucleus round Rye and Sedlescombe, near Battle, 'the seat of government'. An entrance fee of 2s and a weekly subscription of 4d deterred a wide membership, however, and splits soon appeared between the Maule-Goddard faction which favoured open strike action and a more conservative group, based on Seaford, who saw the main function as being to replace dependence on paternalistic village friendly societies.

Paradoxically, it was the latter organisations which proved the undoing of the movement, together with a concerted farmers' lockout of any members of the union. Appeals for help received scant support from urban unions, and the movement had gone underground by December 1835.[7]

The unions owed no direct inspiration to religious movements, although the more apocalyptic parts of the New Testament were apparent favourites at branch meetings.[8] They were strongest in 'open' villages. Its main influence, apart from fostering a short-lived hope, was that it brought its members into contact with the mainstream of contemporary working class radicalism, fed by speakers and pamphlets from London and Birmingham. After its collapse, its members appear to have maintained a presence of consciousness in such Wealden villages as Burwash where they hosted Chartists and others for the next decade whilst the more covert forms, arson, sheep stealing and maiming and poaching, continued unabated into the late 1840s.[9] The establishment of the East Sussex Police in 1839 and the Kent and West Sussex forces in 1857 was some deterrent, but a crisp memory of protest survived to provide a base for the 'Revolt of the Field' in the 1870s (see section 7.5).

Notes

1. Lowerson (1978), pp. 19-23.
2. *Kent Herald*, May and June 1835; PRO, HO 52/26, letters from Rev Dr Poore.
3. East Sussex County Record Office, *Battle Union Minute Book*, 24 July 1835.
4. PRO, HO 52/27, letter from Goring, 13 September 1835.
5. PRO, HO 52/15, letters from Sir Godfrey Webster, 28 March and 9 November 1831.
6. *Brighton Patriot*, 1835, *passim*.
7. PP (1835), vol. XXXV, pp. 207ff.
8. See PRO, HO 52/27, letter from Rev J. Carnegie, 7 July 1835.
9. Kemnitz (1969).

6.9 PROTEST IN EAST ANGLIA AGAINST THE IMPOSITION OF THE NEW POOR LAW   Anne Digby

The number of anti poor law disturbances in East Anglia, as with those in the south-east, necessitates a modification of the conventional view that protest against the implementation of the New Poor Law was mainly confined to the north of England.[1] It is noticeable that this opposition involved violence to people as well as the damage to property which had marked earlier resistance to changes in relief administration in this region. This suggests the worsening social relationships between the labourer and those who had either administered poor relief or who had paid low wages which needed supplementation by poor law allowances to bring them up to subsistence level. The widespread incidence of disturbances showed that they were not confined to the heavy-soil areas where underemployment and low wages had produced exceptionally high levels of pauperism. Antagonism was most marked in Norfolk, in east Suffolk, and in those parts of Essex continuous to the disturbed parts of Suffolk.

In responding to this hostility the central poor law authority learned from its initial mistakes in implementing the new system in east Suffolk where the provisions of the Poor Law Amendment Act of 1834 were first imposed. Here the attempt to introduce sudden changes in relief administration in adjoining areas sparked off a violent conflagration in the second half of 1835 which culminated in an attack on Ipswich Workhouse in December 1835. At the same time workhouses to the west of our region at Saffron Walden and Bishop's Stortford were set on fire. This effective challenge forced the poor law inspectors to adopt a gradualist approach elsewhere, phasing in the new system parish by parish, and union by union, so that any resistance that was produced would be isolated and more easily contained. The predominantly rural nature of this area, with its scattered population and its preponderance of ill-educated and unpoliticised agricultural workers, made it difficult to organise sustained resistance, even had leaders emerged who had attempted to do so. Ironically, such shortlived riotous assemblies as did occur were the result of the geography of the New Poor Law itself since poor law unions were often centred round market towns where workhouses were located. These symbols of an oppressive system provided a focus for the disaffection of the labouring poor; not least because it was at the workhouse that the guardians' meetings were held and poor relief was given to or withheld from the paupers who had been summoned there. Several riots occurred spontaneously outside the guardians' board room: these caused intense, but needless, alarm to the local administration of the poor law since they were soon dispersed. As these incidents were widely separated in time and place, one from another, they posed no long-term threat to the successful imposition of the 1834 Act.

The New Poor Law's radical departures from the traditional system of poor relief provoked substantial opposition from the East Anglian poor precisely because of their innate conservatism. They wanted the poor law to continue to be administered in their own locality's customary manner. In the west of Norfolk and Suffolk where the workhouse had rarely been set up under the Old Poor Law, the poor protested initially against the changes made in the form of outdoor relief — from money allowances to bread or flour — and later attempted to prevent the erection of workhouses which would have replaced even outdoor relief in kind with a new system of indoor relief. In the east of these counties, where some houses of industry had been built in the second half of the eighteenth century, the labourers in many areas had already accepted the principle of indoor relief, but objected to its conversion from a relatively humane system to one which, after 1834, classified the members of a family so that they were separated one from another within the workhouse.

The main period of protest from 1835 to 1837 coincided with the changes made in outdoor relief, with the erection of workhouses and with the introduction of systematic indoor relief for the able-bodied poor. While the most spectacular conflict took the form of riotous assemblies at guardians' meetings or attacks and fires at workhouses, the more typical hostilities were the sporadic

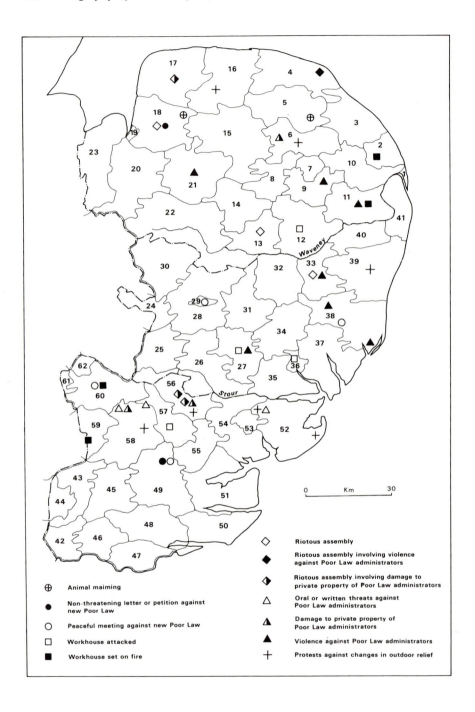

offensives against the property — or, on occasion, the persons — of parish over-seers, poor law guardians, inspectors and union relieving officers. Not all protest was violent and occasionally there was an organised meeting, a petition or a non-threatening letter which expressed local opposition in a more peaceful manner. But the enduring resentment of the poor against the New Poor Law was shown by the threatening letters, the animal maiming and the arson which continued to be directed against the local administrators of the poor law even after the new system had been imposed in the region.

Map 50. Protests Against the New Poor Law in East Anglia

Poor Law Unions or Incorporations (*)

Norfolk

1. Yarmouth
2. E. and W. Flegg*
3. Tunstead and Mapping*
4. Erpingham
5. Aylsham
6. St Faith's
7. Norwich*
8. Forehoe*
9. Henstead
10. Blofield
11. Loddon and Clavering
12. Depwade
13. Guiltcross
14. Wayland
15. Mitford and Launditch
16. Walsingham
17. Docking
18. Freebridge Lynn
19. King's Lynn
20. Downham Market
21. Swaffham
22. Thetford
23. Wisbech (part)

Suffolk

24. Newmarket (part)
25. Risbridge
26. Sudbury
27. Cosford
28. Thingoe
29. Bury St Edmunds*
30. Mildenhall

31. Stow
32. Hartismere
33. Hoxne
34. Bosmere and Claydon
35. Samford*
36. Ipswich
37. Woodbridge
38. Plomesgate
39. Blything
40. Wangford
41. Mutford and Lothingland*

Essex

42. West Ham
43. Epping
44. Edmonton (part)
45. Ongar
46. Romford
47. Orsett
48. Billericay
49. Chelmsford
50. Rochford
51. Maldon
52. Tendring
53. Colchester
54. Lexden
55. Witham
56. Halstead
57. Braintree
58. Dunmow
59. Bishop's Stortford (part)
60. Saffron Walden
61. Royston
62. Linton (part)

Note

1. A further account of these events in Norfolk and Suffolk and the general background to the protests can be found in Digby (1972), ch. 5 and (1978). For the disturbances in Essex see Amos (1971) ch. 8 and Richardson (1977), ch. 7. Dr Richardson also supplied supplementary material, which is gratefully acknowledged.

6.10 THE AGRICULTURAL LABOURERS' PROTESTS IN EAST ANGLIA IN THE 1840s

In the 1840s the labourers' protests appear to have been driven underground. Most studies on why this occurred have focused on the labourers of East Anglia. As Digby has pointed out for Norfolk, the disturbances on 1816, 1822 and 1830-1 gave a fatal blow to the traditional, paternalistic order of rural society. The poor had not responded with the dependent loyalty expected of them by the propertied classes. The gentry and the clergy thus gradually withdrew themselves from active involvement in village life, particularly involvement with what they now regarded as the 'undeserving poor'. The gentry now turned all their attention to tending their 'close' villages.[1] With the old paternalistic framework from which the labourers' collective actions had drawn their legitimation dismantled, but with the labourers still clinging to the now archaic values of that society, they were left 'in a state of general demoralisation and confusion'.[2] With the tight controls of the New Poor Law, now administered by the farmers as poor law guardians, and with a more closely supervised system of charitable doles, victimisation of the troublesome labourer could easily be achieved. Under such circumstances all the labourers could manage by way of protest were arson attacks and, at times, spates of threatening letters.[3]

Harber's study of the covert protests in Suffolk in the 1840s gives us a detailed account of such outbreaks. In the western half of Suffolk between 1840 and 1845 there were 126 fires and a further 70 in east Suffolk. The geography of the attacks was not a reflection of spatial variations in unemployment alone, it also reflected the spatial variations in the severity of poor law implementation. Now that farmers were the poor law guardians it is not surprising that farmers' property was attacked rather than the property of the gentry; indeed, in Suffolk, only one gentleman's property was fired. Yet there was no selectivity for attack on farmers who were poor law guardians, rather blame seems to have been apportioned by farmworkers to farmers as a class for the way the New Poor Law was administered. The peak year for arson was 1844 when unemployment reached high levels.[4] As Harber notes:

> the closest the country came to experiencing public popular disturbances was from March to June 1844. Then not only did threatening letters appear that showed that the fires were much more than the work of isolated individuals but there were refusals to help put the fires out.[5]

Not until the 1860s when the labourers 'had learned the rules of capitalist social relations' did they begin again to fight effectively and openly for their share of prosperity, and then it was, as will be seen, with weapons better fitted for the struggle.[6]

Notes

1. Digby (1978), ch. 11.
2. Harber (1972), p. 54.
3. Ibid., parts II, V.
4. Ibid., part III; see also Jones (1976), pp. 5-44.
5. Harber (1972), p. 57.
6. Obelkevitch (1976), p. 90.

7 RURAL PROTEST IN MID- AND LATE-VICTORIAN BRITAIN

7.1 INTRODUCTION

The final section of this atlas focuses on the divergence of experience between lowland and highland, central and peripheral Britain that clearly emerged from the 1840s onwards. It is perhaps somewhat distracting to the reader that there is an overlap between this period and some of the collective protests examined above. The dichotomy between the two parts of Britain is seen at its starkest in the protests of the last quarter of the nineteenth century. Yet to isolate the events of the Rebecca riots in the 1839-44 period from the collective violence that took place in Wales and the Highlands of Scotland in the later-nineteenth century would be just as problematic. As Carter has pointed out a history of the Celtic periphery and its nineteenth-century revolts, including the Irish experience, is urgently needed.[1] Hopefully the juxtaposition of three of those revolts here will spur on such historical research. For what one has on the Celtic fringes of Britain is an almost continuous series of protests.

Against these massive collective protests one has in lowland Britain during this period what Stevenson has called 'the transition to order': the rise of agricultural trade unionism and the strike weapon and the development of farmers' movements to obtain land reform through legislation.[2] For the countryside the outlines of this transition and the prehistory of these associations has barely been uncovered. Indeed, because of the scattered nature of the research and the consequence lacunae on both these subjects, we have chosen just to focus on the agricultural trade unions in England in this section. In Scotland and northern England farm servants' associations developed commensurate with the greater numbers of such agricultural workers. The same reasons why these areas remained quiescent between 1793 and 1831 equally apply to the lack of the southern British type of agricultural trade unionism. Yet, as Dunbabin points out, working within the framework of the traditional structure of hiring fairs, the Scottish farm servants movement was one of the most successful in achieving its, albeit limited, objectives.[3]

Whereas the agricultural depression of the late 1870s undermined agricultural trade unionism, agricultural depression began to strain the relationship between tenants and landlords and movements by farmers and tenants sprang up. The most noticeable was the Farmers' Alliance founded in England in 1879. Dunbabin has charted its rise and achievements, whilst Carter has uncovered a comparable agitation in north-east Scotland during the same period. On the whole all these movements in lowland Britain were associational. Studies have only just begun to explain why tithes became such a violent issue in Non-conformist Wales in the 1880s and not in those of southern and eastern England, where areas, like the High Weald, had their share of small, Non-conformist farmers. Indeed tithe agitation was to come to the surface in Cornwall and eastern England in the early-twentieth century. Perhaps more than any other period studied in the atlas, this period reveals how major series of protests have cast into shadow areas where agitation certainly did occur but whose geographical extent has not yet been uncovered. Hopefully it will not be too long before this section in particular is in need of revision.[4]

Notes

1. Carter, personal communication.
2. Stevenson (1979), p. 293.
3. Dunbabin (1974), chs. 6, 7, 11; for the Scottish unions, see also Robertson (1979), pp. 90-114.
4. Dunbabin (1974), ch. 8; Carter (1979), ch. 6; Rowe, personal communication.

7.2 THE REBECCA RIOTS 1839-44   David J.V. Jones

The Rebecca riots were the most spectacular manifestation of rural anger in nineteenth-century Wales.[1] During the century there was a whole series of disorders, beginning with the squatter disturbances in the north and west (see section 2.15), encompassing the little known poaching affrays in mid-Victorian Wales (labelled 'the second Rebecca riots'), and culminating in the widespread anti-tithe riots at the turn of the century (see section 7.6). What characterised them all was their community-based nature. The Rebecca riots in particular grew out of a special kind of rural community undergoing rapid social change and economic pressure. This was not a highly-capitalised region; in the hills especially an old peasant economy lingered, with poor farmers and labourers sometimes working closely together. In the last decades of the eighteenth century, and especially in the first 20 years of the next, these small west Wales communities became defiantly Non-conformist, and the gulf between them and the Anglicised landowners, stewards and magistrates visibly widened. As the threatening letters illustrate, Rebecca was the creation of a fractured society.[2]

The grievances of the Rebeccaites were many. At one key meeting, attended by *The Times* reporter Thomas Campbell Foster, the people complained of church-rates, tithes, high rents, the poor law and the activities of insensitive agents and clerical magistrates. The three factors which seemed to have transformed this general unrest into something more serious were the bad seasons of 1839-41, the collapse in prices 1842-3 and the extension on country roads of tollgates operated by turnpike trusts. Just as the small farmers of the area, 'Rebecca's faithful followers', began to experience grave economic difficulties, so the trusts of Cardigan, Carmarthen, Newcastle and Whitland brought in Thomas Bullin to erect more gates and increase charges.

The result was inevitable, and the attacks on the gates along the Carmarthen-Pembrokeshire border in January 1839 mark the first phase of the Rebecca riots proper (Map 55). Thereafter, there were a few scattered incidents, but the next major phase began in the winter of 1842. Over the next two years scores of carefully selected gates were smashed, mainly in Carmarthenshire, Pembrokeshire and south Cardiganshire, though occasionally Rebecca travelled as far as east Glamorgan, Radnorshire and beyond (Map 51). The men who smashed the gates usually numbered 50-100, were well organised and had a formidable range of weapons. As to Rebecca herself, no one person was given that title, although the brains behind some later operations was probably the radical lawyer, Hugh Williams.

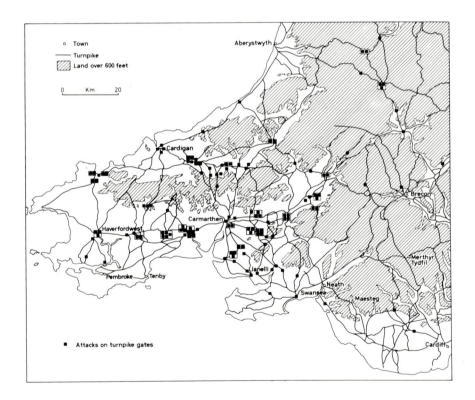

Map 51. Turnpike Gates: 1839-44

Source: The maps in this section are based on Williams (1955) and supplementary material from *The Welshman* 1843 and H.O. 45/265 and 454.

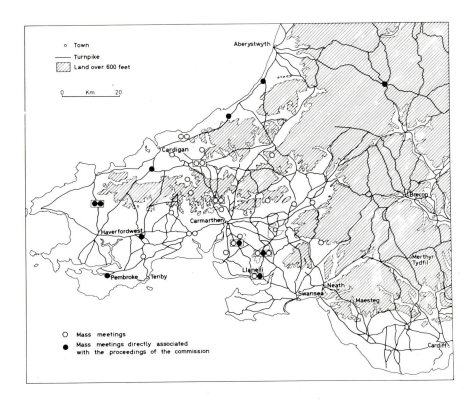

Map 52. Mass Meetings: 1843-4

One of the interesting developments of this rural protest movement was the number of mass meetings held (Map 52), both in secret and in the presence of the general public. At these meetings lists of grievances were drawn up, plans made for future action and petitions to Parliament and Queen signed. For a time, in the late-summer and autumn of 1843, these mass meetings appeared to take the place of nocturnal outrages. In fact, this was just one of the many changing aspects of the movement. In the early 1840s attacks on workhouses, the burning of hayricks and the destruction of salmon weirs were all counter-signed by Rebecca (Map 53), and scores of letters were sent in her name threatening destruction to many people in authority (Map 54).

There is some evidence of a significant shift in the social support for these later Rebecca incidents. As unemployed workmen and iron-workers like Dai' Cantwr and Shoni Sgubor Fawr became more active in west Wales, so the farmers retreated. Fearful of attacks on their own property, some became special constables and others co-operated fully with the commission of enquiry set up by the government in 1843. The tollgate problem was quickly resolved, and

Williams believed that the coming of the railways helped to remove the remaining tension in isolated communities.

Notes

1. The essential book is Williams (1955).
2. See Jones (1973); cf. Howell (1977).

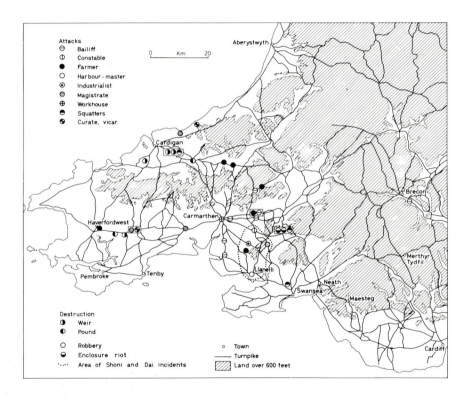

Map 53. Other Collective Protests: 1842-4

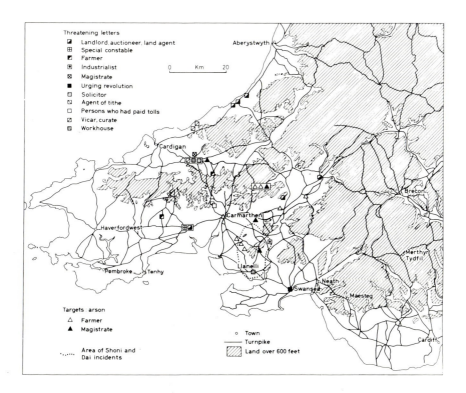

Map 54. Arson and Threatening Letters: 1842-4

7.3 THE SPREAD OF THE REBECCA RIOTS 1842-4

The destruction of tollgates recommenced in south-west Wales at St Clears in mid-November 1842, the provocation being the erection of a new tollgate.[1] The area between St Clears and Narbeth was to be the centre of the disturbance for the next five months, many of the riots being concerned with the demolition of re-erected gates. During February and March 1843 the protests spread sporadically into the adjacent regions but only to the north did this lead immediately to a continuity of disturbances over the next few months. June appears to be the critical month in the evolution of the revolt; the numbers of incidents began to build up from the end of the first week. The authorities had found it difficult enough to contain the situation before June; now their forces were at full stretch. In mid-June the government finally relented and sent troops into the region. By then, however, the protests were very widespread. With the hilly terrain of the region and the decision of Love, the military commander, to concentrate his troops at four centres within the region, it was possible for the rioters to play a cat and mouse game with the troops. Love was inevitably forced to send troops to repress rioting the day after it happened. The only preventive role the troops were used for was in Glamorgan and Monmouthshire. Consequently at the height of the disturbances 1,800 of them were tied down in the region.

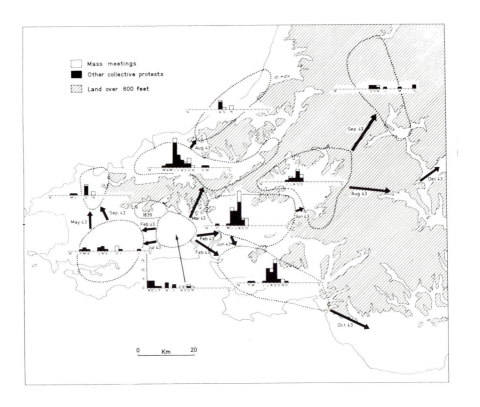

Map 55. The Spread of the Rebecca Riots: 1842-4

Thus initially the momentum of the revolt was not checked by the measures taken by the authorities. More important were factors internal to the movement itself. The first of these was the gradual replacement of the riots by mass meetings to discuss grievances and to petition the government. These were given added importance in October, when the commission of enquiry was set up, for the mass meetings could appoint and brief delegates to appear before the commission. Secondly, the protests were spreading into areas where the abuses of the turnpike trusts were not as blatant and economic conditions were better. Even so in Brecknockshire the trustees removed their nine gates as a precaution. Thirdly, the breakdown of law and order, which had been partly caused by the reluctance of farmers to be enrolled as special constables, and the increase of violent incidents, such as those associated with Shoni and Dai, had frightened many farmers, who now wanted to see the ending of the collective disturbances. Many began to enrol freely as special constables. Finally, dissatisfaction was expressed of Love's handling of the situation. In early October a new strategy was devised by Sir Geoge Brown which dispersed forces throughout the area. By November 1843 the disturbances were very few and far between. The spread of the protests continued, however, in the next month and indeed it was not until September 1844 that the last collective disturbances occurred.

Note

1. The account and map are based on Williams (1955), chs. 7-10 and supplementary material from *The Welshman*, 1843 and H.O. 45/265 and /454.

7.4 AGRICULTURAL TRADE UNIONISM IN ENGLAND 1872-94
John P.D. Dunbabin

In 1872 English agricultural labourers suddenly mounted a movement far larger than any of its predecessors and firmly cast in a trade union format.[1,2] The transition was neither total nor taken for granted, but no serious 'law and order' problems were presented; so central government involvement was very slight. Admittedly scope remained for legal harassment at a local level, and the imprisonment of 15 Oxfordshire women for picketing/intimidation produced a national outcry. Also until 1875 contracts of employment could be enforced by the criminal law. This was used to inhibit strikes by *long-term* employees, but could not reach most southern English agricultural labourers, the great majority of whom were engaged by the week.

Agricultural unionism had two peaks, 1874 (with over 100,000 members) and 1892-3 (with about 40,000); both coincided with periods of general union activism. Among the causes of agricultural organisation in 1872 was the urban agitation for a nine-hour day, while the later East Anglian revival was a direct sequel of the 1889 dock strike. More generally agricultural, like other 'unskilled', unionism surfaced during economic up-swings and fell off in recessions. In the 1860s the earlier endemic rural underemployment began to lift, and occasional combinations were attempted to raise wages. Then the urban boom of the early 1870s multiplied openings for countrymen and held out the prospect of transforming the rural labour market by migration.

Since agricultural unions were formed on a rising market, they were at first gratifyingly successful. Attempts in Warwickshire and Oxfordshire to counter specific strike threats by wider lock-outs proved inconclusive. But in the east farmers were rather more cohesive; about a 1,000 unionists were locked out around Sudbury in April 1873 and could not be supported for much over a month. 1874 saw a larger-scale repetition, as local wage claims were met in Lincolnshire and Suffolk by more extensive lock-outs. The Lincolnshire dispute was eventually resolved by mediation, but in Suffolk the Defence Associations were clearly fighting unionism as such. The struggle became a test case, with the labourers attracting urban sympathy and subscriptions. But after the harvest had been gathered without the locked-out men, their unions abandoned them.

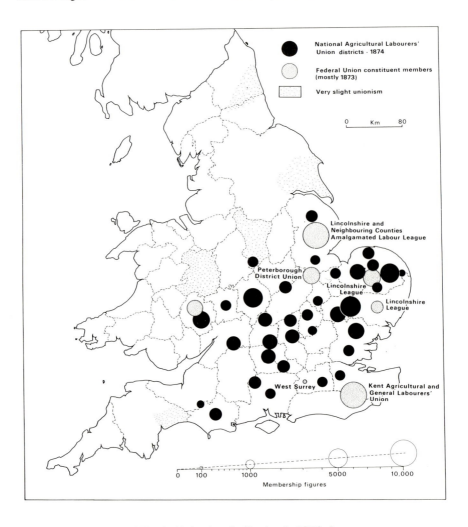

Map 56. Agricultural Trade Unionism in England, 1873-4

Note: The Kent Agricultural and General Labourers' Union later became the Kent and Sussex Labourers' Union.

Only 5,000-6,000 men had been directly involved. But expectations had been high, sometimes even millenarian, and disappointment was proportionate. Also financial irregularities sparked acrimonious disputes. The upshot was splits, inter-union abuse and disillusion. Later, agricultural depression set in, bringing cuts in money (though not generally real) wages. In this climate the unions both dwindled and concentrated increasingly on other matters, notably emigration and the acquisition of the vote. The labourers' enfranchisement in 1885 brought many of their other concerns onto the political agenda and led to exaggerated ideas of the likelihood of state intervention. These ideas informed the new unions that sprouted after 1890, though the National Union continued to look more to direct action. 1891 again saw the formation in Norfolk and Suffolk of a Farmers' Federation. In 1892-3 prices fell, farmers insisted that wages follow, and the unions were seldom able to resist. In 1894 their membership collapsed.

Agricultural unionism had had no single source – rather local combinations mushroomed in 1871-2 and subsequently coalesced. The process was assisted by unprecedented press publicity, which Arch used to establish his Warwickshire combination as the predominant agricultural union, indeed as one of the largest unions of the day. It often enrolled a majority of the labourers in particular villages, but never in a whole county. So the most important determinants of its geographical incidence must have been local ones, which we can only sometimes identify. However, combinations of the southern English variety clearly did not flourish where farm servants were commonly hired on long contracts – not primarily for legal reasons, but because hiring fairs generated a distinctive form of labour relations. Contemporaries also noted that agitation was most marked in arable districts. Lastly, unionism and, still more, disputes, appear to have been features chiefly of large farms. Even in the 1870s these factors inclined the movement towards eastern England. But its revival in the 1890s was a much more exclusively East Anglian affair – wages had suffered more there from the arable depression, and perhaps too the local tradition of adjusting them with the price of corn encouraged combinations and counter-combinations.

Notes

1. For a complete and fully referenced account of agricultural trade unionism during this period, see Dunbabin (1973), ch. 4.
2. For the geography of trade unionism see ibid. and Dunbabin (1968), pp. 114-41.

7.5 THE KENT AND SUSSEX LABOURERS' UNION 1872-95
Felicity Carlton

Guided by its first secretary, Alfred Simmons, the KSLU was the strongest, most stable independent regional combination of agricultural and general workers to oppose Arch's National Union.[1] With Sussex recruitment limited to border areas, it remained essentially a county union for 15 years. Achieving solidarity within the local labouring community, yet avoiding parochialism, it proved so attuned to Kent conditions as to attract 16,000 members by 1879.

Those conditions included comparative freedom from large estates, subdivision of property, a high proportion of 'open' nucleated villages and the traditional presence of small freeholders in numerous market towns which contributed a certain independence and assisted agitation. Distinctions between urban and rural populations were blurred by the wide distribution of commercial and industrial centres, which lessened the impact of rural depopulation (and the relevance of the National Union's almost exclusively agricultural recruitment). Wages had been raised, to a level capable of supporting regular subscriptions, through industrial competition and the demand for specialist skills essential to mixed farming. Most favoured were north, west and mid Kent, and Canterbury: here the KSLU gained its firmest bases. Labourers (and the union) fared worse in areas devoted to arable or livestock, with scattered populations and lacking alternative industries. Yet the whole region benefited from improving communications and high education standards which increased awareness of current events and potential for efficient combination.

A Kent Agricultural Labourers' Protection Association, often judged England's first true labourers' union, had briefly afforded its few hundred members direct experience of combination and fellowship with Maidstone trade unionists and radicals. It established patterns of local self-reliance (Map 57). West Kent farm and general labourers staged first meetings in April, 1872, inviting assistance from Maidstone Trades Council representatives. Such men brought from their craft union backgrounds a careful approach to organisation. Uniquely in 1872, the KSLU was not formed for pay agitation: in west and mid Kent potential members' wages already approached, sometimes exceeded, rates demanded in other counties. As it mobilised (more slowly) in the poorer-paid east, the KSLU recognised the impracticality of fixing a single desirable pay level.

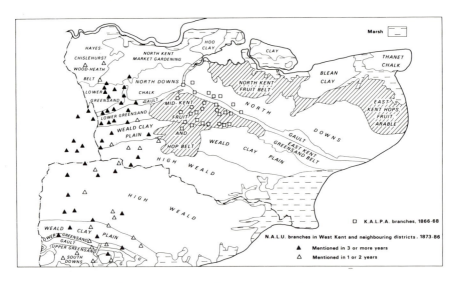

Map 57. Kent and East Sussex: KALPA and NALU Branches

Note: The maps in this section are based on press reports. The author was unable to trace any official records of the KSLU during her research.

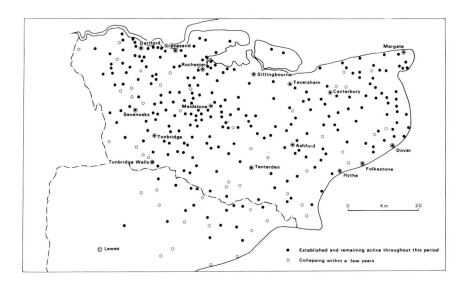

Map 58. Kent and East Sussex: KSLU Branches, 1872-9

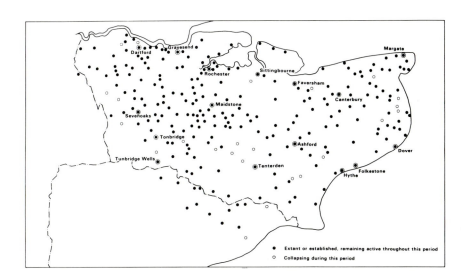

Map 59. Kent and East Sussex: KSLU Branches, 1880-7

Early restraint reassured employers; and deciding to offer 15s a week to victimised members (6s more than the National Union) encouraged the avoidance of unnecessary disputes. Social and moral arguments attracted 8,000 recruits in the first year, from which sound base the KSLU could assume a national role through the short-lived Federation of Agricultural & General Labourers' Unions.

Only after two years' groundwork were rural wage increases sought, through successful 'wages district' sub-committees whose localised negotiations made for flexibility and limited areas of tension, preventing Kent's embroilment in the bitter Eastern Counties Lock-out which destroyed the Federation.

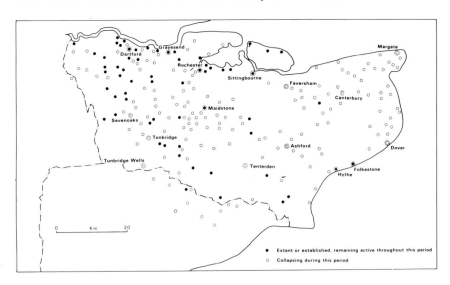

Map 60. Kent and East Sussex: KSLU Branches, 1888-94

KSLU growth and prosperity continued. Besides encouraging voluntary branch benefit collections, it became the first labourers' combination to offer contributory sickness, funeral and confinement payments. It ran a Land and Cottage Fund along balloting building society lines, its own newspaper (*Kent & Sussex Times*) and, briefly, a Co-operative Store. It offered victimised labourers legal protection, and managed successful emigration parties. Strictly non-sectarian and non-party political, it supported general reform campaigns through mass meetings and petitions. Grand anniversaries, attracting attendances of up to 35,000, celebrated the union's progress (Map 58).

The solidarity thus fostered preserved the KSLU through crisis in the winter of 1878-9 when generally hostile east Kent and Sussex farmers locked out 1,000 members who rejected unprecedentedly harsh wage cuts. Thereafter, however, depression settled even on Kent's mixed farming: the KSLU could not realistically continue resisting pay cuts. Its retention of rural members in the difficult 1880s − while the National's never strong West Kent District collapsed (Map 57) − showed what respect and affection the KSLU had earned (Map 59). But the industrial initiative shifted so firmly from the countryside that the carefully balanced county synthesis was upset and eventually destroyed.

Under Simmons' successors the union turned to costly, ultimately unsuccessful urban recruitment on a national basis, restyling itself the London & Counties Labour League and acquiring headquarters in the capital. Neglect and disillusion alienated all but Kent's most enthusiastic agricultural branches: the KSLU's spirit had died before the organisation was formally dissolved in December 1895 (Map 60).

Note

1. For a complete and fully referenced account of the union, see Carlton (1977).

7.6 THE WELSH TITHE WAR 1886-95   John P.D. Dunbabin

From 1886-8 tithe rebates were widely demanded throughout north Wales, and secured in half the beneficies of the Bangor diocese and in three-quarters of those of St Asaph.[1] Even where rebates were conceded, payments were often withheld, and stock were concealed, roads blocked and crowds assembled to prevent recovery by distraint and auction. To distrain tithe-owners needed police, and sometimes military, protection; but (in marked contrast to the Highlands) this was seldom refused. In mid-1887 there were clashes, and anti-tithers forced an inquiry. Although this heard evidence on all aspects of the question, it confined its report to the disturbances and (unlike the 1883-4 Crofters' Commission) gave no handle to further agitation. Distraints were resumed in 1888, 615 farms being visited in Denbighshire alone. Things often went smoothly but at Llanefydd troops had again to be summoned; they proved surprisingly popular and effective. Subsequently a system of 'moral suasion' brought de-escalation: police numbers were limited, while anti-tithers stuck to token refusals to pay and attempted to calm the auction crowds. First violence, then agitation gradually petered out in north Wales before the 1891 Act transferred tithe liability from occupier to owner. In the south-west they lasted longer; but the 1891 Act, together with police abandonment of their policy of 'moral suasion', ended them in Pembrokeshire and Carmarthen. Cardiganshire, however, took no action until 1894, when the Home Secretary threatened to withhold its police grant. Once the authorities there accorded protection to distraint proceedings, resistance crumbled.

Agitation against the tithe in Wales had two sources: economic and politico-religious. What converted passive distaste for tithes into active opposition was the 1885 collapse of livestock prices. This brought rent reductions and several Denbighshire farmers spontaneously demanded comparable tithe cuts. Equally, a mild recovery in livestock prices in 1889 was one reason for the agitation's decline. But it was not simply a question of economics, for Wales was less heavily tithed than eastern England, where sentiment never became so virulent. Moreover, many tithe-payers owed such small sums that they clearly defaulted from principle, not necessity; and few took up the tithe-owners' offer of rebates to individuals in genuine distress.

Secondly, in the 1880s a new Non-conformist small-town elite challenged the

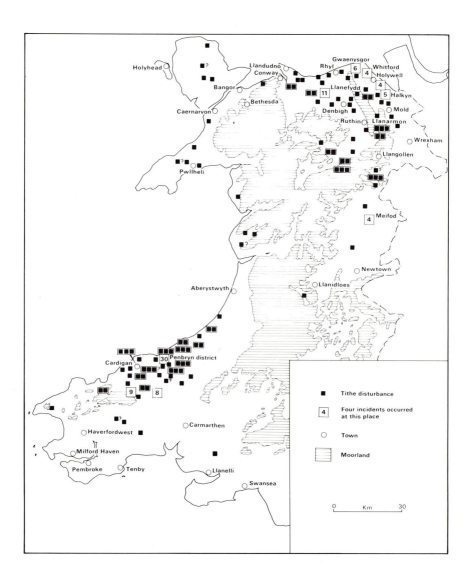

Map 61. The Welsh Tithe War, 1886-95

Source: Based on PP (1887) (xxxviii); the following newspapers for the period *The Times, Daily News, Cambrian News, Caernarvon and Denbigh Herald, Denbigh Free Press, Montgomery Express*; parish questionnaire (diocese of St Asaph), National Library of Wales SA/Tithe/Nos. 1-207; Lewis (n.d.), (NLW 15321).

traditional Welsh ascendancy of Anglicised landlords and the Anglican Church. Most farmers sympathised with the challengers, especially as regards the Church.

Thus when they were refused tithe rebates (partly because tithe had already been cut by a sliding scale), they at once voiced demands for Disestablishment. This was a godsend to politicians, especially Thomas Gee of Denbigh whose prestige had been badly dented over the question of Home Rule. He rapidly set up an Anti-Tithe League, subsequently expanded into a Welsh Land League. This farmers joined and used, and they undoubtedly devoured Gee's rhetoric. They did not, however, necessarily take his advice, particularly when he sought to embroil them with their landlords by advocating Irish-style boycotting. Nor were his further initiatives in 1889 able to prevent the decline of agitation.

Map 61 plots newspaper accounts of tithe *disturbances*. Their incidence was strongly influenced by local factors, for the initiative in demanding rebates lay with the actual tithe-payers. If demands were conceded, trouble was less likely (though not uncommon), and local incumbents were readier to concede (to safeguard the rest of their income) than were external tithe-owners like the Ecclesiastical Commissioners, who owned nearly a fifth of Welsh tithes, but were chiefly concerned to avoid setting precedents for England. Landlords' attitudes were another factor; they might stand aside, but increasingly they assumed part of the tithe burden themselves and/or pressured their tenants, although almost never to the point of eviction. Crowds also differed, labourers and miners being often more given to violence than the tithe-payers themselves. Lastly, police policy varied from county to county, but there were general trends. Tithe fell chiefly on farmers, and the urban south was little involved. It was less unpopular in Anglicised districts — there was a sharp difference between English and Welsh Pembrokeshire. The most heavily tithed counties were Flint, Denbighshire and Anglesey; Flint and Denbighshire were also the territory of Gee. The other main centre of disturbance, Cardiganshire, inherited the tradition of 'Rebecca'. Moreover, especially around Penbryn, the region had unusual numbers of small freeholders, who were exempt from landlord influence and not relieved by the 1891 transfer of tithe liability from occupier to owner.

Note

1. For more details of the disturbances, see Dunbabin (1974), ch. 10 and 11; PP (1887) (xxxviii).

7.7 THE HIGHLAND LAND WAR 1881-96   James Hunter

The emergence of the crofting community was a slow and very painful process.[1] Highlanders' primary loyalties were to their kin-groups, their clans, their chiefs. During the eighteenth century, however, those chiefs had become the agents of social and economic forces originating in southern Britain's rapidly developing industrial society. The people were thus disposed of to make way for sheep and were settled on newly created coastal smallholdings or crofts. There they were

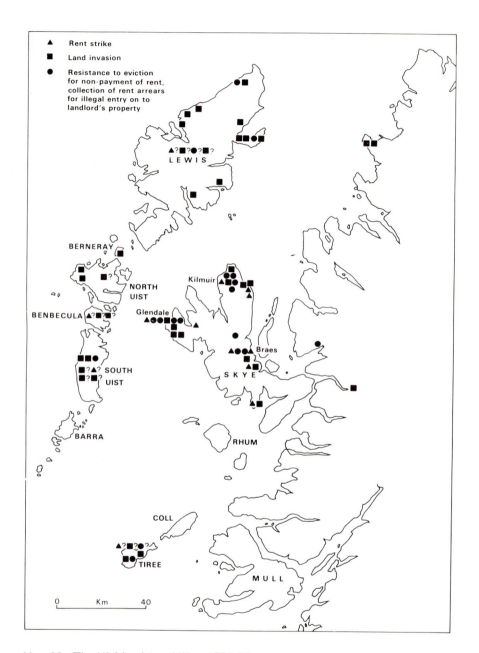

Map 62. The Highland Land War, 1881-96

exposed to renewed removal — and to hunger, destitution and suffering of every kind. But to come to terms with the new situation — representing, as it did, such a sharp and sudden break with the past — was not easy. The mores of the clan were not suited to the exigencies of the capitalist order responsible for the destruction of northern Scotland's traditional way of life, but there was nothing to put in their place.

Eventually a new community of interest was forged among the people whose ancestors had been the commons of the clans. A different outlook on the world was evolved — an outlook which took account of the class animosities engendered by the brutality of eviction, clearance and dispossession. Crucial to this development was the evangelical Presbyterianism which, in the 1840s, became institutionalised as the Free Church of Scotland — and which, from its first appearance in the nineteenth-century's opening decades, was distinctly anti-landlord in tone.

The later protest drew upon the common currency of late-nineteenth century land reform movements — notably on notions associated with the name of Henry George, but there was much that was uniquely Highland in the events which plunged northern Scotland into disorder of a kind not seen since the demise of Jacobitism. Age-old Celtic concepts of the community's stake in the land — concepts clearly inimical to the idea of private property — were resurrected, and much that was illegal was justified by reference to the Bible and the precepts of Presbyterian fundamentalism.

Unrest first broke out at Braes in Skye — where, in 1881, crofters mounted a rent strike and demanded the restoration of grazings added to a sheep farm during the Clearances. An attempt by their laird, Lord MacDonald, to evict the rebellious Braes crofters resulted in the eviction orders being seized and burned. In April 1882, a 50 strong police detachment clashed violently with Lord MacDonald's tenantry — an episode which passed into history and legend as the 'Battle of the Braes'.

Following these events at Braes, lands were occupied illegally at Glendale in northern Skye. In January 1883, an attempt to arrest those responsible resulted in the police being forcibly expelled from the district. A royal commission — the Napier Commission — was set up. The commission's 1884 report recommended reform: no immediate action was taken by Gladstone's government.

During 1884, 1885 and 1886, unrest erupted throughout the Highlands and Islands, with rent strikes becoming general and sheep farms and deer forests being taken over by crofters. The police in Skye were authorised to carry guns, and marines and gunboats were sent north. A political organisation — the Highland Land Law Reform Association, subsequently renamed the Highland Land League — was established. In the general elections of 1885 and 1886, its candidates were all but universally successful in Scotland's crofting constituencies.

It was in response to this pressure that Gladstone's short-lived 1886 administration passed the first Crofters Act. Modelled on the Irish Land Act of 1881, that measure granted crofters security of tenure, set up a rents tribunal called the Crofters Commission and generally brought the Highland Clearances to an end. Discontent continued, however, largely because the 1886 Act contained little provision for reversing the clearances by making more land available to crofters. Later protests — notably the widespread land seizures which followed the First World War — resulted in steps being taken to remedy this deficiency. In the

Hebrides in particular, many of the sheep farms created in the early-nineteenth century were acquired by official agencies and resettled by crofters.

Note

1. A complete and fully referenced account of these matters is to be found in Hunter (1976).

REFERENCES

Allan, D.G.C. (1950) 'Agrarian Discontent Under the Early Stuarts and During the Last Decade of Elizabeth', unpublished MSc(Econ) thesis, University of London
—— (1952) 'The Rising in the West 1628-31', *Economic History Review* (2nd series), *5*
Allison, K.J. (1957) 'The Sheep-corn Husbandry of Norfolk in the Sixteenth and Seventeenth Centuries', *Agricultural History Review, 5*
Amos, S.W. (1971) 'Social Discontent and Agrarian Disturbances in Essex 1795-1850', unpublished MA thesis, University of Durham
Annual Register, various years
Appleby, A.B. (1975a) 'Agrarian Capitalism or Seigneurial Reaction? The North West of England 1500-1700', *American Historical Review, 80*
—— (1975b) 'Common Land and Peasant Unrest in Sixteenth Century England: A Comparative Note', *Peasant Studies Newsletter, 4* (3)
—— (1978) *Famine in Tudor and Stuart England*, Stanford, California
Ashton, T.S. and Sykes, J. (1929; 1956) *The Coal Industry of the Eighteenth Century*, Manchester
Barnes, T.G. (1961) *Somerset 1625-40*, Cambridge, Mass.
Barnsby, G.J. (1977) *The Working Class Movement in the Black Country 1750-1867*, Wolverhampton
Batho, G. (1967) 'Noblemen, Gentlemen and Yeomen' in J. Thirsk (ed.), *The Agrarian History of England and Wales vol. IV: 1500-1640*, Cambridge
Baugh, D.A. (1975), 'The Cost of Poor Relief in South East England 1790-1834', *Economic History Review* (2nd series), *28*
Beloff, M. (1938) *Public Order and Popular Disturbances*, London
Beresford, M.W. and Hurst, J.G. (eds.) (1971) *Deserted Medieval Villages*, London
Bindoff, S.T. (1949) *Ket's Rebellion*, 1549, London
Blanchard, I. (1970) 'Population Change, Enclosure and the Tudor Economy', *Economic History Review* (2nd series), *23*
Bohstedt, J.H. (1972) 'Riots in England 1790-1810 with Special Reference to Devonshire', unpublished PhD thesis, Harvard University
Booth, A. (1977) 'Food Riots in the North West of England 1790-1801', *Past and Present, 77*
Bouch, C.M.L. and Jones, G.P. (1961) *A Short Economic and Social History of the Lake Counties 1500-1830*, Manchester
Bowden, P. (1967) 'Agricultural Prices, Farm Profits and Rents' in J. Thirsk

(ed.), *The Agrarian History of England and Wales vol. IV: 1500-1640*, Cambridge

Boyes, J.H. and Russell, R. (1977) *The Canals of Eastern England*, Newton Abbot

Brenner, R. (1976) 'Agrarian Class Structure and Economic Development in Pre-industrial Europe', *Past and Present, 70*

Brewer, J. and Styles, J. (1980) 'Introduction' in J. Brewer and J. Styles (eds.), *An Ungovernable People*, London

Brighton Patriot (1835)

Brown, A.F.J. (1969) *Essex at Work 1700-1815*, Chelmsford

Bush, M.L. (1975) *The Government Policy of Protector Somerset*, London

Butlin, R.A. (1967) 'Enclosure and Improvement in Northumberland in the Sixteenth Century', *Archaeologia Aeliana* (4th series), *45*

Campbell, M.E. (1942) *The English Yeoman*, New Haven, Conn.

Caple, J.N. (1978) 'Popular Protest and Public Order in Eighteenth Century England: The Food Riots of 1756-7', unpublished MA thesis, Queen's University, Kingston, Canada

Carlton, F. (1977) ' "A Substantial and Sterling Friend to the Labouring Man": The Kent and Sussex Labourers' Union', unpublished MPhil thesis, University of Sussex

Carter, I. (1977) 'Class Culture Among Farm Servants in the North-east, 1840-1914' in A.A. MacLaren (ed.), *Social Class in Scotland: Past and Present*, Edinburgh

—————— (1979) *Farm Life in North-east Scotland*, Edinburgh

Chambers, J.D. and Mingay, G.E. (1966) *The Agricultural Revolution 1750-1880*, London

Charlesworth, A. (1979) *Social Protest in a Rural Society: The Spatial Diffusion of the Captain Swing Disturbances 1830-1831*, Historical Geography Research Series no. 1, Norwich

—————— (1980) 'The Development of the English Rural Proletariat and Social Protest 1700-1850: A Comment', *Journal of Peasant Studies, 8*

Christian, G. (1967) *Ashdown Forest*, Forest Row

Clark, P. (1976) 'Popular Protest and Disturbance in Kent 1558-1640', *Economic History Review* (2nd series), *29* (3)

—————— (1977) *English Provincial Society from the Reformation to the Revolution*, Hassocks

Clifford, H. (1887) *Life of Jane Dormer, Duchess of Feria*, London

Coate, M. (1928) 'The Duchy of Cornwall: Its History and Administration 1640-1660', *Transactions of the Royal Historical Society* (4th series), *10*

Coles, A.J. (1978) 'The Moral Economy of the Crowd: Some Twentieth Century Food Riots', *Journal of British Studies, 18*

Collins, E.J.T. (1970) 'Harvest Technology and Labour Supply in Britain 1790-1870', unpublished PhD thesis, University of Nottingham

Cornwall, J. (1977) *Revolt of the Peasantry 1549*, London

Croot, P. and Parker, D. (1978) 'Agrarian Class Structure and Economic

Development', *Past and Present, 78*

Cust, L.A. (1914) *Chronicles of Erthig on the Dyke*, London

Darby, H.C. (1956) *The Draining of the Fens*, Cambridge

Darvall, F.O. (1969) *Popular Disturbances and Public Order in Regency England*, London

Davies, C.L.S. (1969) 'Les révoltes populaires en Angleterre (1500-1700)', *Annales E.S.C., 24*

Derby Mercury, 20 September 1757

Devine, T. (1978) 'Social Stability and Agrarian Change in the Eastern Lowlands of Scotland 1810-1840', *Social History, 3*

Digby, A. (1972) 'The Operation of the Poor Law in the Social and Economic Life of Nineteenth Century Norfolk', unpublished PhD thesis, University of East Anglia

—— (1978) *Pauper Palaces*, London

Dinwiddy, J. (1979) 'Luddism and Politics in the Northern Counties', *Social History, 4*

Dobson, C.B. (1980) *Masters and Journeymen*, London

Dodd, A.H. (1971) *The Industrial Revolution in North Wales*, 3rd edn, Cardiff

Dodd, J.P. (1965) 'South Lancashire in Transition', *Transactions of Historic Society of Lancashire and Cheshire, 117*

Dodgshon, R.A. (1976) 'The Economics of Sheep Farming in the Southern Uplands During the Age of Improvement 1750-1833', *Economic History Review* (2nd series), *29* (4)

—— (1978) 'Geographical Relationships in the Decline of Feudalism', unpublished paper read at the Institute of British Geographers Historical Geography Research Group Conference, Cambridge

Dunbabin, J.P.D. (1968) 'The Incidence and Organization of Agricultural Trades Unionism in the 1870's', *Agricultural History Review, 16*

—— (1974) *Rural Discontent in Nineteenth Century Britain*, London

Dunkley, P. (1979) 'Paternalism, the Magistracy and Poor Relief in England 1795-1834', *International Review of Social History, 24*

Dyer, C.C. (1977) 'The Estates of the Bishopric of Worcester 680-1540', unpublished PhD thesis, University of Birmingham

—— (1980) *Lords and Peasants in a Changing Society*, Cambridge

East Sussex County Record Office (1835) *Battle Union Minute Book*, 24 July

Edwards, I. ab Owen (1929) *A Catalogue of Star Chamber Proceedings Relating to Wales*, Cardiff

Ellis, W. (1750) *The Modern Husbandman*, 8 vols., London

Emery, F.V. (1967) 'The Farming Regions of Wales' in J. Thirsk (ed.), *The Agrarian History of England and Wales vol. IV: 1500-1640*, Cambridge

Emsley, C. (1979) *British Society and the French Wars 1793-1815*, London

Everitt, A. (1967) 'Farm Labourers' in J. Thirsk (ed.), *The Agrarian History of England and Wales vol. IV: 1500-1640*, Cambridge

Fisher, C. (1978) 'The Free Miners of the Forest of Dean 1800-41' in R. Harrison (ed.), *Independent Collier*, London

Foster, J. (1977) *Class Struggle and the Industrial Revolution*, Methuen edn, London

Gay, E.F. (1904) 'The Midland Revolt and the Inquisitions of Depopulation of 1607', *Transactions of the Royal Historical Society* (3rd series), *18*

Geddes, M. (1979) *Uneven Development and the Scottish Highlands*, Urban and Regional Studies, University of Sussex Working Paper 17

Gentleman's Magazine, various issues

Godber, J. (1970) 'Some Documents Relating to Riots', *Bedfordshire Historical Record Society, 49*

Gould, P.R. (1964) 'A Note on Research Into the Diffusion of Development', *Journal of Modern African Studies, 2*

Gray, M. (1957) *The Highland Economy 1750-1850*, Edinburgh

——— (1973) 'Scottish Emigration', *Perspectives in American History, 7*

Gruffydd, K.L. (1977) 'The Vale of Clwyd Corn Riots of 1740', *Flintshire Historical Publications, 27*

Hadfield, C. (1960) *The Canals of South Wales and the Border*, London

——— (1966a) *The Canals of the East Midlands*, Newton Abbot

——— (1966b) *The Canals of the West Midlands*, Newton Abbot

——— (1967) *The Canals of South West England*, Newton Abbot

——— (1969a) *British Canals*, Newton Abbot

——— (1969b) *The Canals of South and South East England*, Newton Abbot

——— (1972/3) *The Canals of Yorkshire and North East England*, vols. 1 and 2, Newton Abbot

Hadfield, C. and Biddle, G. (1970) *The Canals of North West England*, Newton Abbot

Hammond, J.L. and Hammond, B. (1911) *The Village Labourer*, London

Harber, J. (1972) 'Rural Incendiarism in Suffolk 1840-1845', unpublished MA thesis, University of Warwick

Harris, L.E. (1953) *Vermuyden and the Fens*, London

Harrison, C.J. (1979) 'Fire on the Chase', paper read at the Winter Conference of the British Agricultural History Society, Polytechnic of Central London, December

Hart, C.E. (1951) *The Commoners of Dean Forest*, Gloucester

——— (1953) *The Free Miners of the Royal Forest of Dean*, Gloucester

——— (1966) *Royal Forest*, Oxford

Hatcher, J. (1970) *Rural Economy and Society in the Duchy of Cornwall 1300-1500*, Cambridge

Hay, D. (1975a) 'Crime, Authority and the Criminal Law', unpublished PhD thesis, University of Warwick

——— (1975b) 'Poaching and the Game Laws on Cannock Chase' in D. Hay, P. Linebaugh and E.P. Thompson (eds.), *Albion's Fatal Tree*, London

Hayter, T. (1978) *The Army and the Crowd in Mid-Georgian England*, London

Heaton, H. (1920) *The Yorkshire Woollen and Worsted Industries*, Oxford

Hey, D.G. (1974) *An English Rural Community: Myddle Under the Tudors and Stuarts*, Leicester

———— (1979) 'Agriculture and Social Change: The Cheshire Plain 1600-1760', paper read at the Conference of Teachers of Local and Regional History, University of Sussex

Hill, C. (1974) *Change and Continuity in Seventeenth Century England*, London

Hilton, R.H. (1973) *Bond Men Made Free*, London

Hipkin, G.M. (1930) 'Social and Economic Conditions in the Holland Division of Lincolnshire from 1640 to 1660', *Lincolnshire Architectural and Archaeological Society, 40*

Hobsbawm, E.J. and Rudé, G. (1973) *Captain Swing*, Penguin edn, London

Hodgson, R.I. (1973) 'Agricultural Improvement and Changing Regional Economies in the Eighteenth Century' in A.R.H. Baker and J.B. Harley (eds.), *Man Made the Land*, Newton Abbot

Holderness, B.A. (1968) 'Rural Society in South-east Lindsey, Lincolnshire 1660-1840', unpublished PhD thesis, University of Nottingham

———— (1972) ' "Open" and "Close" Parishes in England in the Eighteenth and Nineteenth Centuries', *Agricultural History Review, 20*

Holmes, C. (1974) *The Eastern Association in the English Civil War*, London

Howell, D.W. (1977) *Land and People in Nineteenth Century Wales*, London

Hughes, J.D. (1954) 'The Drainage Disputes in the Isle of Axholme', *The Lincolnshire Historian, 2* (1)

Hull, F. (1950) 'Agriculture and Rural Society in Essex 1540-1640', unpublished PhD thesis, University of London

Hunter, J. (1976) *The Making of the Crofting Community*, Edinburgh

Huzel, J.P. (1976) 'A Quantitative Approach to the Agricultural Labourers' Riots of 1830 in Kent' (abstract) in J. Bak, 'Conference Report: Peasant Revolts', *Peasant Studies, 5*

Ipswich Journal, 17 and 24 May 1740

Isaac, D.G.D. (1953) 'A Study of Popular Disturbances in Britain 1714-54', unpublished PhD thesis, University of Edinburgh

James, M. (1974) *Family, Lineage and Civil Society*, Oxford

Jenkin, A.K. Hamilton (1962) *The Cornish Miner*, 3rd edn, London

John, A.H. (1967) 'Farming in Wartime 1793-1815' in G.E. Mingay and E.L. Jones (eds.), *Land, Labour and Population in the Industrial Revolution*, London

———— (1976) 'English Agricultural Improvement and Grain Exports 1660-1765' in D.C. Coleman and A.H. John (eds.), *Trade, Government and Economy in Pre-industrial England*, London

Jones, D.J.V. (1965) 'Popular Disturbances in Wales 1790-1832', unpublished PhD thesis, University of Wales

———— (1973) *Before Rebecca*, London

———— (1976) 'Thomas Campbell Foster and the Rural Labourer, Incendiarism in East Anglia in the 1840s', *Social History, 1*

Jones, E.L. (1964) *Seasons and Prices*, London

———— (1965) 'The Agricultural Labour Market in England 1793-1872', *Economic History Review* (2nd series), *17*

Jones Pierce, T. (1967) 'Landlords in Wales' in J. Thirsk (ed.), *The Agrarian History of England and Wales vol. IV: 1500-1640*, Cambridge

Kemnitz, T.M. (1969) 'Chartism in Brighton', unpublished DPhil thesis, University of Sussex

Kent Herald, May and June 1835

Kerridge, E. (1951) 'The Agrarian Development of Wiltshire 1540-1640', unpublished PhD thesis, University of London

————— (1958-9) 'The Revolts in Wiltshire Against Charles I', *Wiltshire Archaeological and Natural History Magazine, 57*

————— (1967) *The Agricultural Revolution*, London

————— (1969) *Agrarian Problems in the Sixteenth Century and After*, London

Kussmaul, A.S. (1978) 'Servants in Husbandry in Early Modern England', unpublished PhD thesis, University of Toronto

Leopold, J. (1980) 'The Levellers Revolt in Galloway in 1724', *Scottish Labour History Society Journal, 14*

Levine, D. (1977) *Family Formation in an Age of Nascent Capitalism*, London

Lewis, Rev R. (n.d.) *The Tithe War in West Wales*, NLW 15321

Lindsay, J. (1968) *The Canals of Scotland*, Newton Abbot

Lipson, E. (1934) *The Economic History of England*, 2nd edn, London

Logue, K.J. (1979) *Popular Disturbances in Scotland 1780-1815*, Edinburgh

London Gazette, various issues

Lowerson, J. (1978) 'Sussex and Industrialisation: Economic Depression and Restrictive Elements, 1700-1840' in M. Palmer (ed.), *The Onset of Industrialisation*, Nottingham

Lynch, G.J. (1973) 'The Risings of the Clubmen in the English Civil War', unpublished MA thesis, Manchester University

Lythe, S.G.E. (1967) 'The Tayside Meal Mobs 1772-3', *Scottish Historical Review, 46*

MacCulloch, D. (1979) 'Kett's Rebellion in Context', *Past and Present, 84*

MacDonald, S. (1975) 'The Progress of the Early Threshing Machine', *Agricultural History Review, 23*

McNair, A.S. (1973) 'History' in H.L. Edlin (ed.), *Queen Elizabeth Forest Park*, Edinburgh

Malcolmson, R.W. (1980) 'A Set of Ungovernable People' in J. Brewer and J. Styles (eds.), *An Ungovernable People*, London

Manchester Mercury, 15 September 1757

Manning, B. (1975) 'The Peasantry and the English Revolution', *Journal of Peasant Studies, 2*

————— (1976) *The English People and the English Revolution*, London

Manning, R.B. (1974) 'Patterns of Violence in Early Tudor Enclosure Riots', *Albion, 5*

————— (1977) 'Violence and Social Conflict in Mid-Tudor Rebellions', *Journal of British Studies, 16*

Marshall, J.D. (ed.) (1967) *The Autobiography of William Stout of Lancaster 1665-1752*, Manchester

Martin, J. (1979) 'Peasant and Landlord in Feudalism and in the Transition to Capitalism in England', unpublished PhD thesis, University of Lancaster

Morrill, J.S. (1974) *Cheshire 1630-60*, London

―――― (1976) *The Revolt of the Provinces*, London

Neave, D. (1976) 'Anti-militia Riots in Lincolnshire, 1757 and 1796', *Lincolnshire History and Archaeology, 11*

Neeson, J.M. (1977) 'Common Right and Enclosure in Eighteenth Century Northamptonshire', unpublished PhD thesis, University of Warwick

Newton, R. (1974) 'The Decay of the Borders: Tudor Northumberland in Transition' in C.W. Chalkin and M.A. Havinden (eds.), *Rural Change and Urban Growth 1500-1800*, London

Northampton Mercury, various issues, 1740

Obelkevitch, J. (1976) *Religion and Rural Society*, Oxford

Pam, D.O. (1974) *The Fight for Common Rights in Enfield and Edmonton 1400-1600*, Edmonton Historical Society Occasional Paper (new series), 27

―――― (1977) *The Rude Multitude*, Edmonton Hundreds Historical Society Occasional Paper (new series), *33*

PP (1834) *Reports of the Commissioners of Poor Laws 1834*

―――― (1887) *Inquiry into Disturbances Connected with the Levying of Tithe in Wales*

Pawson, E. (1977) *Transport and Economy*, London

Peacock, A.J. (1965) *Bread or Blood*, London

―――― (1974) 'Village Radicalism in East Anglia 1800-50' in J.P.D. Dunbabin, *Rural Discontent in Nineteenth Century Britain*, London

Pettit, P.A.J. (1968) *The Royal Forests of Northamptonshire*, Northamptonshire Record Society, vol. 23

Plume, G.A. (1935) 'The Enclosure Movement in Caernarvonshire', unpublished MA thesis, University of Wales

Reaney, B. (1970) *The Class Struggle in Nineteenth Century Oxfordshire*, History Workshop Pamphlets 3, Oxford

Richards, E. (1974) 'Patterns of Highland Discontent 1790-1860' in J. Stevenson and R. Quinault (eds.), *Popular Protest and Public Order*, London

―――― (1981) 'The Last Scottish Food Riots', *Past and Present* (supplement)

Richardson, T.L. (1977) 'The Standard of Living Controversy 1790-1840 with Special Reference to Agricultural Labourers in Seven English Counties', unpublished PhD thesis, University of Hull

Robertson, B.W. (1979) 'The Scottish Farm Servant and his Union' in I. MacDougall (ed.), *Essays in Scottish Labour History*, Edinburgh

Rose, R.B. (1961) 'Eighteenth Century Price Riots and Public Policy in England', *International Review of Social History, 6*

Rowe, A. (1942) 'Food Riots of the Forties in Cornwall', *Royal Cornwall Polytechnic Society Report*

Rowe, J. (1953) *Cornwall in the Age of the Industrial Revolution*, Liverpool

Rudé, G. (1964) *The Crowd in History: A Study of Popular Disturbances in*

France and England 1730-1848, New York

Rule, J.G. (1971) 'The Labouring Miner in Cornwall c. 1740-1820', unpublished PhD thesis, University of Warwick

Russell, F.W. (1859) *Kett's Rebellion in Norfolk*, London

Samuel, R. (1975) 'Quarry Roughs' and 'Village Labour' in R. Samuel (ed.), *Village Life and Labour*, London

Searle, E. (1974) *Lordship and Community*, Toronto

Sharp, B. (1980) *In Contempt of all Authority*, London

Simpson, A. (1958) 'The East Anglian Foldcourse: Some Queries', *Agricultural History Review, 6*

Smout, T.C. (1972) *A History of the Scottish People 1560-1830*, Fontana edn, London

Somerville, R. (1977) 'Commons and Wastes in Northwest Derbyshire − The High Peak New Lands', *Derbyshire Archaeological Journal, 97*

Spufford, M. (1963) *A Cambridgeshire Community*, Leicester Occasional Papers 20, Leicester

────── (1974) *Contrasting Communities*, Cambridge

Stevenson, J. (1974) 'Food Riots in England 1792-1818' in J. Stevenson and R. Quinault (eds.), *Popular Protest and Public Order*, London

────── (1979) *Popular Disturbances in England 1700-1870*, London

Stone, Thomas (1787) *Suggestions for Rendering the Inclosures of Common Fields and Wastelands, a Source of Population and of Riches*, London

Stovin, G. (1752) 'A Brief Account of the Drainage of the Levels of Hatfield Chase and Parts Adjacent', *The Yorkshire Archaeological and Topographical Journal, 37* (1948-51)

Strype, J. (1822) *Ecclesiastical Memorials*, London

Summers, D. (1976) *The Great Level*, Newton Abbot

Tate, W.E. (1944) 'Parliamentary Counter-petitions During the Enclosures of the Eighteenth and Nineteenth Centuries', *English Historical Review, 59*

Tawney, R.H. (1912) *The Agrarian Problem in the Sixteenth Century*, London

Thirsk, J. (1957) *English Peasant Farming*, London

────── (1967) 'The Farming Regions of England' in J. Thirsk (ed.), *The Agrarian History of England and Wales vol. IV: 1500-1640*, Cambridge

────── (1969) 'Horn and Thorn in Staffordshire: The Economy of a Pastoral County', *North Staffordshire Journal of Field Studies, 9*

Thomas, M. (1975) 'The Rioting Crowd in Derbyshire in the Eighteenth Century', *Derbyshire Archaeological Journal, 95*

Thomis, M.I. (1979) *The Luddites*, Newton Abbot

Thompson, E.P. (1968) *The Making of the English Working Class*, Penguin edn, London

────── (1971) 'The Moral Economy of the English Crowd in the Eighteenth Century', *Past and Present, 50*

────── (1975) *Whigs and Hunters*, London

Tilly, C. (1975) 'Food Supply and Public Order' in C. Tilly (ed.), *The Formation of National States in Western Europe*, Princeton, NJ

Trinder, B. (1973) *The Industrial Revolution in Shropshire*, Chichester

Tubbs, C.R. (1965) 'The Development of the Small Holding and Cottage Stock-keeping Economy of the New Forest', *Agricultural History Review, 13*

Turner, M. (1980) *English Parliamentary Enclosure*, Folkestone

Underdown, D. (1973) *Somerset in the Civil War and Interregnum*, Newton Abbot

—— (1980) 'The Chalk and Cheese: Contrasts Among the English Clubmen', *Past and Present, 85*

VCH, *Lancashire, Leicestershire, Warwickshire* and *Worcestershire*

Wadsworth, A.P. (1919-22) 'The Enclosure of the Commons in the Rochdale District in the Sixteenth and Seventeenth Centuries', *Transactions of the Rochdale Literary and Scientific Society, 14*

Walton, J. (1976) 'Aspects of Agrarian Change in Oxfordshire 1750-1880', unpublished DPhil thesis, University of Oxford

Watts, S.J. (1971) 'Tenant Right in Early Seventeenth Century Northumberland', *Northern History, 6*

Wearmouth, R. (1945) *Methodism and the Common People*, London

Wells, R.A.E. (1977a) *Dearth and Distress in Yorkshire 1793-1802*, Borthwick Papers 52, York

—— (1977b) 'The Revolt of the South-west 1800-01', *Social History, 6*

—— (1978a) 'Counting Riots in Eighteenth Century England', *Bulletin of the Society for the Study of Labour History, 37*

—— (1978b) 'The Grain Crises in England 1794-96, 1799-1801', unpublished DPhil thesis, University of York

—— (1979) 'The Development of the English Rural Proletariat and Social Protest 1700-1850', *Journal of Peasant Studies, 6*

The Welshman, 1843

Western, J.R. (1965) *The English Militia in the Eighteenth Century*, London

Whyte, I. (1978) 'The Effects of the Transition from Feudalism to Capitalism on Rural Society in Lowland Scotland in the Seventeenth Century', paper read at the Historical Geography Research Group of Institute of British Geographers Conference, Sydney Sussex College, Cambridge, July

—— (1979) *Agriculture and Society in Seventeenth Century Scotland*, Edinburgh

Willan, T.S. (1936) *River Navigation in England*, London

—— (1938) *The English Coasting Trade 1600-1750*, Manchester

Williams, D. (1955) *The Rebecca Riots*, Cardiff

Williams, D.E. (1978) 'English Hunger Riots in 1766', unpublished PhD thesis, University of Wales (pub. in prep.)

Williams, M. (1970) *The Draining of the Somerset Levels*, Cambridge

Williams, R. (1975) *The Country and the City*, Paladin edn, London

Williams, T. (1928) 'Aspects of the Agrarian Problem in Wales in the Sixteenth Century', unpublished MA thesis, University of Wales

Woodman, A. Vere (1957) 'The Buckinghamshire and Oxfordshire Rising of 1549', *Oxoniensia, 20*

Wrightson, K. and Levine, D. (1979) *Poverty and Piety in an English Village*, London

Yarlott, R. (1963) 'The Long Parliament and Fear of Popular Pressure 1640-1646', unpublished MA thesis, University of Leeds

LIST OF CONTRIBUTORS

JOHN BOHSTEDT is Assistant Professor of History at the University of Tennessee, Knoxville. He is the author of a forthcoming book entitled *Riots and Community Politics in England and Wales 1790-1810*.

JEREMY N. CAPLE is a doctoral candidate in History at the University of Toronto. He previously completed a Master's thesis on the food riots of 1756-7 at Queen's University, Kingston, Ontario.

FELICITY CARLTON completed a M. Phil thesis on the Kent and Sussex Labourers' Union at the University of Sussex.

ANDREW CHARLESWORTH is Lecturer in Geography at Liverpool University. He is the author of a monograph *Social Protest in a Rural Society: The Spatial Diffusion of the Captain Swing Riots 1830-1*.

ANNE DIGBY is Research Fellow at the Institute of Social and Economic Research, University of York. She is the author of *Pauper Palaces*.

JOHN P.D. DUNBABIN is Fellow of St Edmund Hall, Oxford. He is the author of *Rural Discontent in Nineteenth Century Britain*.

JAMES HUNTER completed a Ph.D thesis at the University of Edinburgh upon which was based his book *The Making of the Crofting Community*.

DAVID J.V. JONES is Senior Lecturer in History, University College of Wales, Swansea. He is the author of *Before Rebecca, Chartism and the Chartists* and *Crime, Protest, Community and Police in Nineteenth Century Britain*.

JOHN W. LEOPOLD was a tutor with the Workers Education Association (West of Scotland District). He is now a Research Fellow in the Department of Social and Economic Research, University of Glasgow.

JOHN LOWERSON is Lecturer in History in the Centre for Continuing Education, University of Sussex. He is editor of *Southern History* and he is the author of *A Short History of Sussex* and co-author of *Time to Spare in Victorian England*.

192

GARRY J. LYNCH completed a Master's thesis on the Clubmen Risings at the University of Manchester.

ROBERT W. MALCOLMSON is Associate Professor of History at Queen's University, Kingston, Canada. He is the author of *Popular Recreations in English Society 1700-1850* and *Life and Labour in England 1700-1780*.

JOHN E. MARTIN completed his doctoral thesis 'Peasant and Landlord During the Development of Feudalism and the Transition to Capitalism in England' at the University of Lancaster. He is now undertaking research for the Department of Scientific and Industrial Research, Wellington, New Zealand.

JEANETTE M. NEESON completed her doctoral thesis 'Common Right and Enclosure in Eighteenth Century Northamptonshire' at the University of Warwick.

ERIC RICHARDS is Professor of History at Flinders University of South Australia. He is the author of *The Leviathan of Wealth: The Sutherland Fortune in the Industrial Revolution* and *A History of the Highland Clearances*.

JOHN WALTER is Lecturer in History at the University of Essex. He is the author of an essay on 'Grain Riots and Popular Attitudes to the Law' in J. Brewer and J. Styles (eds.) *An Ungovernable People*.

DALE E. WILLIAMS is Assistant Professor of History at Loyola University, New Orleans. His doctoral thesis 'English Hunger Riots in 1766' (University College of Wales Aberystwyth) is shortly to be published.

INDEX